Global Adult Tobacco Survey : Thailand Country Report

CENTERS FOR DISEASE CONTROL AND PREVENTION

World Health Organization

Regional Office for South-East Asia

WHO Library Cataloguing-in-Publication data

World Health Organization, Regional Office for South-East Asia.

Global adult tobacco survey : Thailand country report.

1. Tobacco use disorder - prevention and control. 2. Tobacco use cessation.
3. Tobacco industry - economics - legislation. 4. Smoking - prevention and control.
5. Knowledge, Attitudes, Practice. 6. Thailand

ISBN 978-92-9022-353-5 (NLM classification: WM 290)

The publication may be obtained from:

Bureau of Tobacco Control
Department of Disease Control (DDC)
Ministry of Public Health
Nonthaburi, 11000
Thailand
Tel. +662 589 7963
Fax. +662 589 1670

Office of the WHO Representative to Thailand
Office of the Permanent Secretary Building 3, 4th Fl
Ministry of Public Health
Nonthaburi, 11000
Thailand
Tel. +662 590 1524
Fax. +662 591 8199

Printed in Thailand

Foreword

Like any other public health initiative, a good surveillance and evaluation infrastructure is the cornerstone for understanding the trends in tobacco use, and tobacco control policy and programme effectiveness. Availability of reliable, accurate and timely data and their proper analysis and inference are also the key to determining interventions and approaches that are required to improve programme performance and persuade policy-makers to adapt appropriate policy measures. The recognition of the need for a standardized survey to monitor adult tobacco use led WHO and its partners, in particular Centers for Disease Control and Prevention, Atlanta, USA and Centers for Disease Control and Prevention Foundation, USA, to launch the Global Adult Tobacco Survey (GATS) in 2007 under the Bloomberg Initiative. The survey is designed to produce national and subnational estimates on tobacco use, exposure to second-hand smoke and "quit attempts" among adults across countries, and to indirectly measure the impact of tobacco control and prevention initiatives using a standard protocol.

I am pleased to note that Thailand is the first country to have completed the survey in South-East Asia Region. I am also pleased to learn that this is the first report of a completed Global Adult Tobacco Survey in the world under the Bloomberg Initiative.

The report has been able to capture important data on different aspects of tobacco use and of the tobacco control programme in Thailand. The efficient design for data collection and management, and the standardized analysis of data have made the survey report a nationally representative account of the existing situation.

I would like to congratulate the implementing agencies and all those involved for having completed the survey successfully, which I am sure has contributed substantially to capacity building of the country to conduct large and standardized surveys.

Most importantly, the findings mentioned in this report will be useful in designing and implementing effective tobacco control interventions in Thailand.

Samlee Plianbangchang, M.D., Dr.P.H.
Regional Director

Foreword

Tobacco use is a global problem. About a third of the global adult male population smokes. Each year, 5 million smokers are killed by tobacco use. Therefore, the World Health Organization in cooperation with its Member States adopted the WHO Framework Convention on Tobacco Control. Thailand is the thirty-eighth country to ratify the WHO FCTC.

As the Permanent Secretary, Ministry of Public Health, I have strongly supported policies for implementation of the FCTC.

The Global Adult Tobacco Survey (GATS) project is to be implemented under article 20, *Research, surveillance and exchange of information.* The Thai government, and the Ministry of Public Health, supports GATS as the data and evidence for tobacco control evaluation and implementation in Thailand, and for comparison with data of 13 other countries around the world.

This survey would not have been successful if there had not been cooperation from both international and national organizations. These organizations are: Centers for Disease Control and Prevention Atlanta, USA, CDC Foundation, Bloomberg Philanthropies, WHO, National Statistical Office, and Mahidol University. I would like to express my gratitude to all these organizations and institutions.

Dr Paijit Warachit
Permanent Secretary
Ministry of Public Health

Foreword

On behalf of the chair of the GATS Steering Committee and advisor to the Bureau of Tobacco Control of the Ministry of Public Health, I am very grateful that WHO, CDC and Bloomberg Philanthropies have supported Thailand to conduct the GATS.

Although Thailand has carried out national tobacco consumption surveys every two to three years, they did not evaluate the impact of tobacco control measures in detail. When the conference of COP II in Bangkok ended in July 2007, representatives from WHO, CDC, and Bloomberg Philanthropies met the Ministry of Health to plan for GATS in Thailand.

The decision to participate in GATS is very useful for Thailand, not only because the result will be useful for tobacco control planning and evaluation, but also in order to establish a national tobacco surveillance system.

I am very proud of the GATS technical team, which has been responsible for all processes of GATS. They have done many things to make Thailand the first country to finish its pilot study and reporting the survey. I would like to thank all for the efforts that they have made.

Professor Dr Prakit Vathesatogkit
Executive Secretary of Action on Smoking
and Health Foundation Thailand (ASH Thailand)

Advisor to Bureau of Tobacco Control,
Department of Disease Control,
Ministry of Public Health

Preface

In many countries, tobacco use is one of the top five behavioural risks impeding health and quality of life. Thailand is one of 14 countries with a high number of smokers (over 10 million) that were selected to participate in the Global Adult Tobacco Survey (GATS). Though Thailand has had several surveys regarding tobacco use conducted by the NSO, Ministry of Public Health, and other institutions, the variations in survey methodology led to difficulty in comparing them with other countries. The GATS uses a comprehensive, standard protocol, which contributes to globally comparable tobacco use data and also provides an opportunity for more detailed country data on tobacco use prevalence.

This report provides results of the 2009 GATS for Thailand. Data are presented in ten chapters as follows. Chapter 1: Introduction—provides an overview of the global tobacco surveillance system, the burden of tobacco use in Thailand and the survey objectives. Chapter 2: Methodology—describes the survey methods and provides information on the study population, sampling design, questionnaire, data collection and statistical analysis. Chapter 3: Sample and Population Characteristics—describes the Thai population aged 15 years and older.

The following six chapters address key survey findings by topic area covered in the survey questionnaire. These include Chapter 4: Tobacco Use; Chapter 5: Cessation; Chapter 6: Secondhand Smoke; Chapter 7: Economics (examining only manufactured cigarettes); Chapter 8: Media (focusing on smoking tobacco); and Chapter 9: Knowledge, Attitudes, & Perceptions.

Finally, Chapter 10: Conclusion and Recommendations, summarizes the results of the GATS Thailand with useful figures and tables. Throughout the report the MPOWER package—six proven tobacco control measures developed by WHO—were incorporated into the recommendations for effective monitoring of the tobacco epidemic in Thailand.

This publication contributes detailed data on the tobacco epidemic in Thailand and provides opportunities for both national and international tobacco control partners to utilize the survey findings to improve tobacco prevention and control measures in Thailand. We hope our efforts will contribute to the continued effectiveness and increased success of tobacco prevention and control programmes in Thailand.

Core staff of the GATS Thailand Working Group
October 2009

Contributors

We gratefully acknowledge the following consultants who contributed paper reviews.

Reviewers:

Dr Sawat Ramaboot	Consultant of WHO Country Office
Asst.Prof.Dr Lakkhana Termsirikulchai	Faculty of Public Health, Mahidol University
Prof.Dr Prakit Vathesatogkit	Executive Secretary of Action on Smoking and Health Foundation, Thailand (ASH Thailand)
Dr Dhirendra N Sinha	Regional Surveillance Officer, WHO Regional Office for South-East Asia, New Delhi
Dr Jason Hsia Ms Mirza Sara Dr Krishna Mohan Palipudi	Global Tobacco Unit, Office of Smoking and Health, United States Centers for Disease Control and Prevention (CDC), Atlanta, USA

Contributing authors:

Dr Sarunya Benjakul	Department of Disease Control, Ministry of Public Health
Asst.Prof.Dr Mondha Kengganpanich	Faculty of Public Health, Mahidol University
Assoc.Prof Tharadol Kengganpanich	Faculty of Public Health, Mahidol University
Ms Chitrlada Touchchai	National Statistical Office
Ms Hataichanok Puckcharern	National Statistical Office
Ms Areerat Lohtongmongkol	National Statistical Office
Mrs Wanpen Toaditep	National Statistical Office
Mr Apichat Thunyahan	National Statistical Office
Mr Saroj Nakju	GATS Office
Mr Nuttapon Theskayan	GATS Office

Acknowledgements

During the long two-year journey towards implementation and completion of the Global Adult Tobacco Survey (GATS) in Thailand, all our success has been the result of the great dedication and contributions of our partners. First of all, GATS Thailand would like to thank the Bloomberg Philanthropies for initiating this project to strengthen tobacco surveillance in high-prevalence countries. Thanks are also due to the WHO South-East Asia Regional Office (SEARO) and WHO Thailand Office, who kindly and actively facilitated development of the survey proposal and grants procedures, and aided in conducting the survey and preparing this report.

We would like to express our profound gratitude to the core technical staff that served as the team responsible for implementing the survey. This team consisted of researchers and academic officers from the Department of Disease Control, Ministry of Public Health, National Statistical Office, and Faculty of Public Health, Mahidol University, who all kindly cooperated in the completion of this survey. Our first and the highest acknowledgement goes to country policy-makers and tobacco control experts from related government and non-governmental organizations, which acted as supporting agencies.

We also appreciated the excellent cooperation from the National Statistical Office (NSO), Ministry of Information and Communication Technology, Health Systems Research Institute (HSRI), Action on Smoking and Health (ASH), Office of Thailand, Health Examination Survey, Bureau of Non-Communicable Disease Control, Department of Disease Control, Ministry of Public Health, Thailand; Health Promotion Institute and International Health Policy Program, Bureau of Policy and Strategy, Ministry of Public Health.

Our cordial thanks go to all experts, from the Global Tobacco Control Program of Office of Smoking and Health, CDC who stand behind our success.

Our final, most heartfelt acknowledgement goes to the work of Provincial Technical Officers and Field Interviewers from our Provincial Statistical Offices and all respondents who made this survey possible.

Core staff of the GATS Thailand Working Group
October 2009

Contents

Tables

3. Sample and Population Characteristics

4. Tobacco use

5. Cessation

6. Second-hand smoke

7. Economics

8. Media

9. Knowledge, attitudes and perceptions

Executive Summary

The Global Adult Tobacco Survey (GATS), 2009 in Thailand was a nationally representative household survey of all non-institutionalized men and women aged 15 years and older, designed to produce internationally comparable data on tobacco use and tobacco control measures using a standardized questionnaire, sample design, data collection and management procedures.

The survey used a three-stage stratified cluster sampling and was designed to produce key indicators for country as a whole stratified by male/ female and urban/ rural area, and by each of the five regions of the country – Bangkok metropolis, Central, North, Northeast and South. A total sample of 22 768 households were screened and 20 566 individuals aged 15 years and older were interviewed, for an overall response rate of 94.2%. Data were collected from one selected person in each household using an adapted questionnaire administered through an electronic data collection device. GATS provides information on tobacco use, cessation, second-hand smoke, economics, media, knowledge, attitudes and perceptions.

GATS was conducted by Department of Disease Control, Ministry of Public Health, the National Statistical Office, the Faculty of Public Health, at Mahidol University, and Tobacco Control Research and Knowledge Management Centre. Technical assistance was provided by the World Health Organization and the United States Centers for Disease Control and Prevention (CDC). Financial support for the survey was provided by the Bloomberg Philanthropies.

Tobacco use: Overall, 23.7% (12.5 million persons) of the Thai adult population currently smoked tobacco; 46.5% of males and 3.1% of females currently smoked. Current smoking in rural and urban areas were 24.8% and 21.5% respectively. Among the different regions, the prevalence of current smokers varied from 19.0% (Bangkok) to 29.7% (Southern region). Among all adults, 15.0% (7.9 million persons) smoked manufactured cigarettes and 14.1% (7.4 million) smoked hand-rolled cigarettes. The prevalence of hand-rolled cigarette use in rural areas (17.5%) was higher than in urban areas (6.4%).

In Thailand, 3.9% of the adult population (2 million persons) currently use smokeless tobacco. Prevalence is lower among males (1.3%) than females (6.3%).

Among male current tobacco users, 97.1% smoked tobacco only, and 2.9% used smokeless tobacco whereas among female current tobacco users, 30.8% smoked tobacco only and 69.2% used smokeless tobacco products.

Overall current tobacco use among all adults is 27.2% while 46.4% of males and 9.1% of females use tobacco in any form. Tobacco use is more prevalent in rural areas (29.2%), and among persons with a lower (primary or less than primary) education level (33.4%).

Cessation: Among 12.5 million current smokers, almost half of them (49.8 %) made an attempt to quit in the last 12 months. Among current smokers and recent quitters (<12 months) who visited any health facility, 60.2% were asked about their history of tobacco smoking while 51.9% were advised to quit smoking.

Among current smokers who attempted to quit during the past 12 months, a higher proportion of smokers reported trying to quit by their own methods (88.9%), followed by the pharmacotherapy method (10.6%) and counseling (5.8%).

Second-hand smoke (SHS): Among 52.6 million adults, 20.5 million adults (39.1%) were exposed to tobacco smoke at home. Among all employed persons who work in indoor areas, 27.2% (3.30 million) were exposed to SHS at indoor areas of the workplace, and among non-smokers who work at indoor workplaces, 23.6% (2.2 million) were exposed to SHS at these workplaces.

By gender, the estimated number of male workers exposed to SHS in indoor workplaces is twice that of female workers (2.19 million and 1.10 million). The number of non-smoking male workers who are exposed to SHS in indoor workplaces is more than the number of exposed non-smoking female workers (1.14 million and 1.08 million, respectively). The estimated number of workers living in rural areas who are exposed to SHS in indoor workplaces is almost two times that of those living in urban areas (2.01 million against 1.29 million). Similarly, more non-smoking workers from rural areas were exposed to SHS in indoor workplaces compared to non-smoking workers in urban areas (1.33 million and 0.89 million, respectively).

Economics: Among smokers, 91.2% purchased manufactured cigarettes from a grocery store and 2.6% of current smokers of such cigarettes reported that their last cigarette purchase did not have a pictorial health warning. Average cigarette expenditure per month among manufactured cigarette smokers was 575.7 Baht/month. An estimated 3.4% of national income in terms of GDP was spent to purchase manufactured cigarettes.

Media: Findings indicate that 86.9% of all persons noticed anti-smoking information and 15.9% noticed advertisements, sponsorship and promotions of tobacco products. Urban populations (90.6%) were more exposed to anti-smoking information compared to rural populations (85.3%). Exposure to anti-tobacco messages was found to be less common among persons with low socioeconomic status (SES) (lowest SES 81.0%; low SES 85.3%) compared to persons with high SES (high SES 91.5%; highest SES 92.6%). Among current smokers, 93.0% noticed pictorial health warnings on cigarette packages; 67.0% of current smokers thought about quitting smoking because of those pictures; 21.8% of current hand-rolled cigarette smokers and smokeless tobacco users noticed pictorial health warnings on shredded-tobacco packages and 15.1% thought about quitting smoking due to those pictures.

Knowledge, attitude and perceptions: Overall, 98.6% of the adults believed that smoking causes serious illnesses. However, their beliefs differ as to the causation of various diseases. In Thailand, a high proportion of adults believed that smoking causes lung cancer (97.5%), followed by mouth cancer (90.8%) and larynx cancer (91.5%), while only 79.6% of adults believed that smoking causes stroke, heart attack (75.7%) and impotence (65.7%). People in Thailand believed more often that exposure to SHS causes lung cancer in adults (90.7%) and lung illness in children (90.0%) than that it caused heart disease (64.9%), low birth weight (69.2%) and premature birth in infants (58.5%). Among all adults, 39.7% believed smoking manufactured cigarettes is more harmful than smoking hand-rolled cigarettes.

Policy implications: GATS provides critical information on key indicators of tobacco control by socio-demographic characteristics and creates an opportunity for policy-makers and the tobacco control community at different levels to make or modify targeted interventions in different areas of tobacco control. Overall, findings from GATS indicate that there is a positive environment for tobacco control. Based on the findings, the specific recommendations are:

1. Tobacco control awareness programmes should be designed in such a way that all subpopulations have equal access to the activities and information. Public health policy and interventions should cover all types of tobacco products. Periodic monitoring of tobacco use through standard surveys as GATS should be continued and integrated into tobacco control action plans and existing health systems to implement the WHO FCTC and MPOWER policy package.

2. There is a need to build capacity for programmes to foster awareness among health-care providers and to expand cessation facilities in primary health care services.

3. There is a need to formulate a 100% smoke-free policy for all public places and workplaces and to follow through with effective implementation.
4. Given the nearly equal prevalence of smoking of both manufactured and shredded tobacco products, and the large difference in taxes on these two products, there is a need to raise taxes especially for shredded tobacco products to reduce tobacco use prevalence.
5. Efforts toward effective anti-smoking media messages and pictorial health warnings on tobacco products need to be continued and there is a need to modify pictorial health warnings on shredded tobacco products for better impact.

1

Introduction

1. Introduction

Tobacco use is a major cause of preventable disease and premature death. Currently it is the cause of over 5 million deaths globally each year and this figure is expected to cross 8 million annually by 2030. If the current situation prevails, the vast majority of these deaths are projected to occur in the developing world. An efficient and systematic surveillance mechanism to monitor the epidemic is one of the essential components of a comprehensive tobacco control programme.

The World Health Organization (WHO) aims to reduce the global burden of disease and death caused by tobacco, thereby protecting present and future generations from the devastating health, social, environmental and economic consequences of tobacco consumption and exposure to tobacco smoke. This is accomplished through providing global policy leadership – promoting the WHO Framework Convention on Tobacco Control (WHO FCTC) and the MPOWER policy package[1] as a key entry point to the said Convention. The WHO Framework Convention encourages countries to adhere to its principles, and supports countries in their efforts to implement tobacco control measures through the MPOWER package.

The Bloomberg Initiative to Reduce Tobacco Use (BI) offers resources to fill the data gap in measuring adult tobacco use globally and to optimize the reach and results of the ongoing Global Tobacco Surveillance System (GTSS). The GTSS originally comprised three school-based surveys for youth and select adult populations: the Global Youth Tobacco Survey (GYTS), the Global School Personnel Survey (GSPS), and the Global Health Professional Students Survey (GHPSS).

The Global Adult Tobacco Survey (GATS) is a household survey that was launched in February 2007 as a new component of the ongoing GTSS. GATS will enable countries to collect data on adult population tobacco use and key tobacco control measures. Results from GATS will assist countries in the formulation, tracking and implementation of effective tobacco control interventions, and national survey results can be compared with that of other countries implementing GATS.

GATS was initially implemented in 14 countries where about half the world's smokers live and bear the highest burden of tobacco use. These countries are Bangladesh, Brazil, China, Egypt, India, Mexico, Philippines, Poland, the Russian Federation, Thailand, Turkey, Ukraine, Uruguay and Viet Nam.

The Centers for Disease Control and Prevention (CDC), CDC Foundation, Johns Hopkins Bloomberg School of Public Health (JHSPH), RTI International, World Health Organization and countries throughout the world are working together to design and implement GATS.

Thailand has established a tool for monitoring tobacco use over the last 30 years, using national survey data from the National Statistical Office (NSO). Data on smoking among the population aged 15 years and above are available from various surveys. However, these surveys have used different

[1] WHO's MPOWER package is a series of six proven policies aimed at reversing the global tobacco epidemic . These include: **M**onitor tobacco use and prevention policies; **P**rotect people from tobacco smoke; **O**ffer help to quit tobacco use; **W**arn about the dangers of tobacco; **E**nforce bans on tobacco advertising, promotion and sponsorship; and **R**aise taxes on tobacco.

methodology in terms of survey sampling, definitions of terms and questionnaires, etc. Some surveys have no long-term follow-up mechanism for measuring changes or trends, which impedes comparison within the country and between countries. Neither the NSO surveys nor surveys from other institutions included questions on use of smokeless tobacco. Therefore, there is no data on smokeless tobacco use available for Thailand. GATS is a standard global adult tobacco survey of households using standard protocol and produces data on adult tobacco use that can be compared across countries and provides evidence for evaluating tobacco control policies, especially the Framework Convention provisions.

1.1 Burden of tobacco use in Thailand

1.1.1 Prevalence of tobacco smoking and use of smokeless tobacco[1-2]

The Health and Welfare Survey (HWS) of households across the nation conducted by the National Statistical Office (NSO) from 1991 to 2007 showed that current smoking prevalence among adults decreased from 32.0% to 21.2%: a 33.7% decrease over 16 years. By gender, the smoking rate for males decreased from 59.3% to 41.7%, a 29.7% reduction. For females, the smoking rate decreased from 4.9% to 1.9%: a 60.9% reduction. During this period, current smoking rates decreased across respondents from all levels of educational qualifications. Persons with primary education or lesser qualification had the highest rates of current smoking prevalence in every survey, which continued declining from 38.9% in 1991 to 24.9% in 2007, a 36% decrease. Persons with a Bachelor's degree or higher level of education had the lowest current smoking prevalence which continued declining from 21.8% in 1991 to 10.6% in 2007, or a 51.5% fall. For rural areas, the smoking prevalence decreased from 34.2% to 23.4% (31.6% decrease), while the smoking prevalence in urban areas also decreased from 26.4% to 16.4% (37.9% decrease).

During the past 16 years, people in the southern region of the country experienced a decrease in the rate of smoking prevalence of 19.9%. People from the Bangkok metropolis showed had the greatest decrease, of 44.1%. Among females, the highest current smoking rate was found in the northern region (12.5% in 1991 and 5% in 2007) and the lowest rate was found in the north-eastern region (2.1% in 1991 and 0.7% in 2007). Among males, the highest current smoking rate was found in the southern region in every survey (60.9% in 1994 and down to 49.9% in 2007), and the lowest rate was found in Bangkok metropolis (45.7% in 1991 and 26.9% in 2007).

1.1.2 Tobacco consumption patterns and trends [1-2]

According to the same NSO surveys, the number of overall tobacco products smoked per day by regular smokers (including manufactured cigarettes, hand-rolled cigarettes, cigars, pipes and other smoking products) decreased from the equivalent of 12 cigarettes in 1991 to 10 cigarettes in 2007. The number of overall tobacco products smoked by male regular smokers decreased from the equivalent of 12 cigarettes in 1991 to 10 cigarettes in 2007. The number of overall tobacco products smoked by females increased from 7 per day to 8 per day during the same period.

Current tobacco users aged 15 years and above used almost equal proportions (50%) of manufactured cigarettes and hand-rolled cigarettes. Use of other tobacco products was negligible (0.1%–0.3%). Among smokers aged 15–18 years, the ratio of manufactured cigarettes to hand-rolled cigarettes smoked was 7:3. However, smokers aged 60 years and over had a reverse ratio of 2:8 on this score. Smokers with a lower educational level had a higher proportion of consumption of hand-rolled cigarettes than those with a higher educational level. The Northern region used less manufactured cigarettes than hand-rolled cigarettes, with a ratio of 4:6 in 1991 and 4:5 in 2007. Smokers in Bangkok metropolis mostly used manufactured cigarettes (94% in 1991 and 91% in 2007). While the ratio of manufactured cigarettes consumed to hand-rolled cigarettes used was 8:2 in urban areas, it was reversed to 4:6 in rural areas.

1.1.3 Economic impact of tobacco use [(1-2)]

When examining the prevalence of current smoking rates by socioeconomic status, it was observed that the lowest household SES had the highest prevalence of current smoking in every survey. For example, in 2007 the prevalence of current smoking for the lowest quintile was 20.8% and for the highest quintile was 13.9%. Over a 16-year period, the highest quintile experienced a smaller decline in current smoking rate than the lowest quintile, of 53.2% against 51.6%.

In 2001, the lowest quintile spent 16.3% of their annual household incomes on tobacco smoking-related expenditures while the highest quintile spent 3.6%. According to the recent National Survey 2007, the lowest quintile spent 8.04% of their annual household incomes on tobacco smoking expenditures while the highest quintile spent 1.18%.

Several studies in Thailand reported on smoking related morbidity data and its economic impacts. In 1991, Wanchai studied the economic impact of lung cancer, coronary heart disease (CHD), and chronic obstructive pulmonary disease (COPD) related to smoking and found that the average direct treatment costs per patient were 5 777 baht, 4 186 baht and 8 784 baht respectively[(3)]. In 1994, the estimated direct medical cost and the cost of work loss due to lung cancer caused by smoking were 2 233 million baht among a cohort of 7 800 smokers[(4)]. In 2001, Jayanton examined the impact of smoking on COPD and CHD health-care expenditure and on quality of life, and revealed that the average direct medical cost for COPD was 13 265 baht per person per year, and the total expenditure on treatment associated with CHD was 17 746 baht per person per year[(5)].

In 2004, Sathirakorn examined the costs of tobacco-related diseases in 2001 and found that the country spent at least two billion baht on treating lung cancer, CHD and COPD. The costs, including those paid by patients and those provided by government medical institutions for these three diseases were predicted to touch 53.67 billion baht in 2007[(6)]. In 2007, Leartsakulpanitch, Nganthavee and Salole analyzed the economic burden of smoking-related health care, and showed that the number of cases attributable to smoking in 2006 were 5 299 for lung cancer, 624 309 for COPD, and 52 605 for CHD. The out-of-pocket expenditures for treatment were 368.5 million baht for lung cancer, 7 714.9 million baht for COPD, and 1 773.7 million baht for CHD. Total smoking-attributable out-of-pocket costs for medical care amounted to 9 857 million baht, or 0.48% of GDP, in 2006 [(7)]. Although the estimated health-care costs related to smoking tobacco vary among these studies, they provide data to assess the larger economic burden due to tobacco use.

1.1.4 Health impact of tobacco use

Studies in Thailand suggest that tobacco use is an important risk factor for many diseases[8]. Tobacco use and second-hand smoke (SHS) exposure contribute greatly to heart disease, coronary vascular disease (CVD) and all forms of malignant neoplasm. During the post-1996 period, all forms of malignant neoplasm were the leading cause of death in Thailand, with an increase from 78.9 per 100 000 population in 2003 to 84.9 per 100 000 population in 2007[9]. The results of studies in Thailand established an association between cigarette-smoking, lung cancer[4] and laryngeal cancer[10]. Sathirakorn reported on the leading diseases caused by smoking, and found that the death rate of COPD increased from 0.07 per 100 000 population in 1989 to 4.1 per 100 000 population in 2001. In addition, the incidence rate of lung cancer also increased four-fold from 3.9 per 100 000 population in 1995 to 18.3 per 100 000 population in 2003[6].

1.2 Current tobacco control policies in Thailand

1.2.1 WHO FCTC status

Thailand signed the WHO Framework Convention on 20 June 2003 and ratified it on 8 November 2004 [11].

1.2.2 National Legislation

Thailand has a long history of anti-tobacco industry movements and of developing and implementing tobacco control programmes since 1986. Two comprehensive National Tobacco Control Acts were enacted in 1992[12]. In subsequent years, several ministerial orders were issued to improve the implementation of tobacco control policies. Existing laws in Thailand cover most of the provisions of the WHO Framework Convention[13].

1) The Tobacco Products Control Act B.E. 2535 (1992) contains the following important elements:
    a) Ban on all types of tobacco advertisements, direct and indirect, including the display of trademarks.
    b) Prohibiting all forms of sales promotion.
    c) Prohibiting cigarette vending machines.
    d) Banning cigarette sales to persons under 18 years of age.
    e) Requiring the disclosure of cigarette product ingredients to the Ministry of Public Health.
    f) Requiring legible health warning labels, with six different messages, to be placed on the front of cigarette packets.
2) The Non-Smokers' Health Protection Act B.E. 2535 (1992) was drafted with the principal purpose of protecting non-smokers' health by prohibiting smoking in public places, and included a degree of punishment for violators. There were also the 18th Ministry of Public Health Notifications that followed the Act to add to the list of non-smoking public places. The 17th Notification issued in December resulted in a total 38 compulsory smoke-free public places that can be divided into two groups:
    a) Public places that must be totally smoke-free.

b) Public places that are partially smoke-free; that is most of the area must be smoke-free except personal working spaces, personal rooms and areas designated as "smoking areas".

The recent 18th Notification issued on 11 February 2008 indicated that all food shops, restaurants, pubs, bars and marketplaces both with or without an air-conditioner must be smoke-free zones. However, food shops without an air-conditioner could provide for a smoking areas.

1.2.3 Current ongoing tobacco control initiatives

Thailand has applied several tobacco control interventions after the two laws aforementioned were enforced. These include increasing cigarette tax rates from 75% of ex-factory price to 79% in 2006 and 80% in 2008, prohibiting the sale of single sticks or small packs, prohibiting sale close to religious institutions or in the vicinity of schools, and prohibiting import of flavored cigarettes. In 2006 the pictorial health warnings on cigarette packs were increased from six pictures to nine and the use of misleading words such as "mild" or "light" was prohibited.

On 24 September 2005 Thailand applied a total ban on advertisements including display at the point of sale, and prohibited the government from accepting sponsorships or monetary support from tobacco companies. Thailand has promoted public education and the development of anti-smoking networks that provide information to target groups. The country has enhanced the quality of cigarette addiction treatment and has increased coverage through the development of guidelines for cessation clinics, a national quit helpline of 1600, capacity-building for health personnel, incorporating cessation services into primary care under the national health security system, and promoting research for further improvements[12].

At the end of 2008 the Department of Disease Control (DDC), Ministry of Public Health, launched the project "Towards 100% Smoke-Free Environments", supported by the Bloomberg Philanthropies. Thailand has also been actively involved in GTSS for many years. The first wave of the Thai Global Youth Tobacco Survey (GYTS) and Global School Personnel Survey (GSPS) were conducted in 2004 and the second round is being conducted by the Department of Disease Control (DDC). The Global Health Professions Students Survey (GHPSS), which includes 3rd year medical dentists, pharmacists, nurses, and public health, medical technology and physical therapy students, was conducted in 2006.

The success of tobacco control in Thailand is due to an active collaboration between different ministerial levels under the Bureau of Tobacco Control, including the Department of Disease Control, the Ministry of Public Health (designated as a national focal point for tobacco control), and other ministries such as the Excise Department and Customs Department, the Ministry of Finance, the National Police Office, and the Ministry of Education. The tobacco control programme receives continuous and strong support from various autonomous organizations under government supervision and nongovernment organizations (NGOs) such as the Thai Health Promotion Foundation (THPF), the Tobacco Control Research and Knowledge Management Center (TRC),

Mahidol University, the Action on Smoking or Health (ASH) Foundation, the Thai Health Promotion Institute (THPI), and the Thai Health Professional Alliance Against Tobacco (THPAAT)[(14)].

1.3 Survey objectives

The main objectives of the GATS in Thailand are to systematically monitor adult tobacco use (smoking and smokeless tobacco) and track key tobacco-control indicators in Thailand in line with WHO Framework Convention-recommended policies outlined in the MPOWER package.

2

Methodology

2. Methodology

GATS Thailand is a cross-sectional household survey that aims to produce the national- and regional-level estimates as a whole. The design also allows estimates stratified according to male and female, and urban and rural areas at the national level and only by male and female at the regional level. This chapter focuses on the survey methodology, and includes study population, eligibility criteria, sampling design, questionnaire, data collection and statistical analysis as described below:

2.1 Study population

The target population for the survey is defined as all Thai residents, aged 15 years and above, living in their primary residence prior to the survey date, excluding those living in student dormitories, military barracks, prisons or hospitals.

2.2 Eligibility criteria

The eligible respondents were all non-institutionalized persons aged 15 years and over who resided in the country and agreed to participate in this survey. For respondents aged 15–17 years, the interviewer was required to obtain a parent's or guardian's consent before starting the interview.

The respondents were excluded if their primary place of residences was in a military base or group quarters and if they were institutionalized, such as those residing in hospitals, prisons and nursing homes. Moreover, the eligible respondents were excluded when the interviewers found out later that they were less than 15 years and/or were incapacitated. In addition, the eligible respondents could withdraw from the study at any time. They also had a right to refuse to answer any question without providing any reason.

2.3 Sampling design

A three-stage stratified cluster sampling was adapted to the survey (*see details in Appendix B*). Target population was partitioned into the Bangkok metropolis area and the four regions of Central, North, Northeast and South. Each of the four regions were further stratified into urban and rural areas to create nine strata in all. At the first stage, urban blocks or rural villages were selected using probability proportional to size (PPS). The sample frame was derived from the last National Population and Housing Census data, which was conducted in 2000 by the National Statistical Office (NSO) of Thailand.

The measure of size was the number of households. At the second stage, 16 and 28 households were selected from the selected blocks in urban areas and the selected villages in rural areas respectively, using systematic random sampling. Mapping and listing were performed to update the existing frame of households. Half of the selected households were randomly assigned to be "male" households where only the males were interviewed, and the other half were assigned to "female" households where only the females were interviewed. At the last stage, one individual was randomly picked from each selected household by elementary random sampling.

2.4 Questionnaire

The GATS Thailand Questionnaire was finalized with added optional and additional country-specific questions (*see details in Appendix A*) to the GATS core questionnaire[15]. The GATS questionnaire consisted of two parts: the *household questionnaire* and the *individual questionnaire*. The individual questionnaire included the following nine topics: (i) background characteristics, (ii) tobacco smoking, (iii) smokeless tobacco, (iv) tobacco cessation, (v) second-hand smoke, (vi) economics of manufactured cigarettes, (vii) the media highlighting of both anti- and pro-tobacco information, (viii) knowledge, attitudes and perceptions, and (ix) pictorial warnings.

2.5 Data collection

The implementing agency responsible for the GATS Thailand data collection was the National Statistical Office. The NSO developed the software for the data collection device: HP iPAQ hx2490c. Prior to the data collection fieldwork, four training sessions of a total of 109 field interviewers (FIs) and 78 provincial technical officers (PTOs) were conducted by the Department of Disease Control, Ministry of Public Health, Bangkok along with the Tobacco Research and Knowledge Management Center and the Faculty of Public Health, Mahidol University, on matters of questionnaire and subject matter, and by the NSO for data collection and survey operations. The training comprised presentations, discussions (Q&A), demonstrations and practical sessions.

The fieldwork took place from 1 February 2009 to 31 May 2009. All FIs and PTOs who had participated in the workshop were distributed among all 75 provinces, including the Bangkok metropolis. Those who never attended the training workshop were not allowed to participate in the process of collecting data. Each province had 1-3 assigned FIs, except for Bangkok where there were 16 assigned FIs. Each FI was instructed to complete only 8–12 interviews each day to ensure adequate good-quality data. One PTO supervised 1–3 FIs in each province except Bangkok, which assigned 3 PTOs to supervise 16 FIs. One Field Supervisor (FS) supervised 7–12 provinces, except in the case of Bangkok, which had one dedicated FS. FSs directly coordinated with PTOs and sometimes with FIs to ensure data quality. On account of ineligible households, such as "female" households having only males, being higher than expected during data collection, additional households were selected by simple random sampling.

Several strategies to monitor fieldwork and quality control were used, including regular follow-up on the progress of data collection using NSO-developed monitoring software, and short verification interviews. A total of 1054 sampled interviewees in 75 provinces including Bangkok were selected for verification. The Kappa coefficient indicated that the data from both sources had almost perfect agreement. The value of Kappa was 0.98 for gender, 0.95 for age-group, 0.96 for tobacco smoking status and 0.93 for smokeless tobacco status. These steps greatly improved data quality and reduced non-sampling errors.

All collected data files were saved on a secured digital card (SD card) for the HP iPAQ hx2490c. The household and individual data were saved as text files (.txt) and eXtensible Markup Language (.XML) files. The data from the SD card were synchronized weekly to the provincial statistical office's desktop and then transmitted to the NSO ICT Center in Bangkok by PTOs. The IT specialist of the NSO ICT Center then received weekly output data (text files and XML files) from 75 provinces via the NSO's private e-mail. The aggregation and checking of data accuracy was done every week by using commands on Microsoft Window XP [Version 5.1.2.2600]. The GATS questionnaire program included skip patterns and some validation checks. At the end of June 2009—one month after field completion—the data from the entire Kingdom were completely checked for accuracy and the weighting and analysis process was begun.

Among the interviews, 60% used the central Thai language. About 10–14% used local Thai dialects for the Northern, Northeastern and Southern regions. Pattani, Malay and other languages were used the least.

GATS protocols for this survey were approved by the Ethical Committee of the Faculty of Public Health, Mahidol University. The Institutional Review Board (IRB) is formally designated to approve, monitor and review biomedical and behavioral research involving humans, and aims to protect the rights of the research subjects. During the process of data collection, the GATS questionnaire did not allow interviewers to interview persons aged less than 17 years without formal permission from either their parents or guardians and the consent of the respondents themselves. FIs could not conduct the interview without verbal permission from all respondents aged 18 and over. The interviewers were required to respect the confidentiality of the data collected, and were required to sign the consent form which included the GATS statement on confidentiality.

2.6 Statistical analysis

Complex survey data analysis was performed to obtain population estimates and their 95% of confidence intervals. The sample weights were developed by NSO. For each respondent, a sample weight was computed in the following weighting process. The process (*see details in Appendix B*) for the GATS included three main steps: (1) creation of the base weight or design weight, calculated from all steps of random selection in the sample design; (2) an adjustment for non-response by sample households and sample individuals eligible for the survey; and (3) a post-stratification calibration adjustment of sample totals for the projection of the population aged 15 years and above by region, area, gender and age-group. The final weights attached to each respondent were computed as the product of the base weights, the non-response adjustment and post-stratification calibration adjustment. The final weights were used in all analyses to produce estimates of population parameters and their confidence intervals. All weighting computations were carried out using SAS 9.1 and all computations of estimates and their confidence intervals were performed using the SPSS 17 complex samples module.

3

Sample and Population Characteristics

3. Sample and Population Characteristics

This chapter presents characteristics of selected samples and population. The population estimates are based on the projected population of Thailand in 2009 by the office of the National Economic and Social Development Board (NESDB)[16] in order to present a true value of population characteristics at any given time.

3.1 Household and person-level response rates

Table 3.1 presents the number of households and persons interviewed and the response rates by residence and region. Of the 22 780 sampled households, 21 390 completed the screener for a household response rate of 97.9%. Categorized by residence, 12 979 households were completed for a response rate 97.0% in urban areas and 8 411 household were completed for a response rate of 99.3% in rural areas. In different regions the response rate varied from 99.0% (North) to 94.6% (Bangkok metropolis).

Of the 21 390 sampled persons from completely screened households, 20 566 were interviewed completely for a person-level response rate of 96.2%. Categorized by residence, 12 979 and 8 411 samples were interviewed in urban and rural areas with individual-level response rates of 95.1% and 97.7% respectively. In regions the individual response rate varied from 99.2% in the Northeast to 90.0% in the Bangkok metropolis.

The overall response rate was 94.2%. This was computed as the product of the household response rate and the person-level response rate. By residence, the overall response rates in urban and rural areas were 97.1% and 92.3% respectively. By regions, overall response rates were greater than 95% in all regions except Bangkok metropolis (85.1%).

3.2 Sample and population characteristics

Table 3.2 presents the unweighted sample size and population estimates by selected demographic characteristics. The unweighted sample count (complete responses) was 20 566. The estimated total Thai population aged 15 years and above is 52.6 million in 2009. In classifying sample distribution by gender, the survey enumerated a total of 10 052 males and 10 514 females. These sample counts yield a de facto population estimate of 25.6 million males and 27.0 million females. The proportions of males and females are 48.6% and 51.4% respectively. The number of unweighted samples in urban areas is higher than in the rural areas (12 346 and 8 220 samples respectively). However, the weighted population in the rural areas is higher than urban areas, with the ratio being 7:3. The majority of the population has reported either less than a primary school education (33.7%) or completion of secondary school (33.0%) study. The Northeast represents the largest proportion of the population (33.4%) whereas Bangkok metropolis represents the smallest (10.6%). The question on income was used as a proxy for socioeconomic status (SES). Average monthly income from various sources was used to compute the quintile distribution, and the same was grouped into five exclusive SES categories: lowest, low, middle, high and highest. According to these categories, the majority of population (68.7%) has the lowest to middle SES.

Table 3.1: Number of households and persons interviewed and response rates, by residence and region (unweighted) – GATS Thailand, 2009.

	Residence		Region					Total
	Urban	Rural	Bangkok	Central	North	Northeast	South	
Selected household								
Completed	13 409	8 735	4 502	4 582	4 384	4 359	4 317	22 144
No screening respondent	21	20	0	0	14	9	18	41
Refused	323	8	248	29	14	22	18	331
Unoccupied	83	64	28	31	37	33	18	147
Address not a dwelling	17	2	3	4	8	1	3	19
Other [1]	65	33	9	24	15	18	32	98
Number of sampled households	13 918	8 862	4 790	4 670	4 472	4 442	4 406	22 780
Household response rate(%) [3]	*97.0*	*99.3*	*94.6*	*98.9*	*99.0*	*98.9*	*98.4*	*97.9*
Selected person								
Completed	12 346	8 220	4 028	4 182	4 119	4 121	4 116	20 566
Not eligible	2	1	0	0	2	0	1	3
Refused	327	36	267	54	15	10	17	363
Incapacitated	44	50	16	24	10	3	41	94
Other [2]	260	104	165	86	51	19	43	364
Number of sampled persons	12 979	8 411	4 476	4 346	4 197	4 153	4 218	21 390
Person-level response rate (%) [4]	*95.1*	*97.7*	*90.0*	*96.2*	*98.2*	*99.2*	*97.6*	*96.2*
Total response rate(%) [5]	*92.3*	*97.1*	*85.1*	*95.1*	*97.2*	*98.1*	*96.1*	*94.2*

[1] This category also includes selected households with nobody home.
[2] This category also includes selected persons who were not at home.
[3] Calculate Household Response Rate (HRR) by;

$$\frac{\text{No complete HH*100}}{\text{[No complete HH + No screening respondent + No refused HH + No other]}}$$

[4] Calculate Person-level Response Rate (IRR) by;

$$\frac{\text{No complete person*100}}{\text{[No completed + No refused HH + No incapacitated+ No other]}}$$

[5] Calculate Total Response Rate (TRR) by (HRR x IRR)/ 100

Table 3.2: Unweighted sample counts and weighted population estimates, by demographic characteristics – GATS Thailand, 2009.

Characteristic	Unweighted sample count	Weighted population estimates	
		Number	Percentage (95% CI[1])
Overall	20 566	52 621 493	100
Age (years)			
15-24	2 072	10 506 741	20.0 (18.8, 21.2)
25-44	8 145	21 783 015	41.4 (40.2, 42.7)
45-59	6 210	12 318 324	23.4 (22.6, 24.3)
60+	4 138	8 011 918	15.2 (14.5, 16.0)
Gender			
Male	10 052	25 577 110	48.6 (47.9, 49.3)
Female	10 514	27 044 383	51.4 (50.7, 52.1)
Residence			
Urban	12 346	16 346 377	31.1 (30.1, 32.0)
Rural	8 220	36 275 116	68.9 (68.0, 69.9)
Education level			
Less than primary[2]	7 810	17 722 454	33.7 (32.4, 35.0)
Primary	3 645	11 049 767	21.0 (20.0, 22.1)
Secondary	5 863	17 334 225	33.0 (31.8, 34.2)
University	3 207	6 450 544	12.3 (11.4, 13.2)
Region			
Bangkok	4 028	5 582 072	10.6 (10.1, 11.1)
Central	4 182	12 661 351	24.1 (22.9, 25.3)
North	4 119	9 808 864	18.6 (17.8, 19.5)
Northeast	4 121	17 595 058	33.4 (32.2, 34.7)
South	4 116	6 974 148	13.3 (12.5, 14.0)
Socioeconomic status			
Lowest	3 986	12 766 016	24.3 (22.7, 25.9)
Low	4 235	12 566 402	23.9 (22.5, 25.3)
Middle	4 392	10 810 512	20.5 (19.5, 21.6)
High	3 654	8 272 711	15.7 (14.9, 16.6)
Highest	4 286	8 178 440	15.6 (14.5, 16.7)

Note: The following observations were missing: 1 for age, 41 for education, and 13 for socioeconomic status (SES).

[1] 95 % confidence Interval

[2] less than a primary education level includes the population with no education.

4

Tobacco use

4. Tobacco use

This chapter presents data on tobacco use and includes information on two commonly used tobacco products in Thailand, i.e. smoked tobacco products and smokeless tobacco products. Smoked tobacco products include manufactured cigarettes, hand-rolled cigarettes, pipes, cigars, water-pipes and other smoked tobacco products. Smokeless tobacco products used include nose-/mouth-intake snuff tobacco, chewing tobacco, betel quid with tobacco and other smokeless tobacco products. This chapter presents a detailed overview of smoking status, the number of tobacco products used daily, age at the time of smoking initiation, time of quitting smoking, and first smoke of the day.

Key findings:

- *23.7% (12.5 million adults) currently smoke tobacco and 3.9% (2 million adults) currently use smokeless tobacco products.*
- *31.9% of daily manufactured cigarette smokers smoke 10–14 cigarettes per day.*
- *34.2% of ever daily smokers, 20–34 years old, start smoking daily at the age of 20 years and above.*
- *28.8% of those who have ever smoked on a daily basis have quit smoking.*
- *35.7% of daily smokers have the first cigarette of the day between six and thirty minutes of waking up.*

4.1 Prevalence of tobacco use

4.1.1 Prevalence of smoking tobacco (%):

In Table 4.1 the prevalence of smoking tobacco is presented by "current tobacco smoker" and "non-smoker". Current tobacco smokers are categorized into "daily smokers" and "occasional smokers". Non-smokers are categorized into "former daily smokers" and "never daily smokers". The overall prevalence rate of current smokers is 23.7%. It is particularly high among males who have 15 times the prevalence rate as compared with females (45.6% against 3.1%). Among current smokers, 20.3% are daily smokers and 3.4% are occasional smokers. The daily smoking prevalence rate among males is 16 times that of females (39.2% against 2.4%). The occasional smoker prevalence rate among males is nine times that of females (6.3% and 0.7% respectively).

Non-smokers account for 76.3% of the surveyed population. Among them, 8.9% are former daily smokers and 67.4% are never daily smokers. For those who are never daily smokers, the survey found that 64.2% have never smoked in their lifetime and 3.2% are former occasional smokers.

Table 4.1: Percentage of adults ≥15 years old, by smoking status and gender – GATS Thailand, 2009.

Smoking status	Overall	Male	Female
		Percentage (95% CI)	
Current tobacco smoker	23.7 (22.8, 24.7)	45.6 (43.8, 47.4)	3.1 (2.7, 3.6)
Daily smoker	20.3 (19.4, 21.2)	39.2 (37.5, 41.0)	2.4 (2.0, 2.9)
Occasional smoker	3.4 (3.0, 3.9)	6.3 (5.5, 7.2)	0.7 (0.5, 0.9)
Occasional smoker, formerly daily	1.5 (1.3, 1.9)	2.9 (2.4, 3.6)	0.3 (0.2, 0.4)
Occasional smoker, never daily	1.9 (1.6, 2.2)	3.4 (2.9, 4.1)	0.4 (0.3, 0.6)
Non-smoker	76.3 (75.3, 77.2)	54.4 (52.6, 56.2)	96.9 (96.4, 97.3)
Former daily smoker	8.9 (8.3, 9.5)	16.7 (15.5, 18.0)	1.4 (1.1, 1.7)
Never daily smoker	67.4 (66.4, 68.4)	37.7 (35.8, 39.6)	95.5 (94.8, 96.1)
Former occasional smoker	3.2 (2.8, 3.7)	5.4 (4.7, 6.2)	1.1 (0.9, 1.4)
Never smoker	64.2 (63.2, 65.2)	32.3 (30.4, 34.2)	94.4 (93.6, 95.0)

Note: Current smoked tobacco use includes both daily and occasional (less than daily) use.

Table 4.1.1 presents the prevalence rate of smoking tobacco according to detailed smoking status, residence and region. Current smokers in rural areas have a higher prevalence rate of smoking than those in urban areas (24.8% and 21.5% respectively). Among the different regions, the highest prevalence of current smokers is in the Southern region (29.7%), followed by the Northeast (23.9%). Bangkok metropolis has the lowest prevalence (19.0%). Among current smokers, daily smokers and occasional smokers in rural areas have a higher rate of consumption than those living in urban areas. Non-smokers in rural areas have lower rates than those in urban areas (75.2% and 78.5%).

When examining current smokers by region, the highest prevalence of daily smokers is found in the Southern region (25.7%) and the lowest in the Bangkok metropolis (16.7%). The highest and lowest rates of occasional smokers are found in the Northern region and Bangkok metropolis (4.2% and 2.3% respectively). The highest and lowest prevalence of non-smokers is found in Bangkok metropolis and the Southern region (81.0% and 70.3% respectively).

Classified by gender, residence and region, the prevalence rate of current smokers in rural areas is higher than those in urban areas (47.1% and 41.9%), 40.5% of urban males are daily smokers, 6.6% are occasional smokers, and 52.9% are non-smokers. Among males in rural areas, 36.2% are daily smokers, 5.7% occasional smokers, and 58.1% non-smokers. Males in the Southern region have the highest rate of current smokers (57.5%) while Bangkok metropolis has the lowest (38.0%). Males in the Southern region also have the highest rate of daily smoking (50.0%) while the lowest rate of daily smoking is in the Northern region (32.8%).

Among females, the prevalence rate of current smokers in urban areas is similar to those in rural areas (3.3% and 3%); 2.6% of female urban current smokers are daily smokers, 0.7% are occasional smokers and 96.7% are non-smokers. Among females in rural areas, 2.3% are daily smokers, 0.7% occasional smokers and 97.0% non-smokers. Females living in the Northern region have the highest rate of current and daily smokers (5.8% current and 4.6% daily) and those in the Northeastern region have the lowest rate of current and daily smokers (1% current and 0.8% daily).

Table 4.1.1: Percentage of adults ≥15 years old, by smoking status, residence and region – GATS Thailand, 2009.

Smoking status	Residence		Region				
	Urban	Rural	Bangkok	Central	North	Northeast	South
	Percentage (95% CI)						
Overall adults ≥15 years old							
Current tobacco smoker	21.5 (20.6, 22.4)	24.8 (23.5, 26.1)	19.0 (17.5, 20.5)	23.2 (21.5, 25.0)	22.6 (20.5, 24.8)	23.9 (21.9, 26.0)	29.7 (27.6, 31.9)
Daily smoker	18.5 (17.6, 19.3)	21.2 (19.9, 22.5)	16.7 (15.5, 18.1)	19.4 (17.8, 21.2)	18.4 (16.4, 20.7)	21.0 (19.1, 23.0)	25.7 (23.7, 27.8)
Occasional smoker	3.0 (2.7, 3.5)	3.6 (3.0, 4.3)	2.3 (1.8, 2.8)	3.8 (3.1, 4.6)	4.2 (3.2, 5.4)	2.9 (2.1, 4.0)	4.0 (3.0, 5.4)
Occasional smoker, formerly daily	1.5 (1.2, 1.8)	1.6 (1.2, 2.0)	1.0 (0.7, 1.5)	1.9 (1.4, 2.6)	1.9 (1.3, 2.8)	1.2 (0.7, 2.1)	1.5 (1.1, 2.2)
Occasional smoker, never daily	1.5 (1.3, 1.8)	2.0 (1.6, 2.5)	1.2 (0.9, 1.6)	1.9 (1.4, 2.5)	2.2 (1.6, 3.0)	1.7 (1.1, 2.5)	2.5 (1.8, 3.5)
Non-smoker	78.5 (77.6, 79.4)	75.2 (73.9, 76.5)	81.0 (79.5, 82.5)	76.8 (75.0, 78.5)	77.4 (75.2, 79.5)	76.1 (74.0, 78.1)	70.3 (68.1, 72.4)
Former daily smoker	8.3 (7.8, 8.9)	9.1 (8.3, 10.0)	8.2 (7.3, 9.1)	8.2 (7.3, 9.2)	11.6 (10.1, 13.2)	9.2 (7.9, 10.6)	6.0 (5.2, 7.0)
Never daily smoker	70.2 (69.2, 71.1)	66.1 (64.8, 67.5)	72.9 (71.3, 74.4)	68.6 (66.7, 70.4)	65.9 (63.5, 68.1)	66.9 (64.8, 69.0)	64.3 (62.0, 66.5)
Former occasional smoker	3.1 (2.7, 3.5)	3.3 (2.7, 3.9)	2.7 (2.1, 3.5)	3.6 (2.8, 4.6)	4.0 (3.1, 5.2)	3.3 (2.5, 4.3)	1.6 (1.2, 2.0)
Never smoker	67.1 (66.1, 68.1)	62.9 (61.5, 64.3)	70.1 (68.5, 71.7)	65.0 (63.0, 67.0)	61.8 (59.4, 64.2)	63.6 (61.5, 65.7)	62.7 (60.4, 65.0)
Male							
Current tobacco smoker	41.9 (40.1, 43.7)	47.1 (44.7, 49.6)	38.0 (35.0, 41.0)	43.8 (40.8, 46.8)	40.0 (36.3, 43.9)	47.4 (43.3, 51.5)	57.5 (54.1, 60.8)
Daily smoker	36.2 (34.6, 37.9)	40.5 (38.1, 43.0)	33.6 (30.9, 36.3)	37.1 (34.2, 40.1)	32.8 (29.0, 36.8)	41.7 (37.8, 45.7)	50.0 (46.5, 53.5)
Occasional smoker	5.7 (4.9, 6.5)	6.6 (5.5, 7.9)	4.4 (3.4, 5.6)	6.7 (5.4, 8.3)	7.2 (5.5, 9.5)	5.7 (4.1, 7.8)	7.4 (5.5, 10.0)
Occasional smoker, formerly daily	2.8 (2.3, 3.5)	3.0 (2.2, 3.9)	2.0 (1.4, 2.9)	3.8 (2.7, 5.3)	3.3 (2.2, 4.8)	2.4 (1.4, 4.2)	2.7 (1.9, 3.9)
Occasional smoker, never daily	2.9 (2.4, 3.4)	3.6 (2.9, 4.6)	2.4 (1.7, 3.2)	2.9 (2.1, 3.9)	4.0 (2.8, 5.5)	3.2 (2.2, 4.8)	4.7 (3.3, 6.7)
Non-smoker	58.1 (56.3, 59.9)	52.9 (50.4, 55.3)	62.0 (59.0, 65.0)	56.2 (53.2, 59.2)	60.0 (56.1, 63.7)	52.6 (48.5, 56.7)	42.5 (39.2, 45.9)
Former daily smoker	16.1 (15.0, 17.2)	17.0 (15.4, 18.8)	16.3 (14.4, 18.3)	15.7 (13.9, 17.6)	20.0 (17.3, 23.0)	17.9 (15.2, 21.0)	11.5 (9.8, 13.3)
Never daily smoker	42.1 (40.4, 43.8)	35.8 (33.2, 38.5)	45.8 (42.9, 48.7)	40.5 (37.5, 43.6)	40.0 (35.9, 44.1)	34.7 (30.3, 39.3)	31.1 (27.9, 34.4)
Former occasional smoker	5.0 (4.3, 5.8)	5.6 (4.6, 6.7)	4.4 (3.2, 5.9)	5.9 (4.5, 7.7)	6.4 (4.9, 8.4)	5.9 (4.5, 7.6)	2.7 (2.0, 3.7)
Never smoker	37.0 (35.4, 38.7)	30.2 (27.6, 32.9)	41.4 (38.7, 44.2)	34.6 (31.4, 38.0)	33.5 (29.6, 37.6)	28.8 (24.6, 33.4)	28.3 (25.1, 31.8)
Female							
Current tobacco smoker	3.3 (2.8, 3.8)	3.0 (2.4, 3.8)	3.0 (2.3, 3.9)	4.1 (3.1, 5.3)	5.8 (4.2, 8.0)	1.0 (0.6, 1.6)	2.9 (2.1, 3.9)
Daily smoker	2.6 (2.1, 3.1)	2.4 (1.8, 3.0)	2.6 (1.9, 3.4)	3.0 (2.2, 4.0)	4.6 (3.2, 6.7)	0.8 (0.4, 1.5)	2.2 (1.5, 3.1)
Occasional smoker	0.7 (0.5, 1.0)	0.7 (0.5, 1.0)	0.5 (0.2, 0.9)	1.1 (0.6, 1.9)	1.2 (0.8, 1.9)	0.2 (0.1, 0.4)	0.7 (0.4, 1.3)
Occasional smoker, formerly daily	0.4 (0.2, 0.5)	0.2 (0.1, 0.4)	0.2 (0.1, 0.7)	0.2 (0.1, 0.5)	0.6 (0.4, 1.1)	0.0 (0.0, 0.1)	0.4 (0.2, 0.9)
Occasional smoker, never daily	0.3 (0.2, 0.5)	0.5 (0.3, 0.8)	0.2 (0.1,0.4)	0.9 (0.5, 1.7)	0.6 (0.3, 1.0)	0.1 (0.0, 0.3)	0.3 (0.2, 0.7)
Non-smoker	96.7 (96.2, 97.2)	97.0 (96.2, 97.6)	97.0 (96.1, 97.7)	95.9 (94.7, 96.9)	94.2 (92.0, 95.8)	99.0 (98.4, 99.4)	97.1 (96.1, 97.9)
Former daily smoker	1.4 (1.1, 1.8)	1.4 (1.0, 1.9)	1.3 (0.8, 2.1)	1.2 (0.8, 1.9)	3.4 (2.5, 4.7)	0.7 (0.3, 1.3)	0.8 (0.5, 1.2)
Never daily smoker	95.3 (94.6, 95.9)	95.6 (94.6, 96.3)	95.7 (94.6, 96.5)	94.7 (93.3, 95.8)	90.7 (88.2, 92.7)	98.4 (97.2, 99.0)	96.3 (95.1, 97.2)
Former occasional smoker	1.3 (1.0, 1.8)	1.0 (0.7, 1.5)	1.3 (0.8, 2.3)	1.4 (0.9, 2.1)	1.8 (1.2, 2.5)	0.7 (0.3, 1.7)	0.4 (0.2, 0.8)
Never smoker	94.0 (93.2, 94.7)	94.5 (93.5, 95.4)	94.3 (93.0, 95.4)	93.3 (91.7, 94.5)	89.0 (86.4, 91.1)	97.6 (96.3, 98.5)	95.9 (94.6, 96.8)

Note: Current smoked tobacco use includes both daily and occasional (less than daily) use.

4.1.2 Prevalence of smokeless tobacco use (%)

Table 4.1a shows that smokeless tobacco use in Thailand is mostly in the form of shredded tobacco or chewing tobacco used with betel quid, which is more common among females. Current smokeless tobacco use is quite low with an overall prevalence rate of only 3.9%. Among females, the prevalence of smokeless tobacco use (6.3%) is five times that of use of smoking tobacco (1.3%). Overall daily smokeless tobacco use is 3.4% and the female prevalence rate for this is 6.5 times that of the male prevalence rate (5.8% for females against 0.9% for males). Overall occasional smokeless tobacco consumption is only 0.5% and is distributed equally for both genders.

Table 4.1a: Percentage of adults ≥15 years old, by smokeless tobacco use status and gender – GATS Thailand, 2009.

Smokeless tobacco use status	Overall	Male	Female
		Percentage (95% CI)	
Current smokeless tobacco user	3.9 (3.4, 4.4)	1.3 (1.1, 1.7)	6.3 (5.5, 7.2)
Daily smokeless user	3.4 (3.0, 3.9)	0.9 (0.7, 1.2)	5.8 (5.0, 6.7)
Occasional smokeless user	0.5 (0.4, 0.6)	0.4 (0.3, 0.6)	0.5 (0.4, 0.7)
Occasional smokeless user, formerly daily	0.1 (0.1, 0.2)	0.1 (0.1, 0.2)*	0.1 (0.1,0.3)*
Occasional smokeless user, never daily	0.4 (0.3, 0.5)	0.3 (0.2, 0.5)	0.4 (0.3, 0.6)
Non-smokeless tobacco user	96.1 (95.6, 96.6)	98.7 (98.3, 98.9)	93.7 (92.8, 94.5)
Former daily smokeless user	0.6 (0.4, 0.7)	0.4 (0.3, 0.6)	0.7 (0.5, 1.0)
Never daily smokeless user	95.5 (95.0, 96.0)	98.3 (97.9, 98.6)	92.9 (92.0, 93.8)
Former occasional smokeless user	0.5 (0.4, 0.7)	0.8 (0.6, 1.0)	0.3 (0.2, 0.5)
Never smokeless user	95.0 (94.5, 95.5)	97.5 (97.1, 97.9)	92.7 (91.7, 93.5)

Note: Current use includes both daily and occasional (less than daily) use.
* Indicates that estimate is based on sample size of less than 25.

4.2 Number of tobacco users

4.2.1 Number of smoked tobacco users:

Table 4.2 presents the prevalence figures for smoked tobacco. The estimated number of adult smokers in Thailand is 12.49 million. Among them 11.65 million are male and 0.84 million are female. The number of daily smokers is 10.69 million (10.04 million males and 0.66 million females). The number of occasional smokers is 1.80 million (1.62 million males and 0.18 million females). The number of non-smokers is 40.13 million (13.93 million males and 26.20 million females). Among the non-smokers, 4.66 million are former daily smokers and 35.47 million have never been daily smokers. As for those who never smoked tobacco, the survey found that 33.78 million have never smoked in their lifetime and 1.69 million are former occasional smokers.

Table 4.2: Number (in thousands) of adults ≥15 years old, by smoking status and gender – GATS Thailand, 2009.

Smoking status	Overall	Male	Female
Current tobacco smoker	12 492.3	11 652.0	840.3
Daily smoker	10 691.1	10 035.2	655.9
Occasional smoker	1 801.3	1 616.8	184.5
Occasional smoker, formerly daily	814.2	744.7	69.6
Occasional smoker, never daily	987.0	872.1	114.9
Non-smoker	40 129.1	13 925.1	26 204.1
Former daily smoker	4 663.7	4 282.9	380.8
Never daily smoker	35 465.4	9 642.2	25 823.2
Former occasional smoker	1 688.5	1 385.0	303.4
Never smoker	33 777.0	8 257.1	25 519.8

Note: Current use include both daily and occasional (less than daily) use.
(Note: The sum of the counts across subgroups might not exactly add up to the overall counts due to rounding off.)

4.2.2 Number of smokeless tobacco use:

Based on Table 4.2a, the estimated number of users of smokeless tobacco is 2.05 million (1.71 million females and 0.34 million males). The number of daily smokeless tobacco users is 1.79 million and the number of occasional smokeless tobacco users is 0.25 million. The number of persons who have never used smokeless tobacco is 50.57 million. Among persons who have never used smokeless tobacco, 50 million have never smoked in their lifetime and 0.27 million are former occasional users of smokeless tobacco.

Table 4.2a: Number (in thousands) of adults ≥15 years old, by smokeless tobacco use status and gender – GATS Thailand, 2009.

Smokeless tobacco use status	Overall	Male	Female
Current smokeless tobacco user	2 047.6	339.3	1 708.3
Daily smokeless user	1 797.1	233.7	1 563.4
Occasional smokeless user	250.5	105.6	144.9
Occasional smokeless user, formerly daily	64.6	25.2*	39.5*
Occasional smokeless user, never daily	185.9	80.4	105.4
Non-smokeless tobacco user	50 573.2	25 237.2	25 336.1
Former daily smokeless user	298.8	99.8	199.0
Never daily smokeless user	50 274.4	25 137.4	25 137.0
Former occasional smokeless user	272.1	194.6	77.5
Never smokeless user	50 002.3	24 942.8	25 059.5

Note: Current use includes both daily and occasional (less than daily) use.
(Note: The sum of the counts across subgroups might not exactly add up to the overall counts due to rounding off.)
* Indicates that estimate is based on sample size of less than 25.

4.3 Prevalence of current smokers by smoked tobacco products

Table 4.3 presents data on smoked tobacco products. In Thailand these products include cigarettes and other smoked tobacco products such as pipes, cigars, *khi-yo* (a local cigarette from the Northern region), cheroots (Myanmarese cigarettes), water-pipes, *hookah*s and others. Cigarettes are of two categories: manufactured cigarettes and hand-rolled cigarettes. The overall prevalence rate of current smokers of any smoked tobacco product is 23.7%. The prevalence rate of smokers who use either manufactured or hand-rolled cigarettes is 23.5%. The prevalence rates for manufactured cigarettes and hand-rolled cigarettes are nearly equal at 15% and 14.1% respectively. The prevalence other smoked tobacco products is minimal, at 0.3%.

There is a 14-fold difference between the prevalence rate for current smoking of any smoked tobacco product between males and females (45.6% and 3.1% respectively). Use of manufactured cigarettes is higher than that of hand-rolled cigarettes among both males and females. Classified by age groups, the highest smoking rate is found among persons aged between 25 and 44 years (26.5%), followed by those of the 45–59-year age-group (24%). Use of manufactured cigarettes is mostly found among those of 25–44 years of age (18.7%) and persons aged between 15 and 24 years (17.9%). In contrast, use of hand-rolled cigarettes is more common among persons aged 60 years and older as against younger age groups and the rate is approximately twice that of the 15-24-year age-group (17.1% and 8.7% respectively).

By residence, the prevalence rate for any smoked tobacco product among the rural population is 3% higher than that for the urban population (24.8% and 21.5%). The type of smoked tobacco products used also differs between urban and rural smokers. The results show a higher prevalence of use of manufactured cigarettes in urban areas than rural areas (17.7% and 13.7% respectively) and a higher prevalence of use of hand-rolled cigarettes in rural areas as against urban areas (17.5% and 6.4% respectively). Classified by education, the prevalence rate of any smoked tobacco product is highest among those with a education up to primary level (29.2%), followed by those with education of less than primary level (24.3%). The types of smoked tobacco products used also varies by different educational levels. Persons with primary and secondary education tend to use manufactured cigarettes while persons with primary and less than primary education tend to use hand-rolled cigarettes.

Table 4.3: Percentage of adults ≥15 years old who are current smokers of various smoked tobacco products, by selected demographic characteristics – GATS Thailand, 2009.

Characteristic	Any smoked tobacco product	Any cigarette[1]	Type of cigarette		Other smoked tobacco[2]
			Manufactured	Hand-rolled	
			Percentage (95% CI)		
Overall	23.7 (22.8, 24.7)	23.5 (22.6, 24.5)	15.0 (14.2, 15.8)	14.1 (13.2, 15.0)	0.3 (0.1, 0.5)
Gender					
Male	45.6 (43.8, 47.4)	45.4 (43.6, 47.2)	29.6 (28.1, 31.1)	27.0 (25.2, 28.9)	0.3 (0.1, 0.5)
Female	3.1 (2.7, 3.6)	2.8 (2.4, 3.3)	1.1 (0.9, 1.4)	1.8 (1.5, 2.2)	0.3 (0.1, 0.7)
Age (years)					
15-24	19.8 (17.4, 22.4)	19.7 (17.3, 22.3)	17.9 (15.6, 20.5)	8.7 (7.0, 10.7)	0.3 (0.1, 0.6)*
25-44	26.5 (25.2, 27.9)	26.5 (25.1, 27.9)	18.7 (17.6, 19.9)	14.4 (13.1, 15.9)	0.1 (0.0, 0.2)*
45-59	24.0 (22.6, 25.5)	23.7 (22.3, 25.1)	12.0 (11.0, 13.1)	16.0 (14.6, 17.5)	0.4 (0.2, 0.8)*
60+	21.0 (19.3, 22.7)	20.5 (18.8, 22.2)	5.4 (4.6, 6.3)	17.1 (15.5, 18.8)	0.6 (0.3, 1.3)*
Residence					
Urban	21.5 (20.6, 22.4)	21.4 (20.5, 22.4)	17.7 (16.9, 18.6)	6.4 (5.9, 7.1)	0.1 (0.1, 0.3)*
Rural	24.8 (23.5, 26.1)	24.5 (23.2, 25.8)	13.7 (12.7, 14.8)	17.5 (16.2, 18.9)	0.3 (0.2, 0.7)
Education level					
Less than primary	24.3 (22.9, 25.8)	23.8 (22.4, 25.2)	8.1 (7.4, 9.0)	19.5 (18.2, 20.9)	0.6 (0.3, 1.3)
Primary	29.2 (26.9, 31.5)	29.1 (26.9, 31.4)	18.6 (16.8, 20.6)	19.7 (17.7, 22.0)	0.1 (0.0, 0.4)*
Secondary	23.3 (21.5, 25.1)	23.2 (21.5, 25.0)	20.2 (18.7, 21.8)	9.1 (7.9, 10.5)	0.1 (0.0, 0.1)*
University	14.3 (12.5, 16.2)	14.3 (12.5, 16.2)	13.4 (11.6, 15.3)	2.8 (2.0, 3.9)	0.1 (0.0, 0.3)*
Region					
Bangkok	19.0 (17.5, 20.5)	19.0 (17.5, 20.5)	17.5 (16.2, 18.9)	2.6 (2.1, 3.2)	0.1 (0.0, 0.2)*
Central	23.2 (21.5, 25.0)	23.2 (21.5, 25.0)	15.8 (14.5, 17.2)	10.8 (9.2, 12.7)	0.1 (0.0, 0.3)*
North	22.6 (20.5, 24.8)	21.5 (19.6, 23.6)	10.9 (9.5, 12.6)	12.9 (11.0, 15.0)	1.3 (0.6, 2.6)
Northeast	23.9 (21.9, 26.0)	23.9 (21.9, 26.0)	14.2 (12.6, 15.9)	17.2 (15.2, 19.3)	0.0 (0.0, 0.1)*
South	29.7 (27.6, 31.9)	29.7 (27.6, 31.9)	19.0 (16.9, 21.2)	23.0 (20.9, 25.2)	0.1 (0.0, 0.2)*
Socioeconomic status					
Lowest	17.9 (16.2, 19.8)	17.4 (15.7, 19.2)	7.5 (6.2, 9.1)	13.4 (11.9, 15.2)	0.6 (0.3, 1.6)
Low	23.7 (21.8, 25.8)	23.5 (21.6, 25.5)	11.9 (10.4, 13.6)	16.8 (15.2, 18.6)	0.3 (0.0, 0.8)*
Middle	29.2 (27.2, 31.4)	29.2 (27.1, 31.3)	20.5 (18.6, 22.5)	17.1 (15.3, 19.0)	0.1 (0.0, 0.3)*
High	28.4 (26.2, 30.7)	28.4 (26.2, 30.7)	21.4 (19.5, 23.4)	14.4 (12.4, 16.7)	0
Highest	20.9 (19.2, 22.7)	20.9 (19.2, 22.7)	17.6 (16.0, 19.2)	6.5 (5.3, 7.9)	0.1 (0.0, 0.2)*

Note: Current use includes both daily and occasional (less than daily) use.
[1] Includes manufactured cigarettes and hand-rolled cigarettes.
[2] Includes pipes, cigars/cheroots/cigarillos, water-pipes and others.
* Indicates that estimate is based on sample size of less than 25.

The prevalence rate for current smokers who use any smoked tobacco products also differs among regions. The highest prevalence of any smoked tobacco product is in the Southern region (29.7%) and the lowest is in Bangkok metropolis (19.0%). The highest rate of use of manufactured cigarettes is in the Southern region (19.0%) followed by Bangkok metropolis (17.5%). The lowest rate is in the Northern region (10.9%). Use of hand-rolled cigarettes is also highest in the South (23.0%), followed by the Northeast and North (17.2% and 12.9% respectively). The lowest prevalence of hand-rolled cigarettes is found in Bangkok metropolis (2.6%). The highest rate of consumption of any smoked tobacco products is found among the moderate and high SES categories (29.2% and 28.4%). These findings are in contrast to the findings of the national surveys conducted by the NSO during 1991-2007. Survey findings indicate that smokers with a higher socioeconomic status tend to use manufactured cigarettes while users with moderate and lower SES tend to use hand-rolled cigarettes.

4.4 Number of current smokers by smoked tobacco products

Table 4.4 (based on Table 4.3) presents the estimated number of current smokers who smoked various tobacco products: 12.49 million persons. This indicates a very high national burden of tobacco use. The number of hand-rolled cigarette users (7.40 million) is almost the same as the number of users of manufactured cigarettes (7.87 million). The number of smokers who use other smoked tobacco products such as pipes, cigar, *khi-yo*, cheroots, water-pipes, *hookah*s and the like is relatively low (0.14 million).

By gender, the number of male smokers who use any smoked tobacco product is 11.65 million. The number of male smokers who use manufactured cigarettes is higher than the number of those who use hand-rolled cigarettes (7.56 million and 6.91 million). The number of female current smokers (0.84 million) is about 12 times less than male current smokers. However, female smokers use more hand-rolled cigarettes than manufactured cigarettes (0.49 million and 0.31 million).

The 25–44 year age group has the highest number of smokers in all categories of smoked tobacco products, i.e. any smoked tobacco product (5.78 million), manufactured cigarettes (4.07 million) and hand-rolled cigarettes (3.15 million).

The overall number of smokers in rural areas (8.98 million) is almost thrice that in urban areas (3.51 million). The results also show that hand-rolled cigarettes are more common in rural than urban areas. By residence, the number of smokers of manufactured cigarettes in rural areas (4.98 million) is approximately twice that in urban areas (2.89 million). The number of hand-rolled-cigarette smokers in rural areas (6.35 million) is about six times the number found in urban areas (1.05 million).

By education, the overall number of smokers is quite high among persons with an education of less than primary level (4.31 million) and those with only secondary-level education (4.03 million). The highest number of smokers of manufactured cigarettes is found among those with at least a secondary education level (3.51 million) while highest use of hand-rolled cigarettes is found among those with an education level of less than primary (3.45 million). The lowest degree of use of hand-rolled cigarettes is found among those with university-level education (0.18 million).

Table 4.4: Number (in thousands) of adults ≥15 years old who are current smokers of various smoked tobacco products, by selected demographic characteristics – GATS Thailand, 2009.

Characteristic	Any smoked tobacco product	Any cigarette[1]	Type of cigarette		Other smoked tobacco[2]
			Manufactured	Hand-rolled	
Overall	12 492.3	12 381.6	7 873.0	7 401.3	144.7
Gender					
Male	11 652.0	11 615.5	7 565.0	6 905.9	64.6
Female	840.3	766.0	308.0	495.3	80.1
Age (years)					
15-24	2 081.4	2 064.6	1 883.2	912.4	27.4
25-44	5 775.9	5 763.0	4 075.9	3 145.5	19.3*
45-59	2 954.8	2 914.1	1 481.3	1 970.9	50.8*
60+	1 680.2	1 639.9	432.6	1 372.4	47.3*
Residence					
Urban	3 513.7	3 504.7	2 892.9	1 053.6	21.6*
Rural	8 978.6	8 876.9	4 980.1	6 347.6	123.1
Education level					
Less than primary	4 308.1	4 210.7	1 443.0	3 453.4	114.0
Primary	3 223.4	3 215.5	2 058.1	2 180.7	14.8*
Secondary	4 032.6	4 027.1	3 505.1	1 582.7	8.7*
University	921.1	921.1	862.5	181.7	7.2*
Region					
Bangkok	1 060.2	1 059.8	975.6	144.8	3.7*
Central	2 940.7	2 938.5	2 005.4	1 367.4	8.3*
North	2 216.3	2 113.2	1 073.7	1 262.9	123.0
Northeast	4 204.5	4 200.4	2 495.8	3 023.8	5.2*
South	2 070.6	2 069.6	1 322.5	1 602.3	4.6*
Socioeconomic status					
Lowest	2 288.5	2 216.5	955.0	1 716.5	83.0
Low	2 982.4	2 949.8	1 497.0	2 113.6	43.1*
Middle	3 161.2	3 156.1	2 214.0	1 844.0	11.2*
High	2 348.9	2 348.3	1 767.8	1 194.4	0.0
Highest	1 707.0	1 706.6	1 437.7	530.0	7.5*

Note: Current use includes both daily and occasional (less than daily) use.

(Note: The sum of the counts across subgroups might not exactly add up to the overall counts due to rounding off and/or missing data.)

* Indicates that estimate is based on sample size of less than 25.

[1] Includes manufactured cigarettes and hand-rolled cigarettes.

[2] Includes pipes, cigars, cheroots, cigarillos, water-pipes and others.

Based on Table 4.4, the number of smoked tobacco users also differ by regions. The highest number of smokers is found in the Northeast (4.2 million) followed by the Central region (2.94 million). The number of users of manufactured cigarettes is highest in the Northeast (2.49 million) followed by the Central region (2.01 million) whereas the number of users of hand-rolled cigarettes is high in the Northeast (3.02 million), followed by the Southern region (1.60 million). Classified by SES status, the highest number of smoked tobacco users is among those with moderate SES (3.16 million) followed by those with low SES (2.98 million). Classified by type of smoked cigarettes, use of manufactured cigarettes is highest among those with middle SES (2.21 million) and that of hand-rolled cigarettes is the highest among those with low SES (2.11 million).

4.5 Smoking frequency

Table 4.5 reports smoking frequency as three standard categories: "daily smokers", "occasional smokers" and "non-smokers". The percentages of adults aged 15 years and above who are daily smokers, occasional smokers and non-smokers are 20.3%, 3.4% and 76.3% respectively. The percentage of male daily smokers is 39.2% and of female daily smokers is 2.4%. The percentage of male occasional smokers is nine times that of females (6.3% and 0.7% respectively). When classified by age-group, the highest percentages of daily smokers are found in the 25–44 year and 45–59 year age-groups (22.7% and 21.8%). The highest percentages of occasional smokers are in the age-group of 15–24 years and 25–44 years (5.2% and 3.8% respectively).

Classified by residence, the percentage of daily smokers in rural areas (21.2%) is higher than that in urban areas (18.5%), which is similar in the case of occasional smokers (rural 3.6% and urban 3.0%). Classified by educational levels, the percentage of daily smokers is high among those with primary and less-than-primary education levels (25.6% and 22.4% respectively) while the percentage of occasional smokers is higher among secondary and primary education levels (5.0% and 3.6% respectively). Classified by region, the percentage of daily smokers is higher in the South (25.7%) and Northeast (21.0%) while the percentage of occasional smokers is higher in the North (4.2%) and South (4.0%). Viewed by socioeconomic status, the percentage of daily smokers is high in middle and high SES (25.1% and 24.6% respectively) categories. This is similar among occasional smokers with 4.2% and 3.8% being in the middle and high SES categories respectively.

Table 4.5: Percentage distribution of adults ≥15 years old who are daily, occasional or non-smokers, by selected demographic characteristics – GATS Thailand, 2009.

Characteristic	Smoking frequency			Total
	Daily	Occasional[1]	Non-smoker	
	Percentage (95% CI)			
Overall	20.3 (19.4, 21.2)	3.4 (3.0, 3.9)	76.3 (75.3, 77.2)	100
Gender				
Male	39.2 (37.5, 41.0)	6.3 (5.5, 7.2)	54.5 (52.6, 56.2)	100
Female	2.4 (2.0, 2.9)	0.7 (0.5, 0.9)	96.9 (96.4, 97.3)	100
Age (years)				
15-24	14.6 (12.4, 17.2)	5.2 (3.9, 6.8)	80.2 (77.6, 82.6)	100
25-44	22.7 (21.4, 24.0)	3.8 (3.2, 4.5)	73.5 (72.1, 74.8)	100
45-59	21.8 (20.4, 23.3)	2.2 (1.8, 2.6)	76.0 (74.5, 77.4)	100
60+	19.0 (17.5, 20.7)	1.9 (1.5, 2.5)	79.1 (77.3, 80.7)	100
Residence				
Urban	18.5 (17.6, 19.3)	3.0 (2.7, 3.5)	78.5 (77.6, 79.4)	100
Rural	21.2 (19.9, 22.5)	3.6 (3.0, 4.3)	75.2 (73.9, 76.5)	100
Education level				
Less than primary	22.4 (21.0, 23.8)	1.9 (1.6, 2.3)	75.7 (74.2, 77.1)	100
Primary	25.6 (23.5, 27.8)	3.6 (2.7, 4.6)	70.8 (68.5, 73.1)	100
Secondary	18.2 (16.7, 19.9)	5.0 (4.1, 6.1)	76.8 (74.9, 78.5)	100
University	11.3 (9.8, 13.0)	3.0 (2.2, 4.1)	85.7 (83.8, 87.5)	100
Region				
Bangkok	16.7 (15.5, 18.1)	2.3 (1.8, 2.8)	81.0 (79.5, 82.5)	100
Central	19.4 (17.8, 21.2)	3.8 (3.1, 4.6)	76.8 (75.0, 78.5)	100
North	18.4 (16.4, 20.7)	4.2 (3.2, 5.4)	77.4 (75.2, 79.5)	100
Northeast	21.0 (19.1, 23.0)	2.9 (2.1, 4.0)	76.1 (74.0, 78.1)	100
South	25.7 (23.7, 27.8)	4.0 (3.0, 5.4)	70.3 (68.1, 72.4)	100
Socioeconomic status				
Lowest	15.1 (13.4, 16.9)	2.9 (2.2, 3.7)	82.0 (80.2, 83.8)	100
Low	20.3 (18.3, 22.4)	3.4 (2.6, 4.6)	76.3 (74.2, 78.2)	100
Middle	25.1 (23.2, 27.1)	4.2 (3.2, 5.5)	70.7 (68.6, 72.8)	100
High	24.6 (22.5, 26.9)	3.8 (2.9, 4.8)	71.6 (69.3, 73.8)	100
Highest	17.9 (16.3, 19.6)	3.0 (2.3, 3.7)	79.1 (77.3, 80.8)	100

[1] Occasional refers to less than daily use.

4.6 Average number/frequency of smoking of manufactured cigarettes

4.6.1 Number of manufactured cigarettes smoked daily:

Table 4.6 presents the average number of manufactured cigarettes smoked per day among daily manufactured-cigarette smokers aged 15 years and over in five categories, i.e. <5, 5-9, 10-14, 15-24, and ≥25 cigarette sticks per day. Among daily manufactured-cigarette smokers, 31.9% smoked 10-14 cigarettes/day, followed by 23.2% who smoked 5-9 cigarettes/day. The smallest group was of those who smoked ≥25 cigarettes/day (2.3%).

The percentage of smokers taking an average of 10 to 14 manufactured cigarettes per day is highest for overall smokers as well as among smokers from all regions. This group of smokers is also the highest prevalent when classified by residence. The largest percentage of smokers of manufactured cigarettes among males smoked 10-14 cigarettes per day (32.1%) whereas for females the highest percentage group smoked less than five cigarettes per day (29.4%).

By residence, the highest proportion of both urban and rural smokers smoked 10-14 cigarettes/day (32.5% and 31.5% respectively). By educational levels, in all groups except for smokers with less than a primary education level, the highest proportion are reported to smoke an average of 10-14 cigarettes/day among those with primary education (28.8%), secondary education (35.8%) and university (36.2%). The highest percentages are also found for the 10-14 cigarettes/day category in all regions, except in the North, with Bangkok metropolis, Central, Northeast and South providing figures of 36.6%, 38%, 27.9% and 30.4% respectively.

By socioeconomic status, three out of the five groups (i.e. low, middle and high SES) have high proportions of smokers reported smoking 10-14 cigarettes/day (31.5%, 32.9% and 31.3% respectively). Among the lowest and highest SES categories, the lowest SES has the highest proportion of smoking 5-9 cigarettes/day (29.8%) and the highest SES has the highest proportion of smoking 15-24 cigarettes/day (33.9%).

4.6.2 Number of hand-rolled cigarettes smoked daily:

In Table 4.6.1, the average number of hand-rolled cigarettes smoked per day is also divided into five categories: <5, 5-9, 10-14, 15-24 and ≥25 hand-rolled cigarettes per day. Among daily hand-rolled cigarette smokers, 28.9% smoke 10-14 cigarettes/day, followed by 25% who smoke 15-24 cigarettes/day. Only 5.4% smoked ≥25 cigarettes/day.

Classified by gender, a higher proportion of males smoked hand-rolled cigarettes at an average of 10-14 cigarettes/day (29.7%) whereas the majority of females smoked an average of <5 cigarettes/day (43.6%).

Table 4.6: Percentage distribution of daily manufactured-cigarette smokers ≥15 years old, by manufactured cigarettes smoked per day and selected demographic characteristics – GATS Thailand, 2009.

Characteristic	Number of manufactured cigarettes smoked on average per day[1]					Total
	<5	5-9	10-14	15-24	≥25	
	Percentage (95% CI)					
Overall	20.5 (17.9, 23.3)	23.2 (20.4, 26.1)	31.9 (29.3, 34.6)	22.1 (19.8, 24.6)	2.3 (1.7, 3.3)	100
Gender						
Male	20.1 (17.4, 23.1)	23.2 (20.4, 26.3)	32.1 (29.4, 34.8)	22.2 (19.9, 24.7)	2.4 (1.8, 3.4)	100
Female	29.4 (21.3, 39.1)	22.2 (15.5, 30.7)	27.5 (18.7, 38.5)	20.0 (13.9, 27.9)	0.9 (0.2, 3.9)*	100
Age (years)						
15-24	27.6 (21.1, 35.1)	31.3 (23.0, 41.0)	28.3 (21.2, 36.6)	12.4 (7.9, 19.0)	0.4 (0.1, 1.7)*	100
25-44	17.3 (14.1, 21.1)	22.6 (19.5, 26.0)	35.1 (31.5, 38.8)	23.0 (19.9, 26.4)	2.0 (1.2, 3.5)	100
45-59	19.0 (14.4, 24.8)	15.3 (12.2, 19.1)	30.4 (26.1, 35.1)	29.9 (25.9, 34.3)	5.4 (3.3, 8.4)	100
60+	25.6 (18.3, 34.5)	23.9 (17.9, 31.0)	22.6 (16.7, 29.8)	25.0 (18.2, 33.4)	2.9 (1.4, 6.0)*	100
Residence						
Urban	16.4 (14.3, 18.7)	21.0 (18.8, 23.5)	32.5 (29.8, 35.2)	27.6 (25.0, 30.2)	2.5 (1.9, 3.5)	100
Rural	23.2 (19.2, 27.9)	24.6 (20.3, 29.4)	31.5 (27.6, 35.7)	18.4 (15.2, 22.1)	2.3 (1.3, 3.8)*	100
Education level						
Less than primary	26.7 (21.2, 33.0)	18.7 (14.8, 23.4)	24.9 (20.7, 29.6)	26.3 (22.2, 30.8)	3.4 (1.8, 6.3)*	100
Primary	24.9 (19.5, 31.1)	23.3 (18.6, 28.7)	28.8 (24.4, 33.6)	21.4 (16.9, 26.6)	1.6 (1.0, 2.9)*	100
Secondary	16.5 (13.6, 19.7)	25.2 (20.7, 30.3)	35.8 (31.3, 40.6)	20.5 (17.0, 24.5)	2.0 (1.1, 3.6)	100
University	14.8 (8.7, 24.2)	22.1 (16.4, 29.2)	36.2 (28.8, 44.3)	23.2 (17.6, 29.9)	3.7 (1.5, 8.4)*	100
Region						
Bangkok	12.6 (9.8, 15.9)	19.3 (15.9, 23.1)	36.6 (32.5, 41.0)	28.8 (24.6, 33.4)	2.7 (1.7, 4.4)*	100
Central	11.9 (8.9, 15.7)	19.1 (14.3, 25.0)	38.0 (33.5, 42.6)	27.3 (22.8, 32.2)	3.7 (2.0, 7.1)*	100
North	20.2 (14.7, 27.1)	32.9 (25.3, 41.4)	26.3 (20.1, 33.5)	19.7 (14.6, 26.1)	0.9 (0.3, 2.6)*	100
Northeast	26.7 (20.2, 34.3)	25.0 (18.8, 32.4)	27.9 (22.1, 34.4)	18.5 (13.8, 24.5)	1.9 (1.0, 3.6)*	100
South	28.7 (23.6, 34.5)	21.9 (17.4, 27.2)	30.4 (25.0, 36.5)	17.1 (13.5, 21.3)	1.9 (1.0, 3.4)*	100
Socioeconomic status						
Lowest	25.6 (16.9, 36.7)	29.8 (20.7, 40.9)	28.3 (19.9, 38.4)	14.7 (7.7, 26.4)	1.6 (0.7, 3.6)*	100
Low	26.7 (20.3, 34.3)	25.0 (17.5, 34.3)	31.5 (24.6, 39.5)	15.6 (11.4, 21.1)	1.2 (0.5, 2.5)*	100
Middle	21.3 (16.5, 27.0)	24.3 (19.2, 30.4)	32.9 (27.3, 39.1)	19.6 (15.4, 24.7)	1.9 (0.9, 3.5)*	100
High	19.8 (15.5, 25.0)	23.1 (18.2, 28.9)	31.3 (26.5, 36.5)	23.1 (18.8, 28.1)	2.7 (1.6, 4.4)*	100
Highest	12.0 (8.8, 16.1)	16.5 (13.1, 20.6)	33.3 (28.7, 38.3)	33.9 (29.0, 39.1)	4.3 (2.3, 8.0)	100

[1] Among daily manufactured-cigarette smokers.

* Indicates that estimate is based on sample size of less than 25.

Table 4.6.1: Percentage distribution of daily hand-rolled-cigarette smokers ≥15 years old, by number of hand-rolled cigarettes smoked per day and selected demographic characteristics – GATS Thailand, 2009.

Characteristic	Number of hand-rolled cigarettes smoked on average per day[1]					Total
	<5	5-9	10-14	15-24	≥25	
	Percentage (95% CI)					
Overall	19.1 (16.4, 22.2)	21.6 (19.2, 24.2)	28.9 (26.0, 32.0)	25.0 (22.4, 27.8)	5.4 (4.1, 6.8)	100
Gender						
Male	17.6 (14.9, 20.6)	21.4 (18.9, 24.2)	29.7 (26.6, 32.9)	26.0 (23.2, 28.9)	5.3 (4.1, 6.8)	100
Female	43.6 (33.5, 54.2)	24.7 (17.6, 33.4)	15.9 (10.5, 23.3)	10.4 (6.1, 17.0)*	5.4 (2.1, 13.6)*	100
Age (years)						
15-24	36.0 (24.0, 50.1)	20.3 (11.0, 34.4)	27.8 (17.1, 41.8)	15.6 (7.9, 28.3)*	0.3 (0.0, 1.6)*	100
25-44	16.1 (12.6, 20.5)	21.5 (17.9, 25.5)	30.0 (25.8, 34.6)	27.2 (22.8, 32.1)	5.2 (3.3, 8.1)	100
45-59	14.6 (11.6, 18.3)	19.1 (15.7, 22.9)	28.5 (24.2, 33.3)	29.6 (25.6, 34.1)	8.2 (6.0, 11.1)	100
60+	22.5 (18.1, 27.7)	26.4 (22.2, 31.0)	27.5 (22.9, 32.5)	19.1 (15.2, 23.8)	4.5 (2.8, 7.2)	100
Residence						
Urban	22.9 (19.3, 27.0)	23.2 (20.0, 26.8)	28.2 (24.4, 32.3)	22.6 (19.1, 26.7)	3.1 (2.0, 4.8)	100
Rural	18.5 (15.4, 22.1)	21.4 (18.7, 24.4)	29.0 (25.7, 32.5)	25.4 (22.5, 28.6)	5.7 (4.3, 7.4)	100
Education level						
Less than primary	17.0 (13.7, 21.0)	23.3 (20.1, 26.8)	26.3 (22.9, 30.0)	26.9 (23.5, 30.7)	6.5 (4.9, 8.4)	100
Primary	13.1 (9.7, 17.5)	19.2 (15.0, 24.2)	34.6 (28.3, 41.5)	28.2 (22.7, 34.4)	4.9 (2.6, 9.0)	100
Secondary	31.3 (23.7, 40.1)	20.1 (14.5, 27.2)	27.4 (21.1, 34.9)	17.3 (12.8, 22.8)	3.9 (2.2, 6.6)*	100
University	32.4 (17.6, 51.6)	31.7 (19.8, 46.5)	23.5 (13.5, 37.8)*	12.4 (6.1, 23.6)*	0	100
Region						
Bangkok	23.6 (15.7, 33.8)	23.4 (16.0, 32.8)	23.0 (14.9, 33.6)	23.9 (16.6, 33.1)	6.1 (2.3, 15.4)*	100
Central	12.6 (8.9, 17.6)	18.8 (14.9, 23.4)	30.4 (26.1, 35.1)	29.5 (24.8, 34.7)	8.7 (5.8, 12.7)	100
North	34.4 (26.0, 43.8)	23.6 (18.5, 29.5)	20.5 (15.0, 27.3)	18.1 (12.9, 24.8)	3.4 (1.8, 6.5)*	100
Northeast	17.7 (13.1, 23.4)	20.4 (16.2, 25.3)	31.5 (26.0, 37.7)	26.3 (21.5, 31.7)	4.1 (2.2, 7.4)*	100
South	14.9 (11.7, 18.8)	24.8 (20.2, 30.1)	29.7 (25.0, 34.8)	24.3 (20.2, 28.9)	6.3 (4.5, 8.7)	100
Socioeconomic status						
Lowest	24.1 (18.2, 31.1)	25.4 (19.8, 32.0)	23.7 (18.5, 29.9)	21.6 (15.9, 28.7)	5.2 (3.3, 7.9)	100
Low	14.9 (11.5, 19.1)	19.9 (15.9, 24.7)	31.8 (26.0, 38.1)	27.9 (23.2, 33.2)	5.5 (3.2, 9.1)	100
Middle	18.7 (13.6, 25.1)	19.0 (15.5, 23.1)	30.9 (25.5, 36.8)	26.8 (22.1, 32.1)	4.6 (2.7, 8.0)	100
High	20.5 (14.4, 28.3)	23.2 (16.8, 31.2)	27.7 (21.4, 35.1)	21.2 (16.6, 26.6)	7.4 (4.7, 11.6)	100
Highest	19.7 (13.2, 28.4)	22.7 (15.4, 32.1)	28.8 (21.2, 37.8)	26.4 (18.9, 35.5)	2.4 (1.0, 6.3)*	100

[1] Among daily hand-rolled cigarette smokers.

* Indicates that estimate is based on sample size of less than 25.

The percentage of smokers of hand-rolled cigarettes smoking 10-14 cigarettes per day is highest for overall smokers of this category (28.9% of all smokers). It is also highest in rural (28.2%) and urban (29%) areas and among males (29.7%). However, the highest percentage of smokers of hand-rolled cigarettes among females were those who smoked less than five a day (43.6%).

Classified by socioeconomic status, all SES levels except the lowest have a higher proportion of average cigarettes smoked being 10-14 cigarettes/day (31.8% in low SES, 30.9 in middle SES, 27.7 in high SES and 28.8% in highest SES) .The lowest SES has a consumption range of 5-9 cigarettes/day (25.4%).

4.7 Age at smoking initiation

Table 4.7 presents the distribution of age at smoking initiation (years) among ever daily smokers aged between 20 and 34 years. The highest proportion was of those smokers who were initiated into their daily smoking habit at the age of 20 years and over (34.2%), followed by those at the age of 17 to 19 years (29.0%). The lowest proportion started their daily smoking habit at less than 15 years of age (14.1%).

The majority of male daily smokers initiated smoking at 20+ years (32.7%) and 17–19 years (29.8%) while most females started at 20+ years (53.4%). By residence, both urban and rural daily smokers have the same proportions of age at initiation (20+ years old at 34.5% and 34% respectively). Smokers with an age of initiation of <15 years are four per cent higher in rural areas (15.1%) than urban areas (11.6%). In all regions, the majority of the ever daily smokers reported their age of smoking initiation to be 20+ years, followed by 17–19 years. The age of initiation of <15 years is also higher in the Northern region (17.8%) followed by the Northeastern region (15.9%). Irrespective of the SES, the highest proportion of age at smoking initiation is 20+ years.

Table 4.7: Percentage distribution of ever daily smokers 20-34 years old, by age at smoking initiation (years) and selected demographic characteristics – GATS Thailand, 2009.

Characteristic	Age at smoking initiation (years)[1]				
	<15	15-16	17-19	20+	Total
	Percentage (95% CI)				
Overall	14.1 (12.6, 15.8)	22.8 (21.0, 24.6)	29.0 (27.2, 30.8)	34.1 (32.4, 36.0)	100
Gender					
Male	14.1 (12.5, 15.8)	23.4 (21.5, 25.3)	29.8 (27.9, 31.7)	32.7 (31.0, 34.6)	100
Female	13.9 (10.3, 18.4)	14.4 (10.9, 18.7)	18.3 (14.0, 23.4)	53.4 (46.9, 59.9)	100
Residence					
Urban	11.6 (10.3, 13.0)	23.0 (21.3, 24.7)	30.9 (29.2, 32.7)	34.5 (32.6, 36.5)	100
Rural	15.1 (13.0, 17.4)	22.7 (20.4, 25.2)	28.2 (25.9, 30.7)	34.0 (31.7, 36.5)	100
Region					
Bangkok	10.4 (8.6, 12.5)	23.2 (20.5, 26.1)	30.9 (27.7, 34.3)	35.5 (32.1, 39.0)	100
Central	11.8 (9.3, 14.7)	20.5 (17.8, 23.5)	30.1 (26.8, 33.6)	37.6 (33.8, 41.6)	100
North	17.8 (14.3, 21.9)	22.9 (20.1, 26.0)	28.7 (25.2, 32.4)	30.6 (27.0, 34.6)	100
Northeast	15.9 (12.7, 19.8)	23.4 (19.4, 28.0)	26.8 (23.1, 30.8)	33.9 (30.4, 37.5)	100
South	10.7 (8.6, 13.4)	24.3 (21.1, 27.8)	31.7 (28.5, 35.0)	33.3 (30.0, 36.8)	100
Socioeconomic status					
Lowest	18.9 (15.1, 23.4)	24.4 (20.7, 28.6)	21.6 (18.4, 25.3)	35.1 (31.2, 39.1)	100
Low	16.2 (12.9, 20.1)	24.8 (20.6, 29.4)	27.6 (24.1, 31.4)	31.4 (28.2, 34.8)	100
Middle	13.1 (10.6, 16.2)	22.6 (19.4, 26.2)	31.6 (28.2, 35.1)	32.7 (29.1, 36.5)	100
High	12.9 (10.2, 16.1)	22.7 (19.4, 26.3)	30.7 (27.2, 34.5)	33.7 (30.1, 37.6)	100
Highest	8.2 (6.5, 10.2)	18.3 (15.2, 21.9)	33.9 (30.7, 37.2)	39.6 (36.0, 43.3)	100

[1] Among respondents 20-34 years of age who are ever daily smokers.

4.8 Former daily smoking prevalence and quit ratio[2]

Table 4.8 presents the prevalence rate of former daily smokers among all adults aged 15 years and over and the quit rate among ever daily smokers. The prevalence rate of those who are former daily smokers among adults aged 15 years and over is 8.9% and the quit rate is 28.8%. By demographic status, the prevalence rate among male former daily smokers is 12 times that of females (16.7% and 1.4%). However female former daily smokers have a higher quit rate than male daily smokers (34.4% against 28.4%). By age group, ages 15–24 have the lowest and the age group of 60+ years has the highest number of former daily smokers (1.1% and 18.2% respectively). They also have the lowest and highest quit rates of 6.2% and 47.5% respectively.

[2] Quit ratio is the percentage of ever daily tobacco smokers who currently do not smoke tobacco. The indicator indicates the success of efforts to encourage cessation among established tobacco smokers.

Table 4.8: Percentage of adults and ever daily smokers ≥15 years old who are former daily smokers (current non-smokers), by selected demographic characteristics – GATS Thailand, 2009.

Characteristic	Former daily smokers (among all adults)[1]	Former daily smokers (among ever daily smokers)[1,2]
	Percentage (95% CI)	
Overall	8.9 (8.3, 9.5)	28.8 (27.0, 30.7)
Gender		
Male	16.7 (15.5, 18.0)	28.4 (26.6, 30.4)
Female	1.4 (1.1, 1.7)	34.4 (29.0, 40.3)
Age (years)		
15-24	1.1 (0.7, 1.9)	6.2 (3.7, 10.2)
25-44	7.0 (6.2, 7.9)	22.4 (20.0, 25.0)
45-59	12.7 (11.4, 14.0)	35.6 (32.6, 38.7)
60+	18.2 (16.7, 19.8)	47.5 (44.1, 50.8)
Residence		
Urban	8.3 (7.8, 8.9)	29.4 (27.6, 31.3)
Rural	9.1 (8.3, 10.0)	28.6 (26.2, 31.2)
Education level		
Less than primary	12.9 (11.9, 14.0)	35.5 (32.9, 38.2)
Primary	7.5 (6.4, 8.8)	21.7 (18.5, 25.2)
Secondary	6.0 (5.2, 6.9)	22.7 (19.8, 25.9)
University	7.8 (6.5, 9.2)	38.3 (33.1, 43.8)
Region		
Bangkok	8.2 (7.3, 9.1)	31.4 (28.2, 34.9)
Central	8.2 (7.3, 9.2)	27.7 (24.8, 30.8)
North	11.6 (10.1, 13.2)	36.2 (31.8, 40.8)
Northeast	9.2 (7.9, 10.6)	29.2 (25.4, 33.4)
South	6.0 (5.2, 7.0)	18.2 (15.7, 20.9)
Socioeconomic status		
Lowest	7.9 (6.9, 9.0)	32.8 (29.0, 36.8)
Low	7.8 (6.8, 8.9)	26.3 (23.0, 29.9)
Middle	8.6 (7.4, 10.1)	24.1 (21.0, 27.5)
High	9.0 (7.9, 10.4)	25.6 (22.4, 29.0)
Highest	12.2 (10.7, 13.8)	38.6 (34.6, 42.7)

[1] Current non-smokers.
[2] Also known as the quit ratio for daily smoking.

Rural areas have a slightly higher percentage for former daily smokers than urban areas (9.1% and 8.3% respectively), but urban areas have a slightly higher quit rate than rural areas (29.4% and 28.6% respectively). By educational level, the highest and lowest percentages of former daily smokers are found among those with less than primary and secondary education (12.9% and 6% respectively). Persons with a university education have the highest quit rate (38.3%).

Classified by regions, the highest and lowest percentages of former daily smokers are found in the Northern and Southern regions (11.6% and 6% respectively). Those who were ever daily smokers in the Northern and Southern regions also have the highest and lowest quit rates (36.2% and 18.2%) respectively. By socioeconomic status, the high proportion of former daily smokers is found in the highest SES (12.2%) category who also have the highest quit rate (38.6%), while the middle SES has the lowest quit rate (24.1%).

4.9 Time since quitting smoking

Table 4.9 presents the time since quitting among former daily smokers aged 15 years and above who was classified into four categories according to the time since they quit smoking: less than 1 year, 1 to less than 5 years, 5 to less than 10 years, and, 10 years or more. Among these categories the majority are in the group who quit for 10 years or more (53.4%), followed by 1 to less than 5 years (21.3%), 5 to less than 10 years (18.1%), and less than 1 year (7.2%).

When classified by demographic characteristics such as sex, age (except young smokers), residence, educational status, region and economic status, most of the former daily smokers from all categories reported quitting smoking for more than 10 years. Female former daily smokers have a higher prevalence of those having quit for more than 10 years than males (56% and 53.1% respectively). Former daily smokers who are 60+ years old have the highest proportion of those having quit smoking for more than 10 years (71.2%). The proportion of those having quit smoking for more than 10 years among former daily smokers in urban areas is slightly higher than those in rural areas (55.1% and 52.7% respectively).

The highest and lowest proportions of those having quit smoking for more than 10 years are found among former daily smokers who have less than primary-level education, and those with primary-level education (63.7% and 40.4% respectively). In all regions, there are similar proportions of former daily smokers who had quit smoking for more than 10 years (51.0% to 55.5%). Among all SES levels the majority had quit smoking for more than 10 years with the highest being reported in the highest SES category (58.5%).

Table 4.9: Percentage distribution of former daily smokers ≥15 years old, by time since having quit smoking (years) and selected demographic characteristics – GATS Thailand, 2009.

Characteristic	Time since quitting smoking (years)[1]				Total
	<1	1 to <5	5 to <10	≥10	
	Percentage (95% CI)				
Overall	7.2 (5.7, 9.1)	21.3 (19.0, 23.7)	18.1 (15.8, 20.6)	53.4 (50.6, 56.2)	100
Gender					
Male	7.3 (5.6, 9.5)	21.2 (18.8, 23.8)	18.4 (16.0, 21.1)	53.1 (50.3, 55.9)	100
Female	6.3 (3.6, 10.5)*	22.0 (15.9, 29.7)	15.7 (9.6, 24.7)	56.0 (47.7, 64.0)	100
Age (years)					
15-24	32.6 (17.8,52.0)*	42.2 (27.4, 58.5)	23.9 (11.0,44.4)*	1.3 (0.3, 4.9)*	100
25-44	7.6 (5.4, 10.7)	26.9 (22.5, 31.8)	26.7 (22.3, 31.7)	38.8 (34.0, 43.7)	100
45-59	4.2 (2.9, 6.0)	17.6 (14.6, 21.1)	13.6 (11.0, 16.6)	64.6 (60.4, 68.8)	100
60+	4.3 (2.8, 6.6)	13.5 (10.7, 16.8)	11.0 (8.0, 14.8)	71.2 (67.1, 75.1)	100
Residence					
Urban	5.2 (3.7, 7.1)	22.8 (20.1, 25.8)	16.9 (14.7, 19.4)	55.1 (51.9, 58.3)	100
Rural	8.1 (6.0, 10.7)	20.6 (17.7, 23.8)	18.6 (15.6, 22.1)	52.7 (49.0, 56.4)	100
Education level					
Less than primary	5.0 (3.5, 7.1)	17.9 (15.2, 21.0)	13.4 (10.4, 17.0)	63.7 (59.9, 67.4)	100
Primary	10.4 (6.6, 15.9)	26.7 (19.9, 34.9)	22.5 (16.7, 29.5)	40.4 (33.3, 48.0)	100
Secondary	9.9 (5.8, 16.4)	23.7 (18.9, 29.3)	23.2 (17.8, 29.5)	43.2 (37.8, 48.8)	100
University	4.8 (2.2, 10.1)*	20.8 (15.4, 27.5)	18.9 (13.8, 25.3)	55.5 (48.4, 62.3)	100
Region					
Bangkok	5.9 (3.8, 9.1)	23.3 (19.1, 28.1)	18.7 (14.6, 23.5)	52.1 (46.5, 57.6)	100
Central	5.5 (3.3, 9.2)*	24.5 (20.0, 29.6)	18.9 (14.9, 23.7)	51.0 (45.5, 56.6)	100
North	5.3 (3.5, 7.7)	21.5 (16.9, 26.8)	17.7 (13.6, 22.6)	55.5 (49.7, 61.3)	100
Northeast	9.9 (6.4, 15.0)	18.0 (14.0, 22.8)	18.7 (14.0, 24.4)	53.4 (47.9, 58.9)	100
South	7.9 (4.8, 12.6)	22.8 (18.3, 27.9)	14.2 (10.3, 19.1)	55.1 (49.2, 61.0)	100
Socioeconomic status					
Lowest	9.6 (6.0, 15.0)	23.6 (18.4, 29.7)	12.6 (8.4, 18.4)	54.1 (47.8, 60.6)	100
Low	7.1 (3.8, 12.9)	18.3 (13.8, 23.9)	20.6 (15.4, 26.9)	54.0 (47.8, 60.0)	100
Middle	7.1 (4.5, 10.9)	20.8 (15.9, 26.6)	21.7 (16.0, 28.7)	50.4 (44.1, 56.9)	100
High	9.0 (4.9, 16.1)*	23.7 (18.7, 29.5)	18.5 (13.7, 24.3)	48.8 (42.2, 55.4)	100
Highest	3.5 (2.1, 5.8)*	20.4 (16.1, 25.5)	17.6 (14.0, 21.9)	58.5 (53.4, 63.4)	100

[1]Among former daily smokers (current non-smokers).

* Indicates that estimate is based on sample size of less than 25.

4.10 Type of current tobacco users

Current tobacco users include current tobacco smokers who are daily and occasional tobacco smokers as well as smokeless tobacco users. Table 4.10 presents the prevalence of current tobacco users aged 15 years and over by selected demographic characteristics. The overall prevalence of tobacco use among current tobacco users is 27.2%.

Classified by gender, it is found that the proportion of current tobacco users among males is five times that of females (46.4% and 9.1% respectively). By age groups, the 60+ years and 15-24-year age-groups have the lowest and highest percentages of current tobacco users (19.8% and 37.7% respectively). By residence, rural areas have a higher percentage of current tobacco users than urban areas (29.2% and 22.9%). By educational status, the highest and lowest percentages of current tobacco users are found among those with less than primary education (34.3%) and university-level education (14.4%) respectively. By regions, the highest and lowest percentages of current tobacco users are found in the Southern region (33.2%) and Bangkok metropolis (19.5%) respectively. By socioeconomic status, the highest and lowest percentages of current tobacco users are found in middle and highest SES categories with 30.7% and 21.6% respectively.

Type of tobacco use is classified into three categories: "smoked only", "both smoked and smokeless"; and "smokeless only". Thai current tobacco users mostly use smoked tobacco (85.7%), followed by smokeless tobacco (12.9%), and both smoked and smokeless tobacco (1.4%). By gender, most male current tobacco users use smoked tobacco (97.1%). In contrast, most female current tobacco users use smokeless tobacco (66.0%). Among the lowest age group (15-24 years), the smoked tobacco use rate is the highest (99.7%) while in the oldest age group (60+ years) this use rate is 52.4%. Among the oldest age group, smokeless tobacco use rate is 44.4% while it is 1.4% among those aged 25 to 44 years.

Classified by residence, the smoked tobacco use rate in urban areas is higher than that in rural areas (93.3% and 83.1% respectively) and the smokeless tobacco use rate in rural areas is three-fold that in urban areas (15.3% and 6.1%). By educational status, the smoked tobacco use rate is highest among those with a university education (99.3%) and the rate among those with less than primary-level of education is 68.1%. The smokeless tobacco use rate among those with less than primary-level of education is 29.1%.

Viewed by regions, Bangkok metropolis has the highest rate of smoked tobacco use (96.8%). The Northeastern region has the lowest (80.3%) smoked tobacco use rate while the same region has the highest (18.7%) smokeless tobacco use rate compared to other regions. By socioeconomic status, the smoked tobacco use rate is highest among those in the highest SES category (95.9%) and the smokeless tobacco use rate is high among those in the lowest SES category (31.1%).

Table 4.10: Percentage of adults who are current tobacco users ≥15 years old, by tobacco use patterns and selected demographic characteristics – GATS Thailand, 2009.

Characteristic	Current tobacco users[1]	Type of current tobacco use			Total
		Smoked only	Both smoked and smokeless	Smokeless only	
	Percentage (95% CI)				
Overall	27.2 (26.2, 28.3)	85.7 (84.1, 87.2)	1.4 (1.0, 2.0)	12.9 (11.5, 14.4)	100
Gender					
Male	46.4 (44.6, 48.2)	97.1 (96.4, 97.7)	1.0 (0.7, 1.5)	1.9 (1.4, 2.4)	100
Female	9.1 (8.2, 10.2)	30.8 (26.9, 34.9)	3.2 (1.9, 5.7)	66.0 (61.4, 70.2)	100
Age (years)					
15-24	19.8 (17.4, 22.5)	99.7 (98.8, 99.9)	0.2 (0.0, 1.1)*	0.1 (0.0, 0.9)*	100
25-44	26.9 (25.5, 28.3)	97.8 (96.6, 98.6)	0.8 (0.4, 1.8)*	1.4 (0.8, 2.3)	100
45-59	27.4 (25.8, 29.1)	85.9 (83.0, 88.3)	1.6 (0.9, 2.9)*	12.5 (10.1, 15.3)	100
60+	37.7 (35.3, 40.2)	52.4 (48.6, 56.3)	3.2 (2.1, 4.8)	44.4 (40.7, 48.1)	100
Residence					
Urban	22.9 (21.9, 23.9)	93.3 (91.9, 94.4)	0.8 (0.5, 1.3)	6.1 (4.9, 7.3)	100
Rural	29.2 (27.7, 30.8)	83.1 (81.0, 84.9)	1.6 (1.1, 2.4)	15.3 (13.5, 17.2)	100
Education level					
Less than primary	34.3 (32.4, 36.1)	68.1 (65.3, 70.8)	2.8 (1.9, 4.1)	29.1 (26.4, 31.8)	100
Primary	29.5 (27.2, 31.9)	98.5 (97.4, 99.2)	0.4 (0.2, 0.9)*	1.1 (0.6, 2.0)*	100
Secondary	23.5 (21.7, 25.3)	98.7 (97.8, 99.3)	0.5 (0.2, 1.0)*	0.8 (0.4, 1.6)*	100
University	14.4 (12.6, 16.4)	99.3 (97.6, 99.8)	0	0.7 (0.2, 2.4)*	100
Region					
Bangkok	19.5 (18.0, 21.0)	96.8 (94.8, 98.0)	0.6 (0.2, 1.8)*	2.6 (1.5, 4.5)*	100
Central	25.6 (23.7, 27.6)	89.3 (86.9, 91.4)	1.4 (0.8, 2.5)*	9.3 (7.4, 11.6)	100
North	25.7 (23.2, 28.3)	84.8 (80.3, 88.3)	3.2 (1.8, 5.7)	12.0 (9.3, 15.4)	100
Northeast	29.4 (27.1, 31.9)	80.3 (77.0, 83.3)	1.0 (0.4, 2.1)*	18.7 (15.8, 22.1)	100
South	33.2 (31.0, 35.4)	88.6 (86.2, 90.6)	0.9 (0.5, 1.7)*	10.5 (8.5, 13.0)	100
Socioeconomic status					
Lowest	26.0 (23.7, 28.4)	66.4 (62.3, 70.3)	2.5 (1.5, 4.2)	31.1 (27.3, 35.1)	100
Low	27.8 (25.7, 30.0)	84.0 (81.0, 86.5)	1.4 (0.8, 2.4)*	14.6 (12.2, 17.5)	100
Middle	30.7 (28.6, 32.8)	94.2 (92.2, 95.7)	1.1 (0.4, 2.7)*	4.7 (3.5, 6.4)	100
High	29.4 (27.2, 31.7)	95.6 (93.7, 97.0)	0.9 (0.3, 2.6)*	3.5 (2.4, 5.1)	100
Highest	21.6 (19.9, 23.4)	95.9 (93.5, 97.4)	0.8 (0.4, 1.7)*	3.3 (2.0, 5.6)*	100

[1] Includes daily and occasional (less than daily) smokers or smokeless users.

* Indicates that estimate is based on sample size of less than 25.

4.11 Time to first cigarette of the day

One measure of evaluating nicotine dependence is the time taken to smoke the first cigarette of the day upon waking. Table 4.11 presents the time to the first smoke or first cigarette of the day. The survey found that most daily smokers have their first cigarette of the day between 6-30 minutes after waking (35.7%) up, followed by those who had it after more than 60 minutes (26.7%). The average time to the first cigarette of the day differs by gender: 36.2% of male daily smokers have their first smoke between 6-30 minutes after waking up whereas 39.8% of female daily smokers have their first cigarette more than 60 minutes after waking up. A high percentage of daily smokers in the age-group of 15-24 years and the oldest age-group of 60+ years have their first cigarette more than 60 minutes after waking up (32.9% and 32.7%). On the other hand, those in the 24-44 year and 45-59 years age-groups have their first cigarette between 6-30 minutes after waking up (37.4% and 36.8%).

When classified by residence, most daily smokers both in urban and rural areas have their first cigarette between 6-30 minutes after waking up (33.9% and 36.4%). By educational level, most daily smokers among all educational levels have their first cigarette at 6-30 minutes after waking up (34.8% to 37.3%). Similar patterns were observed with respect to regions and SES categories as well. A high percentage of daily smokers, irrespective of region and SES category, have their first cigarette 6-30 minutes after waking up. The highest and lowest proportions of smokers who have their first smoke between 6-30 minutes of waking up are found in the Southern region and Bangkok metropolis (42.7% and 32.6%) respectively. The highest and lowest proportions of smokers having their first smoke between 6-30 minutes of waking up are found in the highest and low SES categories (38.5% and 33.3%).

Table 4.11: Percentage distribution of daily smokers ≥15 years old, by time to smoke the first cigarette of the day and selected demographic characteristics – GATS Thailand, 2009.

Characteristic	Time to first smoke				Total
	≤5 minutes	6-30 minutes	31-60 minutes	>60 minutes	
	Percentage (95% CI)				
Overall	24.4 (22.0, 26.9)	35.7 (33.0, 38.4)	13.2 (11.3, 15.2)	26.7 (24.4, 29.4)	100
Gender					
Male	24.7 (22.2, 27.4)	36.2 (33.4, 39.0)	13.1 (11.3, 15.3)	26.0 (23.4, 28.7)	100
Female	19.2 (14.7, 24.7)	27.9 (20.9, 36.1)	13.1 (9.0, 18.8)	39.8 (32.3, 47.8)	100
Age (years)					
15-24	18.0 (12.1, 25.9)	31.2 (23.7, 39.9)	17.9 (10.9, 27.9)	32.9 (25.4, 41.5)	100
25-44	25.3 (21.9, 28.9)	37.4 (33.8, 41.2)	12.5 (10.4, 15.1)	24.8 (21.6, 28.3)	100
45-59	27.0 (23.8, 30.5)	36.8 (33.3, 40.5)	12.5 (10.3, 15.0)	23.7 (20.8, 26.9)	100
60+	23.2 (19.1, 27.9)	32.5 (28.1, 37.1)	11.6 (9.1, 14.7)	32.7 (28.6, 37.1)	100
Residence					
Urban	28.0 (25.5, 30.5)	33.9 (31.5, 36.4)	12.7 (11.2, 14.4)	25.4 (23.1, 27.8)	100
Rural	22.9 (19.8, 26.4)	36.4 (32.8, 40.0)	13.3 (10.9, 16.2)	27.4 (24.1, 30.9)	100
Education level					
Less than primary	26.2 (22.9, 29.7)	34.8 (31.2, 38.6)	11.7 (9.7, 14.0)	27.3 (24.2, 30.6)	100
Primary	23.6 (19.5, 28.4)	37.3 (32.5, 42.4)	16.0 (12.1, 21.0)	23.1 (19.1, 27.4)	100
Secondary	23.1 (19.2, 27.6)	35.2 (30.8, 39.8)	13.2 (10.4, 16.7)	28.5 (24.0, 33.4)	100
University	22.9 (17.8, 29.1)	35.8 (28.3, 44.2)	9.5 (6.7, 13.4)	31.8 (24.4, 40.1)	100
Region					
Bangkok	32.1 (27.8, 36.8)	32.6 (28.5, 37.0)	11.5 (9.0, 14.7)	23.8 (19.9, 28.0)	100
Central	28.1 (24.3, 32.3)	34.6 (30.2, 39.3)	15.0 (11.7, 19.1)	22.3 (18.7, 26.3)	100
North	21.2 (16.9, 26.2)	36.7 (30.8, 43.1)	13.8 (10.2, 18.4)	28.3 (23.1, 34.2)	100
Northeast	24.9 (19.4, 31.3)	33.2 (27.6, 39.3)	11.2 (7.5, 16.3)	30.7 (25.3, 36.8)	100
South	17.4 (14.2, 21.1)	42.7 (37.7, 47.9)	14.9 (11.9, 18.6)	25.0 (20.3, 30.3)	100
Socioeconomic status					
Lowest	22.5 (18.1, 27.6)	34.4 (28.4, 40.9)	12.1 (8.7, 16.8)	31.0 (25.5, 37.1)	100
Low	25.6 (20.6, 31.3)	33.3 (28.8, 38.1)	18.8 (14.0, 24.7)	22.3 (18.4, 26.8)	100
Middle	22.2 (18.0, 27.0)	37.6 (32.9, 42.5)	12.9 (10.5, 15.8)	27.3 (22.7, 32.5)	100
High	25.9 (21.0, 31.5)	35.4 (30.8, 40.2)	9.5 (7.4, 12.1)	29.2 (24.6, 34.2)	100
Highest	26.4 (22.2, 31.2)	38.5 (33.6, 43.6)	10.3 (7.9, 13.2)	24.8 (20.4, 29.7)	100

In short, considering only current tobacco users, males were the predominant users of smoked tobacco products and females of smokeless tobacco products. Among smoked tobacco products, the survey found that users of manufactured cigarettes were mostly from the following categories: male, aged 25–44 years, living in urban areas, with secondary-level education, living in the Southern region, and belonging to the high-income category. In contrast, hand-rolled-cigarette users were mostly from the 60 years and over age groups, living in rural areas, having a primary-level education, and belonging to the middle SES category. The average smoking frequency among those who daily smoke manufactured cigarettes as well as hand-rolled cigarette smokers was 10-14 cigarettes/day.

5

Cessation

5. Cessation

Thailand has a tobacco control policy in place to set up and support smoking cessation clinics in various health service settings and to provide counseling through national quit-lines all over the country. In 2005 Thailand had 1 120 smoking cessation clinics, 127 of these in Bangkok and 993 in other provinces. Most of them are in governmental settings. In the private sector, smoking cessation services are available in clinics rather than in hospitals[(17)]. Tobacco cessation clinics registered with the Department of Disease Control follow all steps of the 5 A's of smoking cessation[3] according to tobacco control policy. The multidisciplinary agency-level teams are responsible for implementation of the tobacco cessation programmes, and use both mass media and individual groups for promoting cessation.

The range of pharmacotherapy used for smoking cessation includes: 1) nicotine replacement therapy (NRT) in the form of nicotine chewing gum or polacrilex, and the nicotine patch, both of which are restricted for sale under a pharmacist's supervision only, 2) non-nicotine tablets such as Bupropion HCL (Amfebutamone) and Nortriptyline are lately included in the National Essential Drug List so that people under universal health-care insurance can obtain it free of charge[(18)]. Quit-lines have been initiated by Action on Smoke or Health (ASH) Thailand since 1993. The phone number 1600 is currently the quit-line number for the national quit-line center established in June 2009.

This chapter presents findings on smoking cessation practices and health-care seeking behaviour, cessation methods and the degree of interest in quitting smoking.

Key findings:

- *6 in 10 current smokers plan to or are thinking of quitting.*
- *6 in 10 current smokers were asked if they smoked tobacco by a doctor or health-care provider in the last 12 months.*
- *5 in 10 current smokers received advice to quit smoking by a doctor or health-care provider in the last 12 months.*
- *"Quitting on your own" was the most common cessation method reported by current smokers who had made an attempt to quit in the past 12 months*

5.1 Smoking cessation and health-care seeking behaviours

A quit attempt in GATS is defined as current tobacco smokers and former tobacco smokers who have been abstinent for less than 12 months. Table 5.1 reports the proportion of adult smokers who made a quit attempt, visited a health-care provider (HCP), were asked about smoking and received advice by an HCP on quitting smoking.

---

[3] **5 A's** of smoking cessation clinics are: 1) Ask about smoking habits, 2) Advise, 3) Assess readiness, 4) Assist and 5) Arrange the follow-up.

5.1.1 Made quit attempt:

Among current tobacco smokers and former tobacco smokers who have been abstinent for less than 12 months, approximately half of all smokers (49.8%) had made an attempt to quit. The proportion is slightly higher among males than females (49.9% and 47.4%). Smokers aged 15-24 years have the highest rate of quit attempts (60.6%) and the rate is lowest in smokers aged 60 years and over (42.3%). Smokers who live in urban areas have a slightly higher rate of quit attempts than those in rural areas (51.7% and 49% respectively). Classified by education levels, smokers with university education have the highest percentage of quit attempts (56.5%) and the rate is lowest among smokers with education level less than primary (43.5%). Smokers in the Central region have the highest rate of quit attempts (55.5%). The rate is lower among smokers who live in the Southern region (43.0%). By socioeconomic status, smokers with middle SES level have a high rate of quit attempts (54.7%); the rate being lower among smokers with the lowest SES level (44.7%).

5.1.2 Visited health-care providers:

The percentage of smokers (including current tobacco smokers and recent quitters, <12 months) who visited a health-care provider during the past 12 months is 34.9%. Female smokers have higher proportion of HCP visits than male smokers (47.3% against 33.9%). Smokers aged 60 years and over have the highest rate of HCP visits (58.0%). The percentages are similar in both urban and rural areas (35.8% and 34.5% respectively). By education level, smokers with the less than primary education have the highest rate of HCP visits (44.3%). HCP visit rate is lowest among smokers in Bangkok metropolis and in the Southern region, being about 31% in both regions. Smokers in the lowest and the highest SES range have approximately the same rate of HCP visits (40.2% and 39.4% respectively).

5.1.3 Asked about smoking tobacco by HCP:

Among the smokers who have visited an HCP during the previous 12 months 60.2% were asked about their history of tobacco smoking. The proportion asked about tobacco smoking by the HCP among female smokers is slightly higher than that among male smokers (63.9% and 59.9% respectively). The proportion is the highest among smokers aged 60 years and over (73.7%). The proportions do not differ between urban and rural areas (59.2% and 60.7% respectively). By education levels, smokers with the less than primary educational level have the highest rate of being asked about smoking tobacco by an HCP (69.3%). Classified by region, the proportions in every region are similar, being approximately 60%. In addition, 68.0% of smokers among the lowest SES level reported that they were asked about smoking history by an HCP.

5.1.4 Getting advised to quit by HCP:

Approximately half of all smokers (51.9%) ever received advice to quit smoking by the HCP. The rate of getting advice from the HCP is slightly higher among male smokers (52.3%) than among female (48.7%). The proportion of receiving advice on quitting smoking is highest among smokers aged 60 years and over (67.6%). The lowest proportion is found among younger smokers aged 15-24 years (24.2%).

The proportions are similar in urban and rural areas (48.8% and 53.2%). Classified by educational level, smokers with less than primary education have the highest proportion of getting advice on quitting smoking (62.2%). The rate of smokers receiving such advice does not differ greatly by region. Classified by socioeconomic status, smokers in the lowest SES level have reported a higher rate of getting advice (58.7%).

Table 5.1: Percentage of smokers[1] ≥15 years old who made a quit attempt and received health-care provider assistance in the past 12 months, by selected demographic characteristics – GATS Thailand, 2009.

Characteristic	Smoking cessation and health-care seeking behaviour			
	Made quit attempt[2]	Visited an HCP[2]	Asked by HCP if a smoker[3]	Advised to quit by HCP[3]
	Percentage (95% CI)			
Overall	49.8 (47.0, 52.5)	34.9 (32.7, 37.1)	60.2 (56.7, 63.6)	51.9 (48.4, 55.4)
Gender				
Male	49.9 (47.1, 52.7)	33.9 (31.7, 36.3)	59.9 (56.1, 63.5)	52.3 (48.5, 56.0)
Female	47.4 (40.5, 54.4)	47.3 (41.0, 53.8)	63.9 (55.3, 71.6)	48.7 (40.1, 57.4)
Age (years)				
15-24	60.6 (52.8, 67.8)	20.8 (16.0, 26.7)	38.0 (27.0, 50.4)	24.2 (15.3, 36.0)
25-44	49.3 (45.8, 52.8)	30.6 (27.6, 33.8)	56.5 (50.8, 62.1)	48.2 (42.4, 54.1)
45-59	47.1 (43.5, 50.7)	39.9 (36.4, 43.6)	63.1 (58.2, 67.7)	54.9 (50.1, 59.7)
60+	42.3 (37.9, 46.7)	58.0 (53.5, 62.3)	73.7 (68.4, 78.3)	67.6 (62.0, 72.7)
Residence				
Urban	51.7 (49.2, 54.2)	35.8 (33.6, 38.1)	59.2 (55.2, 63.1)	48.8 (44.8, 52.8)
Rural	49.0 (45.4, 52.6)	34.5 (31.6, 37.5)	60.7 (56.0, 65.1)	53.2 (48.5, 57.8)
Education level				
Less than primary	43.5 (40.1, 47.0)	44.3 (40.9, 47.8)	69.3 (65.2, 73.2)	62.2 (57.8, 66.4)
Primary	49.4 (44.3, 54.4)	27.7 (23.7, 32.1)	57.9 (48.5, 66.8)	50.6 (41.5, 59.6)
Secondary	55.2 (50.6, 59.7)	30.3 (26.8, 34.0)	48.9 (42.4, 55.4)	38.0 (32.3, 44.0)
University	56.5 (49.8, 63.0)	35.5 (29.7, 41.9)	55.7 (44.5, 66.4)	47.9 (37.6, 58.4)
Region				
Bangkok metropolis	45.6 (41.4, 50.0)	31.5 (27.7, 35.5)	60.6 (53.3, 67.5)	51.0 (44.1, 58.0)
Central	55.5 (50.6, 60.2)	34.2 (30.3, 38.3)	57.8 (52.1, 63.3)	47.3 (41.5, 53.1)
North	46.8 (40.6, 53.0)	40.6 (35.2, 46.1)	60.4 (53.4, 67.0)	51.7 (45.0, 58.3)
Northeast	51.6 (45.7, 57.6)	34.8 (30.2, 39.7)	60.1 (52.2, 67.5)	55.7 (47.4, 63.6)
South	43.0 (38.9, 47.3)	31.4 (27.6, 35.5)	63.9 (56.8, 70.5)	51.4 (45.2, 57.6)
Socioeconomic status				
Lowest	44.7 (39.0, 50.5)	40.2 (35.1, 45.4)	68.0 (60.7, 74.5)	58.7 (51.0, 66.0)
Low	45.0 (39.3, 51.0)	31.3 (26.9, 36.1)	62.3 (55.6, 68.6)	55.9 (48.9, 62.7)
Middle	54.7 (50.2, 59.1)	31.3 (27.3, 35.7)	54.1 (46.3, 61.7)	46.4 (39.0, 54.0)
High	52.6 (47.7, 57.5)	35.4 (31.3, 39.7)	55.9 (48.3, 63.2)	44.2 (36.9, 51.8)
Highest	51.9 (47.8, 56.0)	39.4 (35.2, 43.9)	60.8 (53.6, 67.5)	54.4 (47.3, 61.4)

HCP = health-care provider.

[1] Includes current tobacco smokers and former smokers who have been abstinent for less than 12 months.

[2] Among current tobacco smokers and former smokers who have been abstinent for less than 12 months.

[3] Among current tobacco smokers and former smokers who have been abstinent for less than 12 months, and who visited an HCP during the past 12 months.

5.2 Cessation method

The cessation methods for smokers (current tobacco smokers and recent quitters of <12 months) covered in GATS Thailand are: (1) pharmacotherapy, including nicotine replacement therapy and other prescribed medications; (2) counseling and advice, including counseling at a cessation clinic and through quit-line, (3) quitting on one's own, including the cold turkey method (stop smoking all at once), or gradual reduction of the number of cigarettes per day or self-change techniques such as chewing gum without nicotine replacement or the use of a sour/sweet candy, (4) others including traditional medicine and other types of smokeless products.

Table 5.2 shows that a higher proportion of smokers reported quitting on their own methods (88.9%), as most of them had attempted some method to quit smoking in the past 12 months, followed by the pharmacotherapy method (10.6%). The least used cessation method was counseling (5.8%). The distribution is equal for the two genders: quit on your own is 89% among male smokers and 87.4% among female smokers. In every group classified by age, residence, education level, region and socioeconomic status, the quit on your own method was reported to be the most commonly used cessation method by smokers in Thailand. Smokers aged 25-44 years have the highest rate of use of pharmacotherapy (12.2%). Smokers in urban areas used pharmacotherapy methods more than smokers in rural areas (the figures being 14.8% and 8.9% respectively). Smokers with secondary-level education have the highest use of pharmacotherapy methods (13.7%) and smokers with less than a primary level of education have the lowest use of pharmacotherapy method (5.4%). Smokers in the Northern and Northeastern regions have the lowest rate of using the pharmacotherapy method (7.7% and 8.9%). The prevalence of the pharmacotherapy method is also low among smokers with lower socioeconomic status, i.e. the low and the lowest SES level (6.7% and 8.0%).

Table 5.2: Percentage of smokers[1] ≥15 years old who attempted quit attempts in the past 12 months, by cessation methods used and selected demographic characteristics – GATS Thailand, 2009.

Characteristic	Use of cessation method[2]			
	Pharmacotherapy[3]	Counseling/advice[4]	Quit on your own	Other[5]
	Percentage (95% CI)			
Overall	10.6 (8.7, 12.9)	5.8 (4.5, 7.5)	88.9 (86.1, 91.2)	2.9 (2.1, 3.9)
Gender				
Male	10.6 (8.5, 13.1)	5.6 (4.2, 7.3)	89.0 (86.1, 91.4)	2.8 (2.0, 3.8)
Female	10.5 (6.5, 16.7)	9.0 (5.1, 15.4)*	87.4 (81.6, 91.6)	4.3 (2.2, 8.0)*
Age (years)				
15-24	11.3 (7.3, 17.0)	3.7 (2.0, 6.8)*	88.5 (79.7, 93.7)	2.8 (1.2, 6.7)*
25-44	12.2 (9.3, 15.7)	5.8 (4.0, 8.3)	90.2 (87.1, 92.6)	1.8 (1.2, 2.9)
45-59	9.6 (7.1, 13.0)	7.0 (4.8, 10.0)	88.1 (84.3, 91.1)	3.9 (2.3, 6.5)
60+	4.9 (3.0, 8.1)*	7.0 (4.0, 12.0)*	86.3 (80.7, 90.5)	5.0 (3.1, 8.1)*
Residence				
Urban	14.8 (12.4, 17.5)	6.3 (4.9, 8.2)	89.0 (86.4, 91.2)	3.7 (2.6, 5.4)
Rural	8.9 (6.5, 12.1)	5.6 (3.9, 7.9)	88.9 (85.0, 91.9)	2.5 (1.6, 3.9)
Education level				
Less than primary	5.4 (4.0, 7.2)	5.6 (3.8, 8.3)	90.2 (86.7, 92.8)	4.0 (2.5, 6.2)
Primary	12.2 (8.2, 17.9)	6.9 (4.0, 11.4)	91.9 (88.0, 94.6)	1.8 (0.9, 3.7)*
Secondary	13.7 (10.1, 18.4)	5.4 (3.9, 7.5)	84.8 (78.9, 89.3)	2.9 (1.7, 4.9)
University	11.1 (7.0, 17.3)	4.9 (2.9, 8.1)*	92.7 (88.3, 95.5)	2.1 (0.9, 4.8)*
Region				
Bangkok	12.6 (9.0, 17.3)	6.0 (3.5, 9.9)*	92.2 (88.1, 94.9)	2.9 (1.3, 6.5)*
Central	13.2 (9.9, 17.4)	6.3 (4.1, 9.7)	92.7 (89.1, 95.2)	2.9 (1.4, 5.9)*
North	7.7 (4.3, 13.6)	2.5 (1.3, 4.9)*	92.7 (89.6, 95.0)	4.6 (2.8, 7.5)
Northeast	8.9 (5.3, 14.5)	7.3 (4.5, 11.5)	85.8 (78.2, 91.0)	1.5 (0.7, 3.5)*
South	12.4 (8.9, 17.0)	4.8 (3.2, 7.1)	83.6 (78.9, 87.4)	3.9 (2.5, 6.2)
Socioeconomic status				
Lowest	8.0 (5.0, 12.5)	7.5 (4.3, 12.5)*	90.1 (84.1, 94.0)	3.2 (1.8, 5.8)*
Low	6.7 (4.2, 10.5)	5.4 (3.2, 8.9)	88.5 (81.9, 92.9)	2.8 (1.3, 6.0)*
Middle	14.2 (9.9, 20.0)	6.6 (3.9, 10.9)	88.0 (83.2, 91.6)	2.2 (1.2, 4.2)*
High	9.6 (7.0, 13.0)	4.1 (2.6, 6.4)	89.2 (81.5, 93.9)	2.9 (1.8, 4.8)*
Highest	13.8 (9.9, 19.0)	5.2 (3.5, 7.8)	89.5 (85.4, 92.5)	3.7 (2.1, 6.5)

[1] Includes current smokers and former smokers who have been abstinent for less than 12 months.
[2] Among current smokers who made a quit attempt in the past 12 months and former smokers who have been abstinent for less than 12 months.
[3] Pharmacotherapy includes nicotine replacement therapy and prescription medications.
[4] Includes counseling at a cessation clinic and a telephone quit-line/helpline.
[5] 'Other' includes traditional medicines and other products. Categories may be adjusted after reviewing the distributions.
* Indicates that estimate is based on sample size of less than 25.

5.3 Interest in quitting smoking

Interest in quitting smoking in GATS is defined as current tobacco smokers who are planning to quit or thinking about quitting smoking within the next month, 12 months, or some day. Table 5.3 presents five categories of "interest in quitting smoking". Most of current smokers have the same proportion of "not interested in quitting" and "will quit some day, but not in the next 12 months" (36%). It is followed by "thinking about quitting within the next 12 months" (16.1%), "planning to quit within next month" (7.8%) and "don't know" (4.1%).

When classified by gender, age-groups, residence, education levels, regions and socioeconomic status, it is found that the profiles of current smokers are similar, that is, very high proportions are not interested in quitting. About 40.0% of female current smokers have reported that they are not interested in quitting compared to 35.7% of males. By age group, current smokers aged 60 years and over have reported a higher rate of "not interested in quitting" response (43.2%) as compared to other age groups. By residence, there is little difference in the percentage of smokers who are "not interested in quitting" from urban (36.2%) areas and rural (35.9%). Classified by education levels, the highest percentages of smokers who are not interested in quitting belong to those with less than primary education (38.3%). When viewed by regions and socioeconomic status, smokers in Bangkok metropolis and in the low SES group have the highest percentages of "not interested in quitting" figures, of 45.3% and 42.3% respectively.

Comparing between current smokers who are planning to quit within the next month and those who are thinking about quitting within the next 12 months, the former category has a lower proportion of interest in quitting smoking than the latter. Among current smokers who are planning to quit within the next month, female current smokers have a higher rate of planning to quit within the next month than males (12% and 7.5%). Current smokers aged 15–24 years have reported planning to quit within the next month (8.7%) at a higher rate than the other age groups.

Current smokers living in urban areas have higher rates than those living in rural areas (9.1% and 7.3%). Current smokers with a university level of education have a higher rate of planning to quit within the next month (12.2%) compared to current smokers with a primary level education (6.2%). Current smokers in the Central region, followed by those in the Bangkok metropolis, have a higher rate of planning to quit within the next month (13.3% and 9.2%) while the smokers living in the Northern region have the lowest rate (3.5%). By socioeconomic status, current smokers with a high SES level have the highest rate of "planning to quit within the next month" (10.1%) responses than smokers belonging to other SES levels.

Table 5.3: Percentage distribution of current smokers ≥15 years old, by interest in quitting smoking and selected demographic characteristics – GATS Thailand, 2009.

Characteristic	Interest in quitting smoking[1]					
	Planning to quit within next month	Thinking about quitting within next 12 months	Will quit some day but not in the next 12 months	Not interested in quitting	Don't know/Can't say	Total
	Percentage (95% CI)					
Overall	7.8 (6.6, 9.2)	16.1 (14.4, 18.0)	36.0 (33.7, 38.5)	36.0 (33.6, 38.5)	4.1 (3.1, 5.2)	100
Gender						
Male	7.5 (6.3, 8.9)	16.2 (14.4, 18.2)	36.8 (34.3, 39.3)	35.7 (33.2, 38.3)	3.8 (3.0, 4.9)	100
Female	12.0 (8.1, 17.4)	15.1 (10.5, 21.2)	25.8 (21.1, 31.3)	40.0 (33.6, 46.8)	7.1 (3.6, 13.5)*	100
Age (years)						
15-24	8.7 (5.7, 13.1)	15.7 (11.3, 21.4)	37.2 (30.0, 44.9)	34.4 (27.5, 42.1)	4.0 (2.3, 6.9)*	100
25-44	8.3 (6.6, 10.3)	16.1 (13.9, 18.6)	36.6 (33.2, 40.1)	35.2 (31.9, 38.7)	3.8 (2.7, 5.4)	100
45-59	6.9 (5.4, 8.8)	15.2 (12.9, 17.7)	39.2 (35.6, 42.8)	34.4 (31.3, 37.7)	4.3 (3.0, 6.3)	100
60+	6.6 (4.8, 9.0)	18.6 (14.8, 23.0)	27.2 (23.5, 31.4)	43.2 (38.4, 48.1)	4.4 (2.7, 6.9)	100
Residence						
Urban	9.1 (7.6, 10.8)	16.7 (14.9, 18.6)	33.6 (31.0, 36.4)	36.2 (33.9, 38.6)	4.4 (3.4, 5.6)	100
Rural	7.3 (5.8, 9.2)	15.9 (13.7, 18.5)	37.0 (33.8, 40.2)	35.9 (32.7, 39.3)	3.9 (2.8, 5.5)	100
Education level						
Less than primary	6.7 (5.3, 8.4)	15.8 (13.5, 18.3)	34.0 (30.9, 37.4)	38.3 (35.1, 41.7)	5.2 (3.6, 7.4)	100
Primary	6.2 (4.5, 8.4)	15.2 (12.2, 18.8)	37.3 (33.0, 41.8)	37.4 (32.8, 42.1)	3.9 (2.6, 6.0)	100
Secondary	9.3 (7.1, 12.1)	16.9 (13.9, 20.4)	37.1 (33.0, 41.3)	33.5 (29.3, 38.0)	3.2 (2.2, 4.7)	100
University	12.2 (8.1, 18.0)	17.8 (12.9, 23.9)	36.7 (30.7, 43.2)	30.7 (25.0, 37.1)	2.6 (1.0, 6.6)*	100
Region						
Bangkok	9.2 (7.0, 12.0)	11.6 (9.4, 14.3)	30.4 (26.5, 34.7)	45.3 (41.1, 49.5)	3.5 (2.2, 5.4)	100
Central	13.3 (10.1, 17.3)	13.3 (11.1, 15.9)	31.9 (26.8, 37.4)	34.2 (29.9, 38.8)	7.3 (4.9, 10.9)	100
North	3.5 (2.1, 5.8)	18.6 (15.1, 22.7)	38.5 (33.6, 43.7)	33.6 (28.6, 39.0)	5.8 (3.1, 10.4)	100
Northeast	6.6 (4.7, 9.4)	18.1 (14.2, 22.6)	39.7 (35.1, 44.6)	33.9 (28.6, 39.5)	1.7 (0.9, 3.1)*	100
South	6.2 (4.1, 9.3)	16.0 (12.5, 20.2)	34.6 (29.4, 40.1)	40.7 (36.0, 45.6)	2.5 (1.5, 4.3)	100
Socioeconomic status						
Lowest	6.7 (4.6, 9.6)	15.8 (12.0, 20.6)	32.4 (27.3, 37.9)	39.5 (33.7, 45.6)	5.6 (3.3, 9.4)	100
Low	6.1 (4.3, 8.5)	13.0 (10.3, 16.4)	35.4 (30.7, 40.3)	42.3 (37.0, 47.8)	3.2 (1.9, 5.3)	100
Middle	7.3 (5.3, 10.0)	16.6 (13.7, 19.9)	40.8 (36.2, 45.6)	31.2 (27.5, 35.3)	4.1 (2.8, 6.1)	100
High	10.1 (7.5, 13.5)	19.2 (15.7, 23.1)	33.2 (28.6, 38.1)	34.0 (29.7, 38.6)	3.5 (2.3, 5.1)	100
Highest	10.0 (7.5, 13.2)	17.1 (13.9, 20.8)	37.1 (32.7, 41.8)	31.8 (27.7, 36.2)	4.0 (2.4, 6.6)	100

[1] Among current daily or less than daily smokers.

* Indicates that estimate is based on sample size of less than 25.

In short, the survey results suggest that about 60% of current smokers and recent quitters (<12 months) were asked about smoking but only half of them were advised to quit. The smokers aged 15–24 years were least asked for history of smoking and also were advised least to quit smoking. The primary cessation method used in Thailand is quit on your own and the least-used method is counseling. More than one third of all smokers are still not interested in quitting smoking.

6

Second-hand smoke

6. Second-hand smoke

Since the enactment of the Non-Smoker's Health Protection Act 1992, smoke-free environment policies have gradually restricted smoking in most public places. Under this Act, the 18th Ministry of Public Health Notification was enacted in 2007. By law, Thailand has two categories of non-smoking areas: a) public places that must be totally smoke-free, and, b) public places that are partially smoke-free, i.e. most of the area is smoke-free except for personal working spaces, personal rooms, and areas designated as "smoking areas"[13]. Since 2006, Action on Smoking and Health (ASH Thailand) has strongly committed itself to promoting smoke-free home policies through several campaigns. According to the 2006 Global Health Professional Students' Survey, Thailand (GHPSS)[19], 3 out of 10 surveyed students reported that they had been exposed to second-hand smoke (SHS) at home in the week before the survey, and 6 in 10 reported that they were exposed to SHS in public places during the week preceding the survey. About 1% reported that they had smoked while they were on the campus of their educational institution. The Health and Welfare Survey of NSO, on the other hand, shows that the Thai population had experienced a decrease in exposure to SHS in their homes, from 8 of 10 people exposed in 2001 to 6 in 10 people exposed in 2007[1].

This chapter measures exposure to SHS in the following public places which should be smoke-free under the law: indoor workplaces, government buildings, health-care facilities, restaurants, outside markets, and public transport. According to the law, the first five public places are partially banned by excluding the ban on private rooms and assigned smoking areas. Smoking on public transport is completely banned.

Key findings:

- *Among those who work indoors, 3 in 10 were exposed to SHS at indoor workplaces in 30 days preceding the survey.*
- *4 in 10 respondents reported being exposed to SHS at home.*
- *Nearly 1 in 10 of all adults were exposed to SHS in restaurants.*

6.1 SHS exposure in indoor workplaces

Results of the prevalence of exposure to SHS in indoor workplaces over the preceding 30 days are shown in Table 6.1. Table 6.1a shows the number, in thousands of adults, of people exposed to SHS during the same period.

6.1.1 Prevalence of SHS exposure in indoor workplaces:

Exposure to SHS in indoor workplaces was measured among adults aged 15 years and more who work outside of home and usually work indoors. Table 6.1 shows that 27.2% of overall workers are exposed to SHS at indoor workplaces. Exposure to SHS varies across different characteristics of workers. Male workers have higher exposure to SHS than female workers (34.9% and 18.9%). Nearly one third (29.7%) of young (15–24 years of age) workers were exposed to SHS at workplaces.

Workers living in urban areas have less exposure to SHS at indoor workplaces than those living in rural areas (23.7% and 30.1% respectively). Workers with less than primary- to primary-level education (36.3% and 38.6%) were more exposed to SHS in indoor workplaces than those with a university-level education (19.3%). Classified by region, exposure to SHS in indoor workplaces varied from 40.8% (Southern) to 18.2% (Bangkok metropolis). By socioeconomic status, workers with lowest, low and middle SES were more exposed to SHS in indoor workplaces than those belonging to the higher SES levels (high and highest).

Among non-smoking workers, 23.6% were exposed to SHS in indoor workplaces, and the exposures in all dimensions were the same as that overall. Non-smoking male workers had twice as much exposure to SHS than female workers in indoor workplaces (30.8% and 18.9% respectively). Nearly one fourth (26.2%) of the young (15–24 years of age) non-workers were exposed to the SHS in indoor workplaces. Non-smoking workers living in urban areas were less exposed to SHS at indoor workplaces than those living in rural areas (20.9% and 25.8% respectively). Non-smoking workers with lower educational levels (less than primary-level and primary-level education at 29.1% and 33.1% respectively) are more exposed to SHS at indoor workplaces than the other two higher educational levels (secondary- and university-level education with 23.2% and 18.5% respectively).

Classified by region, exposure in indoor workplaces is the highest among non-smoking workers living in the Southern region (32.1%) and lowest among workers in Bangkok metropolis (15.9%). Classified by socioeconomic status, the lowest, low and middle SES groups are more exposed to SHS in indoor workplaces than the higher SES groups.

Table 6.1: Percentage of adults ≥15 years old who are exposed to SHS in indoor workplaces, by smoking status and selected demographic characteristics – GATS Thailand, 2009.

Characteristic	Adults exposed to SHS in indoor workplaces[1]	
	Overall	**Non-smokers**
	Percentage (95% CI)	
Overall	27.2 (24.9, 29.7)	23.6 (21.1, 26.2)
Gender		
Male	34.9 (31.2, 38.8)	30.8 (26.0, 36.1)
Female	18.9 (16.8, 21.2)	18.9 (16.8, 21.2)
Age (years)		
15-24	29.7 (21.7, 39.3)	26.2 (17.6, 37.2)
25-44	25.3 (23.2, 27.6)	22.3 (20.1, 24.8)
45-59	29.5 (26.0, 33.2)	24.3 (20.9, 27.9)
60+	35.6 (26.4, 46.0)	27.7 (18.7, 38.9)
Residence		
Urban	23.7 (21.9, 25.5)	20.9 (19.0, 22.9)
Rural	30.1 (26.3, 34.3)	25.8 (21.8, 30.4)
Education level		
Less than primary	36.3 (31.3, 41.8)	29.1 (23.7, 35.1)
Primary	38.6 (33.5, 44.0)	33.1 (27.3, 39.5)
Secondary	26.4 (21.9, 31.3)	23.2 (18.2, 29.1)
University	19.3 (16.9, 21.9)	18.5 (15.9, 21.4)
Region		
Bangkok	18.2 (15.4, 21.3)	15.9 (13.0, 19.4)
Central	24.0 (20.2, 28.2)	21.0 (17.7, 24.8)
North	27.6 (23.5, 32.1)	24.8 (20.3, 30.0)
Northeast	31.1 (24.4, 38.5)	28.0 (20.6, 36.8)
South	40.8 (36.0, 45.8)	32.1 (27.3, 37.4)
Socioeconomic status		
Lowest	31.2 (22.4, 41.5)	29.6 (20.3, 41.0)
Low	37.6 (29.6, 46.3)	28.9 (20.6, 38.9)
Middle	31.6 (27.4, 36.1)	28.4 (23.7, 33.7)
High	22.5 (19.3, 26.0)	17.6 (14.5, 21.3)
Highest	22.8 (20.1, 25.7)	21.6 (18.6, 24.8)

[1] During the preceding 30 days and among those respondents who work outside of home and usually work in indoors.

6.1.2 Number of workers exposed to SHS in indoor workplaces:

Table 6.1a presents the estimated number of overall workers who are exposed to SHS at indoor workplaces. Overall 3.30 million workers are exposed to SHS in the indoor areas of their workplaces. Considering by gender, the estimated number of male workers exposed to SHS in indoor workplaces is twice that of female workers (2.2 million and 1.1 million respectively). Classified by number of adults, the workers in the 25–44 age-group are most prominently (1.8 million) exposed to SHS in indoor workplaces.

The estimated number of workers living in rural areas who are exposed to SHS in indoor workplaces is almost twice that of those living in urban areas (2.01 million against 1.29 million). Classified by educational level, the highest estimated number of workers who are exposed to SHS in indoor workplaces is to be found among those with a secondary-level education (1.27 million). The Central region has the highest number of exposed workers (0.95 million) and Bangkok metropolis has the lowest (0.35 million). Classified by socioeconomic status, the middle SES has the highest number of those who among all workers were exposed to SHS in indoor workplaces (0.86 million) compared with the lowest SES that has the least number of workers exposed to SHS in the same (0.24 million).

The estimated number of non-smoking workers who are exposed to SHS at indoor workplaces is 2.22 million. The number of non-smoking male workers who are exposed to SHS in indoor workplaces is higher than the number of non-smoking female workers similarly exposed (1.14 million and 1.08 million respectively). Similar to adults overall, non-smoking workers aged 25–44 years have the highest number of persons who are exposed to SHS in indoor workplaces (1.23 million).

The estimated number of rural non-smoking workers who are exposed to SHS in indoor workplaces is higher than the number of those who live in urban areas (1.33 million and 0.89 million). By regions, the Central region has the highest (0.66 million) and Bangkok metropolis has the lowest number (0.24 million) of non-smoking workers exposed to SHS. The non smoking workers in the highest SES category have the highest number of persons exposed to SHS in indoor workplaces (0.69 million).

Table 6.1a: Number (in thousands) of adults ≥15 years old who are exposed to SHS in indoor workplaces, by smoking status and selected demographic characteristics – GATS Thailand, 2009.

Characteristic	Adults exposed to SHS in indoor workplaces[1]	
	Overall	Non-smokers
Overall	3 303.4	2 219.1
Gender		
Male	2 199.2	1 139.3
Female	1 104.3	1 079.8
Age (years)		
15-24	717.6	480.7
25-44	1 800.1	1 234.0
45-59	682.8	443.4
60+	103.0	61.1
Residence		
Urban	1 290.2	890.3
Rural	2 013.2	1 328.8
Education level		
Less than primary	508.1	284.3
Primary	765.2	453.7
Secondary	1 271.0	839.5
University	753.2	636.2
Region		
Bangkok	344.8	241.1
Central	953.9	658.7
North	551.1	409.0
Northeast	900.2	609.4
South	553.3	300.9
Socioeconomic status		
Lowest	243.3	205.9
Low	618.8	371.0
Middle	862.2	543.8
High	724.0	413.0
Highest	855.1	685.5

Note: The sum of the counts across subgroups might not exactly sum up to the overall counts due to rounding and/or missing data.

[1] In the preceding 30 days and among those respondents who work outside of the home and usually work indoors.

6.2 SHS exposure at home

Results for prevalence of SHS exposure at home in the past 30 days are shown in Table 6.1.1. The number (in thousands) of adults exposed to SHS at home (either occurs daily, weekly, monthly or less than monthly) are shown in Table 6.1.1a.

6.2.1 Prevalence of SHS exposure at home:

Overall exposure to SHS at home for adults aged 15 years and above is 39.1%. The prevalence rate reported for males exposed to SHS at home is higher than that for females (43.4% and 35.1% respectively). The age-group of 15–24 years has the highest exposure at home (43.2%) while the remaining three age categories have similar rates of exposure of about 38%. Adults living in rural areas have higher exposure to SHS at home than those who live in urban areas (43.7% and 29.1%). Adults with a lower educational level (less than a primary level and primary level) have similar levels of exposure to SHS (43.3% and 46.0%). Those with a university level of education have the lowest level of exposure to SHS at home (22.2%).

Classified by regions, exposure to SHS at home is the highest among adults who live in the Southern region (58.1%) and the lowest among those who live in Bangkok metropolis (22.8%). As far as socioeconomic status is concerned, adults with the lowest and low SES have higher exposure to SHS at home than those from any other SES level. Adults in the highest SES report the lowest exposure level at home (25.6%).

Prevalence rate of SHS exposure at home for non-smokers is 32.4%. Female non-smokers have a higher exposure to SHS at home than male non-smokers (33.9% and 29.4%). In addition, exposure to SHS at home is higher among non-smokers aged 15–24 years (38.4%) while the remaining three age-groups report similar exposure levels (29.6% to 31.5%).

Non-smokers living in urban areas are less exposed to SHS at home than those living in rural areas (21.8% and 37.3% respectively). When looking at other demographic characteristics such as education level, SES and region, the pattern of exposure to SHS among non-smokers is similar to that of overall population. For example, exposure to SHS at home is the highest among non-smokers living in the Southern region (51.0%) and is the lowest in Bangkok metropolis (16.3%). Similarly, non-smokers belonging to the lowest (38.9%) and low (36.3%) SES levels have exposed themselves to SHS at a higher rate than those from either the high (29.3%) or highest (19.3%) SES levels.

Table 6.1.1: Percentage of adults ≥15 years old who are exposed to SHS at home, by smoking status and selected demographic characteristics – GATS Thailand, 2009.

Characteristic	Adults exposed to SHS at home[1]	
	Overall	Non-smokers
	Percentage (95% CI)	
Overall	39.1 (37.3, 41.0)	32.4 (30.5, 34.3)
Gender		
Male	43.4 (41.1, 45.7)	29.4 (26.8, 32.2)
Female	35.1 (33.1, 37.3)	33.9 (31.8, 36.1)
Age (years)		
15-24	43.2 (39.2, 47.3)	38.4 (33.9, 43.0)
25-44	38.2 (36.0, 40.5)	31.2 (28.9, 33.5)
45-59	37.5 (35.2, 39.8)	29.6 (27.3, 32.1)
60+	38.9 (36.3, 41.5)	31.5 (28.8, 34.3)
Residence		
Urban	29.1 (27.8, 30.5)	21.8 (20.5, 23.2)
Rural	43.7 (41.0, 46.3)	37.3 (34.6, 40.1)
Education level		
Less than primary	43.3 (40.9, 45.6)	35.4 (33.0, 37.9)
Primary	46.0 (42.8, 49.1)	37.9 (34.6, 41.4)
Secondary	36.9 (34.2, 39.7)	31.9 (28.8, 35.1)
University	22.2 (19.9, 24.7)	18.4 (16.1, 21.0)
Region		
Bangkok	22.8 (20.7, 25.1)	16.3 (14.4, 18.4)
Central	36.1 (33.3, 38.9)	27.2 (24.7, 29.9)
North	39.4 (35.5, 43.4)	32.9 (29.3, 36.7)
Northeast	38.8 (34.5, 43.3)	34.4 (29.9, 39.1)
South	58.1 (54.5, 61.6)	51.0 (47.1, 54.8)
Socioeconomic status		
Lowest	43.6 (40.2, 47.0)	38.9 (35.4, 42.6)
Low	43.4 (40.3, 46.6)	36.3 (33.1, 39.7)
Middle	40.6 (38.0, 43.2)	31.7 (29.0, 34.5)
High	37.2 (34.4, 40.0)	29.3 (26.3, 32.5)
Highest	25.6 (23.4, 27.9)	19.3 (17.2, 21.7)

[1] Respondents who reported that smoking inside their homes occurs daily, weekly, monthly, or less than monthly.

6.2.2 Number of adults exposed to SHS at home:

By Table 6.1.1a the estimated overall number of adults aged 15 years and over who were exposed to SHS at home is 20.5 million. Classified by gender, the estimated number of males exposed to SHS at home is higher than females (11.04 million and 9.46 million). Classified by age group, adults aged 25–44 years have the highest number of persons exposed to SHS at home (8.28 million). The estimated number of adults living in rural areas who are exposed to SHS at home is about three times that of those living in urban areas (15.76 million and 4.74 million respectively).

Classified by education levels, the estimated number of adults who are exposed to SHS at home is highest among those with less than a primary level of education (7.64 million) and is lowest among adults with a university-level education or degree (1.43 million). By regions, the Northeastern region has the highest number (6.81 million) and Bangkok metropolis has the lowest number (1.27 million) of adults exposed to SHS at home. By socioeconomic status, the lower SES levels have the highest numbers of adults overall who are exposed to SHS at home (5.54 million and 5.43 million for lowest and low, respectively). The highest SES category has the lowest number of overall adults who are exposed to SHS at home (2.08 million).

The estimated number of non-smokers who are exposed to SHS at home is 12.91 million. The number of non-smoker females who are exposed to SHS at home is about twice as many males (8.85 million and 4.06 million). The pattern of exposure to SHS at home among non-smokers followed a similar pattern observed for overall adult population. By age groups, non-smokers aged 25–44 years have the highest number of persons exposed to SHS at home (4.95 million). The estimated number of rural non-smokers exposed to SHS at home is about 3.6 times more than urban non-smokers (10.13 million against 2.79 million). By regions, the Northeast region has the highest number (4.59 million) and Bangkok metropolis (0.73 million) have the lowest number of non-smokers exposed to SHS at home. By socioeconomic status, the highest number of persons exposed to SHS at home among non-smokers lies in the lowest SES category (4.06 million) and the lowest number is to be found among the highest SES (1.24 million).

Table 6.1.1a: Number (in thousands) of adults aged ≥15 years who are exposed to SHS at home, by smoking status and selected demographic characteristics – GATS Thailand, 2009.

Characteristic	Adults exposed to SHS at home[1]	
	Overall	Non-smokers
Overall	20 498.0	12 911.9
Gender		
Male	11 036.6	4 057.3
Female	9 461.4	8 854.6
Age (years)		
15-24	4 521.0	3 216.6
25-44	8 276.5	4 953.6
45-59	4 600.4	2 759.0
60+	3 100.1	1 982.8
Residence		
Urban	4 742.3	2 786.9
Rural	15 755.7	10 125.0
Education level		
Less than primary	7 637.2	4 723.5
Primary	5 051.0	2 944.9
Secondary	6 363.0	4 212.2
University	1 428.9	1 014.5
Region		
Bangkok	1 274.0	734.8
Central	4 506.1	2 600.8
North	3 861.4	2 496.9
Northeast	6 811.4	4 586.9
South	4 045.0	2 492.6
Socioeconomic status		
Lowest	5 542.2	4 059.0
Low	5 434.1	3 465.6
Middle	4 361.4	2 405.8
High	3 062.0	1 724.1
Highest	2 079.4	1 240.5

Note: The sum of the counts across subgroups may not exactly add up to the overall count due to rounding of and/or missing data.

[1] Respondents who reported that smoking inside the home occurs daily, weekly, monthly, or less than monthly.

6.3 SHS exposure in public places

Common sites of exposure to SHS in public places are government buildings, health-care facilities, restaurants, public transport and outside markets. Table 6.2 and Table 6.2a present the prevalence rate of SHS exposures in these public places for the preceding 30 days for all adults and for non-smokers aged 15 years and over, respectively.

6.3.1 Prevalence of adults exposed to SHS in public places:

Table 6.2 reveals that outside markets are the most common sites for the highest exposure to SHS among adults aged 15 years and over (53.5%). Second-hand smoke exposures in other public places are lower, such as with restaurants (9.0%), public transport (6.3%), government buildings (3.9%) and health-care facilities (2.0%).

Going by demographic characteristics, exposure to SHS in all sites is similar to overall exposure. When factoring in gender, males are more exposed to SHS in restaurants than females (10.8% and 7.2% respectively). Exposure levels to SHS in other public places are quite similar for males and females. Classified by age-group, adults aged 15–24 years have the highest exposures to SHS in all public places, and especially in marketplaces (62.1%). Exposure in urban areas is higher than in rural areas for all public places. By educational level, adults with a university educational level are more exposed to tobacco smoke in all public places (except in outside markets) than adults with other educational levels. By regions, adults living in the Southern region are more exposed to SHS in all public places (except in public transportation) than adults in other regions. Those who live in the Bangkok Metropolis area have the highest exposure to SHS on public transport (14.8%). By socioeconomic status, adults with the highest SES are more exposed to SHS in public places than all other SES levels, except for the exposure on public transport, where the highest exposure is among the high SES group (7.6%).

Table 6.2: Percentage of adults ≥15 years old who were exposed to SHS in public places in the past 30 days, by selected demographic characteristics – GATS Thailand, 2009.

Characteristic	Adults exposed to SHS[1] in...				
	Government buildings	Health-care facilities	Restaurants	Public transport	Outside markets
			Percentage (95% CI)		
Overall	3.9 (3.4, 4.5)	2.0 (1.8, 2.4)	9.0 (8.2, 9.8)	6.3 (5.7, 7.1)	53.5 (52.0, 55.0)
Gender					
Male	4.8 (4.1, 5.7)	2.0 (1.6, 2.6)	10.8 (9.8, 12.0)	5.1 (4.4, 5.8)	54.4 (52.6, 56.3)
Female	3.1 (2.5, 3.9)	2.1 (1.7, 2.5)	7.2 (6.4, 8.1)	7.5 (6.5, 8.7)	52.7 (50.8, 54.6)
Age (years)					
15-24	5.9 (4.1, 8.5)	2.1 (1.3, 3.4)	11.9 (9.7, 14.4)	10.9 (8.6, 13.9)	62.1 (58.7, 65.4)
25-44	3.7 (3.2, 4.2)	2.1 (1.7, 2.5)	11.2 (10.1, 12.4)	6.3 (5.5, 7.1)	59.9 (57.9, 61.8)
45-59	3.9 (3.3, 4.6)	1.9 (1.5, 2.3)	6.8 (6.0, 7.6)	4.5 (3.9, 5.2)	50.9 (48.8, 53.0)
60+	2.1 (1.6, 2.7)	2.2 (1.7, 2.9)	2.4 (1.9, 3.1)	3.3 (2.7, 4.0)	28.9 (27.0, 30.9)
Residence					
Urban	4.5 (4.0, 5.0)	2.4 (2.1, 2.8)	12.6 (11.6, 13.6)	9.5 (8.5, 10.5)	57.4 (56.0, 58.8)
Rural	3.7 (3.0, 4.5)	1.9 (1.5, 2.3)	7.4 (6.4, 8.5)	4.9 (4.1, 6.0)	51.8 (49.7, 53.9)
Education level					
Less than primary	2.0 (1.6, 2.5)	1.9 (1.5, 2.4)	2.8 (2.3, 3.4)	3.5 (3.0, 4.1)	38.9 (36.9, 40.8)
Primary	2.9 (2.2, 3.9)	1.6 (1.1, 2.3)	6.9 (5.7, 8.3)	6.1 (4.9, 7.7)	59.3 (56.3, 62.3)
Secondary	5.3 (4.2, 6.7)	2.2 (1.6, 2.9)	12.8 (11.4, 14.4)	8.3 (6.8, 10.1)	62.0 (59.7, 64.2)
University	7.4 (6.2, 8.8)	2.9 (2.3, 3.8)	19.3 (17.4, 21.3)	9.1 (7.5, 11.1)	61.1 (58.6, 63.5)
Region					
Bangkok	4.3 (3.5, 5.2)	2.7 (2.0, 3.5)	11.5 (9.9, 13.3)	14.8 (12.8, 17.0)	55.0 (52.4, 57.6)
Central	2.6 (2.0, 3.4)	2.0 (1.5, 2.6)	10.7 (9.0, 12.7)	6.2 (5.0, 7.6)	57.8 (55.5, 60.1)
North	3.2 (2.4, 4.3)	1.5 (1.0, 2.3)	6.8 (5.7, 8.0)	2.9 (2.0, 4.0)	44.0 (40.1, 47.9)
Northeast	4.0 (2.8, 5.5)	1.3 (0.8, 2.2)	4.3 (3.4, 5.5)	4.8 (3.4, 6.6)	49.9 (46.6, 53.1)
South	6.9 (5.7, 8.3)	4.3 (3.4, 5.3)	18.8 (16.0, 22.1)	8.7 (6.9, 10.8)	67.4 (64.4, 70.2)
Socioeconomic status					
Lowest	3.5 (2.3, 5.2)	1.8 (1.2, 2.8)	4.4 (3.6, 5.4)	6.4 (4.9, 8.2)	40.3 (37.7, 43.0)
Low	2.8 (2.0, 3.9)	1.3 (1.0, 1.7)	6.6 (5.2, 8.2)	5.9 (4.7, 7.2)	52.6 (49.9, 55.3)
Middle	3.1 (2.5, 4.0)	2.1 (1.5, 2.9)	9.1 (7.8, 10.5)	5.7 (4.7, 6.8)	58.1 (55.3, 60.7)
High	4.6 (3.6, 5.7)	2.5 (1.9, 3.3)	12.2 (10.6, 13.9)	7.6 (6.3, 9.1)	61.5 (58.7, 64.3)
Highest	6.7 (5.8, 7.8)	3.1 (2.5, 3.9)	16.6 (15.0, 18.2)	6.6 (5.6, 7.8)	61.7 (59.3, 64.0)

[1] In the past 30 days.

6.3.2 Prevalence of non-smokers exposed to SHS in public places:

Table 6.2a indicates that outside markets are the most common place of exposure to SHS for non-smokers (54.2%), followed by restaurants (8.8%), public transport (6.9%), government buildings (3.8%) and health-care facilities (2.2%).

Table 6.2a: Percentage of non-smokers ≥15 years old who were exposed to SHS in public places in the past 30 days, by selected demographic characteristics – GATS Thailand, 2009.

Characteristic	Adults exposed to SHS[1] in...				
	Government buildings	Health-care facilities	Restaurants	Public transport	Outside markets
	Percentage (95% CI)				
Non-smokers	3.8 (3.2, 4.4)	2.2 (1.8, 2.5)	8.8 (8.0, 9.6)	6.9 (6.1, 7.7)	54.2 (52.6, 55.9)
Gender					
Male	5.1 (4.1, 6.3)	2.4 (1.8, 3.1)	11.6 (10.2, 13.1)	5.7 (4.8, 6.7)	56.7 (54.4, 59.0)
Female	3.1 (2.5, 3.9)	2.1 (1.7, 2.5)	7.3 (6.5, 8.2)	7.5 (6.5, 8.7)	53.0 (51.0, 54.9)
Age (years)					
15-24	5.7 (3.7, 8.7)	1.9 (1.1, 3.3)	11.3 (9.3, 13.8)	12.0 (9.4, 15.2)	63.0 (59.3, 66.6)
25-44	3.5 (2.9, 4.1)	2.3 (1.9, 2.9)	11.1 (9.9, 12.4)	6.7 (5.8, 7.8)	61.6 (59.4, 63.8)
45-59	3.7 (3.0, 4.6)	2.0 (1.6, 2.5)	6.7 (5.8, 7.7)	4.8 (4.1, 5.6)	51.6 (49.3, 53.9)
60+	2.2 (1.6, 2.9)	2.4 (1.8, 3.2)	2.5 (1.9, 3.3)	3.4 (2.7, 4.2)	27.6 (25.5, 29.9)
Residence					
Urban	4.4 (3.8, 5.0)	2.7 (2.3, 3.1)	12.2 (11.2, 13.3)	9.8 (8.7, 10.9)	57.2 (55.6, 58.7)
Rural	3.5 (2.8, 4.4)	1.9 (1.5, 2.5)	7.2 (6.2, 8.4)	5.5 (4.5, 6.7)	52.9 (50.6, 55.1)
Education level					
Less than primary	1.8 (1.4, 2.4)	2.1 (1.6, 2.8)	2.6 (2.1, 3.2)	3.7 (3.1, 4.4)	38.3 (36.3, 40.4)
Primary	2.9 (2.0, 4.1)	1.7 (1.1, 2.7)	6.0 (4.8, 7.5)	6.6 (5.0, 8.6)	61.2 (57.8, 64.4)
Secondary	4.9 (3.7, 6.5)	2.1 (1.6, 2.9)	12.4 (10.9, 14.0)	9.0 (7.3, 11.0)	63.2 (60.6, 65.7)
University	7.3 (6.1, 8.8)	2.9 (2.2, 3.7)	19.1 (17.0, 21.3)	10.0 (8.2, 12.2)	61.4 (58.6, 64.1)
Region					
Bangkok	4.2 (3.3, 5.3)	2.8 (2.1, 3.7)	11.1 (9.5, 13.1)	15.1 (13.0, 17.5)	55.1 (52.2, 58.0)
Central	2.3 (1.8, 3.1)	2.3 (1.8, 3.0)	10.7 (9.0, 12.8)	6.5 (5.2, 8.1)	57.7 (55.2, 60.1)
North	3.0 (2.2, 4.1)	1.7 (1.1, 2.5)	7.3 (6.0, 8.8)	3.0 (2.1, 4.2)	45.9 (42.0, 49.9)
Northeast	4.1 (2.8, 5.8)	1.3 (0.8, 2.3)	4.1 (3.2, 5.4)	5.3 (3.8, 7.4)	51.6 (48.1, 55.1)
South	6.6 (5.4, 8.1)	4.3 (3.3, 5.5)	18.1 (15.1, 21.5)	10.2 (8.1, 12.9)	66.9 (63.6, 70.0)
Socioeconomic status					
Lowest	3.9 (2.5, 6.0)	2.0 (1.2, 3.2)	4.5 (3.6, 5.7)	6.9 (5.2, 9.1)	41.6 (38.7, 44.6)
Low	2.6 (1.7, 3.8)	1.3 (1.0, 1.8)	6.7 (5.3, 8.4)	6.8 (5.4, 8.5)	52.8 (49.7, 56.0)
Middle	2.8 (2.1, 3.8)	2.0 (1.5, 2.7)	8.8 (7.5, 10.4)	6.2 (5.1, 7.6)	59.8 (56.7, 62.9)
High	3.9 (3.0, 4.9)	2.7 (2.0, 3.6)	11.5 (9.8, 13.6)	7.5 (6.1, 9.2)	62.4 (59.3, 65.4)
Highest	6.4 (5.4, 7.7)	3.5 (2.7, 4.4)	16.4 (14.7, 18.1)	7.1 (5.9, 8.5)	62.8 (60.2, 65.4)

[1] In the past 30 days.

In short, home is the most common site of exposure to SHS for adults aged 15–24 years. Adults who live in rural areas, have lower education levels (less than primary or primary), live in the Southern region, and are in the lowest SES category report being exposed to SHS at home. The level of exposure at the workplace was generally lower than that at home. However, workers who were exposed to SHS at indoor workplaces vary across different groups. The rates are higher among males, persons aged 60 years and over, those living in rural areas, living in the Southern region and belonging to lower SES categories compared to other groups. For public places, outside markets are the most common site of exposure to SHS followed by restaurants and public transport for both overall population and non-smokers aged 15 years and above.

7

Economics

7. Economics

The government-owned Thailand Tobacco Monopoly (TTM), established in 1939, is the main domestic producer of cigarettes. Foreign cigarettes are imported by local companies or trade agents such as Phillip Morris Co. Ltd (Thailand), BAT, RJ Reynolds, Tobacco of Japan and others. Nowadays the market share of these companies totals around one fourth of the entire cigarette supply. Thailand has allowed the import of cigarettes since 1991 but domestic cigarettes have always held a larger proportion of the market share. However, the pressure from world trade and taxation policies have led to a gradual erosion in the domestic share while the share of imported cigarettes in the market has continuously increased from 0.6% in 1991 to 24.6% in 2007[18]. The International Tobacco Control (ITC) Project Thailand in 2007 showed that the most three popular domestic cigarettes brands were Krongthip, Saifon and Wonder while the most popular imported cigarettes were of the L&M, Marlboro, Camel and Winston[19] brands.

This chapter focuses on current smokers who used manufactured cigarettes – particularly in the last instance of purchase – source of last purchase, expenditure on cigarettes and pictorial health warnings on the last cigarette package purchased.

Key findings;

- *The most preferred brand was Krongthip.*
- *9 in 10 of current smokers buy manufactured cigarettes from grocery stores.*
- *An average of 575.7 Baht per month was spent for manufactured cigarettes.*
- *2.6% of current manufactured-cigarette smokers reported that their last purchase of a cigarette package did not have a pictorial health warning.*

7.1 Last brand of manufactured cigarettes purchased

GATS Thailand asked respondents to report on the brand names of the last cigarette packet purchased. Among the five most purchased brands, the majority were local except for L&M: Krongthip (51.1%), Wonder (20.0%), Saifon (11.4%), L&M (10.6%) and Krungthong (1.9%). By demographic characteristics, all groups of current manufactured-cigarette smokers mostly bought the Krongthip brand at their last purchase. The largest category of smokers buying this brand of cigarettes were males aged 15-24 years, who lived in rural areas, had a primary education level, lived in the Southern region, and belonged to the lowest SES level (Table 7.1).

Table 7.1: Percentage of current manufactured-cigarette smokers aged ≥15 years, by last brand of manufactured-cigarette purchased and selected demographic characteristics – GATS Thailand, 2009.

Characteristic	Last brand purchased				
	Krongthip	Wander	Saifon	L&M	Krungthong
	Percentage (95% CI)				
Overall	51.1 (47.9, 54.2)	20.0 (17.4, 22.9)	11.4 (9.6, 13.6)	10.6 (09.1, 12.5)	1.9 (1.4, 2.7)
Gender					
Male	52.0 (48.7, 55.2)	19.9 (17.2, 22.8)	11.3 (9.4, 13.5)	10.1 (8.5, 11.9)	2.0 (1.5, 2.8)
Female	29.6 (21.5, 39.2)	22.1 (15.3, 30.8)	15.4 (9.9, 23.1)	24.2 (15.5, 35.9)	0.4 (0.0, 2.5)*
Age (years)					
15-24	64.9 (57.0, 72.1)	11.0 (6.5, 17.9)	8.5 (5.1, 13.8)	12.0 (7.9, 17.7)	0.5 (0.1, 2.2)*
25-44	49.1 (45.3, 52.9)	20.5 (17.5, 24.0)	12.9 (10.5, 15.7)	11.4 (9.5, 13.7)	1.5 (0.9, 2.5)
45-59	43.9 (39.4, 48.4)	27.6 (23.7, 31.8)	10.2 (7.8, 13.2)	7.7 (5.9, 10.0)	4.3 (2.8, 6.6)
60+	31.6 (23.8, 40.5)	29.8 (22.5, 38.3)	15.6 (9.9, 23.7)	7.3 (4.6, 11.2)	4.7 (2.3, 9.4)
Residence					
Urban	44.8 (42.1, 47.6)	17.2 (15.3, 19.4)	14.5 (12.7, 16.6)	15.0 (13.2, 17.1)	2.2 (1.5, 3.0)
Rural	54.9 (50.1, 59.6)	21.6 (17.7, 26.1)	9.6 (7.0, 12.9)	8.0 (5.9, 10.8)	1.8 (1.1, 2.9)
Education level					
Less than primary	48.8 (43.1, 54.6)	29.7(25.0, 34.8)	8.8 (6.5, 11.7)	4.8 (3.0, 7.6)	3.2 (2.0, 5.0)
Primary	55.3 (49.5, 60.9)	20.3 (16.1, 25.2)	10.8 (7.3, 15.6)	7.1 (4.8, 10.5)	1.6 (0.9, 2.7)*
Secondary	54.3 (49.2, 59.2)	17.7 (13.5, 22.9)	11.9 (9.5, 14.9)	11.4 (8.8, 14.6)	1.2 (0.7, 2.1)*
University	32.0 (25.3, 39.6)	12.9 (8.4, 19.1)	15.3 (10.9, 21.0)	25.2 (20.0, 31.3)	3.7 (1.8, 7.6)*
Region					
Bangkok	40.7 (36.6, 45.0)	12.6 (10.0, 15.8)	17.6 (14.5, 21.3)	21.2 (17.4, 25.5)	2.1 (1.3, 3.6)*
Central	50.3 (44.8, 55.8)	22.5 (18.6, 27.0)	11.8 (9.0, 15.2)	9.7 (6.5, 14.4)	1.8 (0.9, 3.6)*
North	43.9 (35.8, 52.4)	32.9 (25.5, 41.2)	6.9 (4.2, 11.2)	10.9 (6.8, 17.1)	0.7 (0.2, 1.8)*
Northeast	56.4 (48.7, 63.8)	22.4 (16.3, 30.0)	14.4 (9.8, 20.5)	2.4 (1.3, 4.6)	1.1 (0.5, 2.4)*
South	56.5 (50.8, 61.9)	6.4 (4.4, 9.3)	4.5 (3.0, 6.8)	18.9 (14.6, 24.1)	4.5 (2.6, 7.8)
Socioeconomic status					
Lowest	56.4 (46.2, 66.1)	22.1 (15.0, 31.2)	11.5 (5.3, 23.3)	2.9 (1.6, 5.2)*	1.1 (0.3, 3.6)*
Low	55.3 (47.3, 62.9)	18.2 (12.8, 25.3)	9.8 (6.6, 14.1)	11.1 (6.5, 18.2)	1.9 (0.9, 4.0)*
Middle	54.4 (48.6, 60.2)	22.7 (17.8, 28.4)	10.7 (7.8, 14.5)	7.0 (5.2, 9.3)	1.8 (0.9, 3.3)*
High	51.1 (45.6, 56.5)	21.1 (17.0, 25.9)	11.3 (8.6, 14.8)	11.1 (8.2, 14.9)	1.6 (0.9, 3.0)*
Highest	38.7 (33.5, 44.1)	14.9 (11.5, 19.2)	14.3 (11.3, 18.0)	19.8 (16.4, 23.7)	3.1 (1.9, 5.3)

Note: Current manufactured-cigarette smokers includes daily and occasional (less than daily) use. The top five reported brands last purchased among all manufactured cigarettes smokers are shown here.

* Indicates the estimate is based on sample size of less than 25.

7.2 Source of last purchase of cigarettes among manufactured-cigarette smokers

Table 7.2 presents the most common source of last purchase of cigarettes among current manufactured-cigarette smokers. The most common were local grocery stores (91.1%), convenience shops (7.1%) and other sources (1.8%) which included wholesale shops/department stores, street vendors, hawkers, flea markets, duty-free shops, purchases made from outside the country, the Internet, military stores, and from another person and others.

Classified by gender, a higher percentage of male smokers buy cigarettes from local groceries than female smokers (91.5% males against 82.2 % females). By age, there is not much of a difference in purchasing trends among the age-groups. Of smokers who bought cigarettes from convenience shops, a high percentage belongs to urban areas (14.1%) when compared with rural areas (2.8%). By regions, most smokers in all regions purchased cigarettes from grocery stores. The proportion of grocery store purchases ranges from a low of 76.8% in Bangkok metropolis to a high 95.9% in the Northeast. About 20.1% of manufactured-cigarette smokers in Bangkok metropolis reported their last purchase from convenience shops. Classified by socioeconomic status, the proportion of manufactured-cigarette smokers purchasing cigarettes from grocery stores who were from the highest SES level is lowest at 81.1% compared with those from the lowest SES level who returned the highest figures of 94.9%.

7.3 Cigarette expenditure

The average expenditure for cigarettes among manufactured-cigarette smokers in Thailand is presented in Table 7.3. On an average a current manufactured-cigarette smoker spends 575.7 Baht per month. By gender, male current-manufactured cigarette smokers spend 579.2 Baht per month, which is about 90 Baht higher than female smokers. The highest-spending age-group is that of smokers aged 45-49 years, who spend 695.1 Baht per month.

Urban current smokers spend 682.8 Baht per month, which is 172 Baht higher than the average amount spent by rural smokers. Smokers with a University education (659.6 Baht per month) spend more compared to smokers with an education level of less than primary (575.2 Baht per month). The cigarette expenditure of smokers living in Bangkok is about 300 Baht higher (759.8 Baht per month) than those living in the Northern region, who spend 460.9 Baht per month. Similarly, smokers with the highest SES level spend on an average 754.0 Baht per month and those in the lowest SES level spend 450.3 Baht per month, which is a difference of 300 Baht.

Table 7.2: Percentage distribution of the source of last purchase of cigarettes among manufactured-cigarette smokers ≥ 15 years old, by selected demographic characteristics – GATS Thailand, 2009.

Characteristic	Grocery	Convenient shop	Other[1]	Total
		Percentage (95% CI)		
Overall	91.1 (89.9, 92.3)	7.1 (6.1, 8.2)	1.8 (1.3, 2.5)	100
Gender				
Male	91.5 (90.2, 92.6)	6.8 (5.8, 7.9)	1.7 (1.2, 2.5)	100
Female	82.2 (74.8, 87.8)	14.5 (9.5, 21.4)	3.3 (1.3, 8.2)*	100
Age (years)[2]				
<18	95.9 (87.0, 98.8)	3.9 (1.1, 13.0)*	0.2 (0.0, 1.6)*	100
18-24	94.6 (92.0, 96.4)	4.5 (3.0, 6.7)	0.9 (0.3, 2.9)*	100
25+	90.0 (88.5, 91.3)	7.9 (6.8, 9.2)	2.1 (1.4, 3.0)	100
Residence				
Urban	83.2 (81.0, 85.2)	14.1 (12.3, 16.2)	2.7 (1.9, 3.7)	100
Rural	96.0 (94.4, 97.1)	2.8 (1.9, 4.0)	1.2 (0.6, 2.5)*	100
Region				
Bangkok	76.8 (73.0, 80.2)	20.1 (16.9, 23.7)	3.1 (2.0, 5.0)	100
Central	91.2 (88.6, 93.2)	6.6 (4.8, 8.9)	2.2 (1.3, 4.0)*	100
North	91.7 (87.5, 94.6)	6.1 (4.2, 8.9)	2.2 (0.5, 8.1)*	100
Northeast	95.9 (93.5, 97.4)	3.3 (2.0, 5.4)	0.8 (0.4, 1.6)*	100
South	93.0 (89.9, 95.2)	5.5 (3.6, 8.3)	1.5 (0.5, 3.9)*	100
Socioeconomic status				
Lowest	94.9 (91.3, 97.0)	3.1 (1.8, 5.5)*	2.0 (0.7, 5.4)*	100
Low	94.7 (91.2, 96.8)	3.8 (2.3, 6.3)*	1.5 (0.5, 4.3)*	100
Middle	95.6 (94.1, 96.8)	2.8 (1.9, 4.1)	1.6 (1.0, 2.7)*	100
High	89.2 (86.4, 91.5)	9.2 (7.1, 11.9)	1.6 (0.9, 2.8)*	100
Highest	81.1 (77.4, 84.3)	16.5 (13.5, 20.1)	2.4 (1.4, 4.1)*	100

[1] Includes: wholesale shop/department store, street vendor, hawker, flea market, duty-free shop, purchase outside the country, purchased on the Internet, military store, purchased from another person, and others.

[2] Age-groups reported in this table have different categories than the standard four reporting age categories due to the national law that prohibits persons below 18 years from access to tobacco products.

* Indicates the estimate is based on sample size of less than 25.

Table 7.3: Average cigarette expenditure per month among manufactured-cigarette smokers ≥15 years old, by selected demographic characteristics – GATS Thailand, 2009.

Characteristic	Cigarette expenditures per month (*Baht*)
	Average (95% CI)
Overall	575.7 (549.5, 602.0)
Gender	
Male	579.2 (551.6, 606.9)
Female	489.9 (405.8, 574.1)
Age (years)	
15-24	458.3 (398.0, 518.7)
25-44	592.0 (557.5, 626.5)
45-59	695.1 (640.1, 750.0)
60+	547.5 (464.8, 630.2)
Residence	
Urban	682.8 (653.7, 711.9)
Rural	510.8 (473.5, 548.2)
Education level	
Less than primary	575.2 (520.9, 629.5)
Primary	566.6 (508.4, 624.8)
Secondary	560.7 (524.7, 596.6)
University	659.6 (586.7, 732.6)
Region	
Bangkok	759.8 (709.9, 809.8)
Central	628.0 (577.7, 678.3)
North	460.9 (398.2, 523.7)
Northeast	523.0 (466.3, 579.7)
South	545.0 (494.2, 595.7)
Socioeconomic status	
Lowest	450.3 (353.2, 547.3)
Low	481.6 (426.7, 536.5)
Middle	564.8 (517.6, 612.0)
High	582.4 (532.3, 632.5)
Highest	754.0 (699.5, 808.6)

7.4 Pictorial health warnings (PHW) on the last cigarette packet purchased

Most current-manufactured cigarette smokers (97.4%) said their last cigarette packet purchased had pictorial health warnings (PHWs) and only 2.6% said it did not have the warnings. This is presented in Table 7.4. Irrespective of the demographic characteristics, the majority of current manufactured-cigarette smokers said that there were PHWs on cigarette packets, with the proportions ranging from a low of 91.4% in the Southern Region to a high of 99.6% in Bangkok metropolis. The highest percentage of current smokers, from different classified categories, who said their last cigarette packet purchased did not have PHWs was: males (2.6%), those belonging to urban areas (2.0%), and those living in the Southern region (8.6%).

Table 7.4: Percentage distribution of current-manufactured cigarette smokers ≥ 15 years old whose last purchased cigarette packet had and did not have a PHW, by selected demographic characteristics – GATS Thailand, 2009.

Characteristic	Cigarette package last purchased that...		Total
	had a PHW	did not have a PHW	
	Percentage (95% CI)		
Overall	97.4 (95.8, 98.4)	2.6 (1.6, 4.2)	100
Gender			
Male	97.4 (95.7, 98.4)	2.6 (1.6, 4.3)	100
Female	97.1 (90.2, 99.2)	2.9 (0.8, 9.8)*	100
Age (years)			
15-24	97.2 (91.6, 99.1)	2.8 (0.9, 8.4)*	100
25-44	97.8 (95.5, 98.9)	2.2 (1.1, 4.5)*	100
45-59	97.7 (95.7, 98.8)	2.3 (1.2, 4.3)*	100
60+	93.4 (86.4, 96.9)	6.6 (3.1, 13.6)*	100
Residence			
Urban	98.0 (96.5, 98.8)	2.0 (1.2, 3.5)	100
Rural	96.9 (94.0, 98.4)	3.1 (1.6, 6.0)*	100
Education level			
Less than primary	96.6 (94.4, 98.0)	3.4 (2.0, 5.6)*	100
Primary	97.0 (93.1, 98.8)	3.0 (1.2, 6.9)*	100
Secondary	98.0 (95.9, 99.0)	2.0 (1.0, 4.1)*	100
University	97.3 (87.9, 99.5)	2.7 (0.5, 12.1)*	100
Region			
Bangkok	99.6 (98.6, 99.9)	0.4 (0.1, 1.4)*	100
Central	98.3 (95.6, 99.4)	1.7 (0.6, 4.4)*	100
North	95.8 (85.6, 98.9)	4.2 (1.1, 14.4)*	100
Northeast	99.0 (97.3, 99.6)	1.0 (0.4 2.7)*	100
South	91.4 (84.2, 95.5)	8.6 (4.5, 15.8)	100
Socioeconomic status			
Lowest	94.7 (85.8, 98.1)	5.3 (1.9, 14.2)*	100
Low	94.3 (86.9, 97.6)	5.7 (2.4, 13.1)*	100
Middle	98.2 (96.5, 99.1)	1.8 (0.9, 3.5)*	100
High	98.1 (96.4, 99.0)	1.9 (1.0, 3.6)*	100
Highest	98.2 (96.3, 99.1)	1.8 (0.9, 3.7)*	100

* Indicates the estimate is based on sample size of less than 25.

In short, the average expenditure for cigarettes among manufactured-cigarette smokers is 575.7 Baht per month. Survey results also show that the average price per pack of manufactured cigarettes is 44.7 Baht. Calculating the average price of 100 packs of manufactured cigarettes (4 470 Baht) and factoring in the gross domestic product (GDP) as of 25 May 2009 (131 246 Baht per capita)[20], this implies that "3.4% of national income in terms of GDP was spent on the purchase of manufactured cigarettes" in the year 2009. Characteristics of persons who bought cigarettes without a PHW on the packet were: males, those belong to urban areas, and those living in the Southern region.

8

Media

8. Media

The Royal Thai Government and the nongovernmental organization (NGO) Action on Smoking and Health (ASH-Thailand) have over the past 20 years extensively conducted education, social marketing and anti-smoking campaigns in the country. Efforts in this direction have also included placing textual health warnings on cigarette packets under the provisions of the Tobacco Products Control Act 1992[(23)].

In 2005 Thailand became only the fourth country in the world to successfully implement the placing of pictorial health warnings (PHWs) on cigarette packets. According to the 11th Notification, issued on 27 March 2007, under the Tobacco Products Control Act 1992[(24)], these pictures should be in colour and cover at least 50% of the total surface area in the front and back of cigarette packets and should be in black-and-white on packets of shredded tobacco[(25)]. This Act also bans all forms of direct and indirect tobacco advertising, sales promotion and sponsorship, and various forms of tobacco promotion including gifts, discounts and the distribution of coupons and free items by tobacco companies. Prohibition of the display of cigarette packets or logos of tobacco brands at the points of sale was also enforced in 2005[(14)]. With such rigorous legislation in place, both the Thailand Tobacco Monopoly (TTM) and the transnational tobacco companies in the country have since shifted their strategy to promoting corporate social responsibility (CSR) activities.

GATS in Thailand provides an opportunity to track tobacco control interventions and focus on awareness through the media for both smokers and non-smokers. The data presented in this chapter relay information on the perception of adults regarding anti-smoking information disseminated through various mass media and in public places, health warnings[4] on different tobacco products, and on pro-tobacco advertising.

Key findings:

- *Nine in 10 adults took note of anti-smoking information in the media and public places.*
- *Nine in 10 current cigarette smokers took note of a pictorial health warning (PHW) on cigarette packets, and seven in 10 current cigarette smokers contemplated quitting because of the PHW.*
- *Two in 10 of current smokers of hand-rolled cigarettes and users of smokeless tobacco took note of a PHW on raw tobacco packets and one in 10 of current hand-rolled cigarette smokers and smokeless tobacco users thought about quitting on account of the PHW.*
- *15.9% of adults noticed any cigarette advertisement, sponsorship or promotion campaign.*

---

[4] Health warning label in Thailand means PHW on the packet which is coloured for cigarette and cigar packs and black-and-white for packets of shredded tobacco for hand-rolled cigarette.

8.1 Noticed anti-smoking information in various media and in public places

This section covers the degree of awareness of anti-smoking information in the media and displayed in public places. This includes newspapers or magazines, television, radio, billboards, leaflets or stickers, the Internet, through campaign and promotional activities, demonstration boards and other media to disseminate information. Table 8.1 reveals that 86.9% of all adults aged 15 years and above noticed any anti-smoking information broadcast through the media or displayed in public places at any location. Of them, 74.4% noted the information on television and 39% saw the information on billboards. Other media vehicles which carried anti-smoking information and were noticed include leaflets or stickers (38.3%), radio (33.5%) and demonstration boards (30.3%).

Classified by smoking status, current smokers noticed and obtained anti-smoking information in the same way as non-smokers in all kinds of media, except in the case of newspapers or magazines (21.7% for current smokers against 29.1% for non-smokers) and demonstration boards (23.8% against 32.4%).

Males and females take equal note of anti-smoking information. Persons aged between 15 and 24 years show a higher proportion of noticing such information than those aged over 25 years, except in the case where radio is the source of information. Urban population notices anti-smoking information more than the rural population, especially on newspapers or magazines, television, billboards, leaflets or stickers and through campaign activities.

Classified by region, most adults (92.2%) in Bangkok metropolis have noticed anti-smoking information while 86% of people in other regions have also been subjected to the same information. Classified by socioeconomic status, the proportion of adults who noticed the anti-smoking information varied from 81.5% in the lowest SES category to 93.3% in highest SES category.

Among current smokers, the proportion of males (85.5%) who were exposed to anti-smoking information in various places is higher than females (79.4%). Current smokers aged between 15 and 24 years and those over 25 years of age can be exposed equally to the information. Urban populations have noticed the information to a greater degree than the rural population for all forms of media, except on the radio in which case the degree of exposure is quite similar for both urban and rural. The proportion of adults exposed to anti-smoking information varied slightly among the regions, with the corresponding figures for each region in descending order being: Bangkok metropolis – 91.6%, South – 88.6%, Central – 85.0%, Northeast – 81.2%, and North – 81.2%. Classified by socioeconomic status, almost 90% of current smokers in the highest SES category and 78.4% in lowest had been exposed to some form of anti-smoking information at any location.

Among non-smokers, approximately 87% of females and 89% of males have noticed anti-smoking information in any location. The pattern is consistent across all media. Non-smokers in the 15–24 year age-group have accessed more information than non-smokers in 25-and-above age-group from all sources except the radio. Non-smokers from urban areas who have accessed information numbered 5% more than those from rural areas. Around 87% of those living in the Central and Northern regions have been exposed to information from any location compared to 92.4% of those living in Bangkok metropolis. Classified by socioeconomic status, only 81.5% of non-smokers from the lowest SES have noticed such information whereas the figure was a high 93.3% among non-smokers from the highest SES category.

Table 8.1: Percentage of adults ≥15years old who noticed anti-cigarette smoking information during the last 30 days in various places, by smoking status and selected demographic characteristics – GATS Thailand, 2009.

Places	Overall	Gender		Age (years)		Residence	
		Male	Female	15-24	≥25	Urban	Rural
Overall							
In newspapers or in magazines	27.4 (26.0, 28.8)	29.1 (27.4, 30.9)	25.7 (24.2, 27.3)	29.8 (26.9, 32.9)	26.8 (25.4, 28.2)	38.2 (36.7, 39.7)	22.5 (20.6, 24.6)
On television	74.4 (72.8, 76.0)	73.9 (72.0, 75.7)	74.9 (73.1, 76.7)	74.5 (71.0, 77.6)	74.4 (72.8, 76.0)	77.8 (76.4, 79.0)	73.0 (70.6, 75.2)
On the radio	33.5 (31.7, 35.3)	34.9 (32.8, 37.2)	32.1 (30.4, 33.9)	28.9 (25.2, 32.8)	34.6 (33.0, 36.3)	32.9 (31.5, 34.4)	33.7 (31.3, 36.3)
On billboards	39.0 (36.9, 41.2)	39.8 (37.4, 42.3)	38.3 (36.1, 40.5)	46.9 (42.8, 51.1)	37.0 (35.0, 39.1)	46.2 (44.4, 48.0)	35.8 (32.8, 38.8)
Leaflet/sticker	38.3 (36.3, 40.3)	39.1 (36.7, 41.6)	37.5 (35.4, 39.7)	48.0 (43.9, 52.1)	35.9 (33.9, 37.9)	43.6 (41.8, 45.4)	35.9 (33.1, 38.8)
Internet	6.3 (5.6, 7.1)	5.5 (4.6, 6.4)	7.1 (6.2, 8.2)	17.7 (15.0, 20.7)	3.5 (3.1, 3.9)	9.0 (8.2, 9.9)	5.1 (4.2, 6.2)
Campaign activity	15.3 (13.7, 17.1)	15.0 (13.3, 16.8)	15.7 (13.9, 17.7)	23.1 (19.6, 27.1)	13.4 (12.0, 14.9)	17.4 (16.1, 18.7)	14.4 (12.2, 17.0)
Demonstration board	30.3 (28.5, 32.3)	30.2 (28.1, 32.4)	30.5 (28.3, 32.6)	46.5 (42.6, 50.4)	26.3 (24.6, 28.2)	30.4 (28.8, 32.0)	30.3 (27.7, 33.1)
Somewhere else	1.0 (0.7, 1.4)	0.9 (0.7, 1.3)	1.0 (0.6, 1.7)	1.3 (0.6, 2.6)	0.9 (0.7, 1.2)	1.3 (1.0, 1.7)	0.8 (0.4, 1.5)
Any location	86.9 (85.7, 88.1)	87.5 (86.1, 88.8)	86.4 (85.0, 87.7)	89.5 (87.1, 91.5)	86.3 (85.0, 87.5)	90.6 (89.8, 91.4)	85.3 (83.5, 86.9)
***Current smokers*[1]**							
In newspapers or magazines	21.7 (20.0, 23.6)	22.2 (20.4, 24.1)	14.6 (10.4, 20.0)	18.1 (14.2, 22.9)	22.4 (20.5, 24.5)	32.7 (30.5, 34.9)	17.4 (15.2, 19.9)
On television	71.4 (68.9, 73.7)	71.7 (69.2, 74.1)	66.3 (58.1, 73.6)	64.4 (56.7, 71.4)	72.8 (70.3, 75.1)	75.7 (73.5, 77.8)	69.7 (66.3, 72.8)
On the radio	32.3 (29.7, 34.9)	32.4 (29.8, 35.2)	30.0 (24.5, 36.3)	25.1 (19.1, 32.2)	33.7 (31.2, 36.3)	30.3 (28.0, 32.8)	33.0 (29.7, 36.6)
On billboards	37.2 (34.4, 40.0)	37.8 (35.0, 40.8)	28.5 (22.8, 34.9)	40.5 (33.3, 48.1)	36.6 (33.8, 39.4)	45.8 (43.1, 48.5)	33.8 (30.2, 37.7)
Leaflet/sticker	36.4 (33.6, 39.2)	37.2 (34.3, 40.1)	25.4 (19.7, 32.0)	47.3 (40.1, 54.6)	34.2 (31.6, 36.9)	43.0 (40.2, 45.9)	33.8 (30.1, 37.6)
Internet	2.4 (1.9, 3.1)	2.5 (1.9, 3.2)	1.3 (0.6, 2.9)*	6.4 (4.2, 9.6)	1.6 (1.2, 2.2)	5.1 (4.1, 6.3)	1.4 (0.8, 2.3)*
Campaign activity	11.9 (10.2, 13.9)	12.0 (10.2, 14.1)	10.2 (6.5, 15.8)	14.6 (10.5, 20.0)	11.4 (9.7, 13.3)	15.2 (13.3, 17.3)	10.6 (8.4, 13.3)
Demonstration board	23.8 (21.4, 26.3)	24.3 (21.9, 27.0)	16.5 (12.0, 22.2)	32.1 (25.4, 39.7)	22.2 (20.0, 24.5)	26.0 (23.5, 28.7)	22.9 (19.8, 26.4)
Somewhere else	0.7 (0.5, 1.0)	0.7 (0.5, 1.0)	0.6 (0.2, 1.9)*	0.5 (0.2, 1.3)	0.7 (0.5, 1.1)	1.7 (1.1, 2.4)	0.3 (0.1, 0.6)*
Any location	85.1 (82.9, 87.0)	85.5 (83.4, 87.3)	79.4 (70.5, 86.2)	85.2 (79.1, 89.8)	85.0 (83.0, 86.9)	89.5 (87.8, 90.9)	83.3 (80.4, 85.9)
***Non-smokers*[2]**							
In newspapers or magazines	29.1 (27.6, 30.7)	34.9 (32.6, 37.4)	26.1 (24.5, 27.7)	32.7 (29.2, 36.3)	28.2 (26.7, 29.8)	39.7 (38.0, 41.3)	24.2 (22.0, 26.5)
On television	75.4 (73.6, 77.1)	75.8 (73.4, 78.0)	75.2 (73.3, 77.0)	76.9 (73.3, 80.2)	75.0 (73.2, 76.7)	78.3 (76.9, 79.7)	74.0 (71.5, 76.4)
On the radio	33.9 (32.0, 35.8)	37.0 (34.2, 39.9)	32.2 (30.4, 34.0)	29.8 (25.7, 34.3)	34.9 (33.2, 36.7)	33.6 (32.1, 35.2)	34.0 (31.3, 36.7)
On billboards	39.6 (37.4, 41.8)	41.5 (38.7, 44.3)	38.6 (36.4, 40.8)	48.5 (44.0, 53.1)	37.2 (35.2, 39.3)	46.4 (44.5, 48.2)	36.4 (33.3, 39.5)
Leaflet/sticker	38.9 (36.8, 41.0)	40.7 (37.7, 43.8)	37.9 (35.8, 40.1)	48.1 (43.6, 52.7)	36.4 (34.4, 38.5)	43.8 (41.9, 45.7)	36.6 (33.7, 39.6)
Internet	7.5 (6.7, 8.5)	7.9 (6.5, 9.6)	7.3 (6.4, 8.4)	20.4 (17.3, 24.0)	4.1 (3.6, 4.6)	10.1 (9.2, 11.1)	6.3 (5.1, 7.7)
Campaign activity	16.4 (14.7, 18.4)	17.5 (15.3, 19.9)	15.9 (14.0, 18.0)	25.2 (21.1, 29.9)	14.1 (12.6, 15.7)	18.0 (16.6, 19.4)	15.7 (13.2, 18.5)
Demonstration board	32.4 (30.4, 34.4)	35.2 (32.6, 37.9)	30.9 (28.8, 33.1)	50.0 (45.8, 54.2)	27.7 (25.8, 29.6)	31.6 (29.9, 33.3)	32.8 (30.0, 35.7)
Somewhere else	1.1 (0.7, 1.6)	1.1 (0.8, 1.7)	1.0 (0.6, 1.7)	1.5 (0.7, 3.2)*	1.0 (0.7, 1.4)	1.2 (0.9, 1.7)	1.0 (0.5, 1.9)
Any location	87.5 (86.3, 88.7)	89.2 (87.5, 90.7)	86.6 (85.2, 87.9)	90.6 (87.9, 92.7)	86.7 (85.4, 87.9)	90.9 (90.1, 91.7)	85.9 (84.1, 87.5)

[1] Includes daily and occasional (less than daily) smokers.
[2] Includes former and never smokers.
* Indicates that estimate is based on sample size of less than 25.

Table 8.1 (continued): Percentage of adults ≥15 years old who noticed anti-cigarette smoking information during the last 30 days in various places, by smoking status and selected demographic characteristics – GATS Thailand, 2009.

Places	Region				
	Bangkok	Central	North	Northeast	South
Overall					
In newspapers or magazines	45.7 (42.7, 48.6)	32.5 (30.0, 35.1)	26.1 (23.1, 29.4)	18.3 (15.5, 21.5)	28.0 (24.5, 31.8)
On television	81.4 (79.6, 83.1)	71.9 (69.0, 74.7)	73.2 (68.7, 77.3)	73.2 (69.7, 76.4)	78.3 (74.7, 81.4)
On the radio	38.2 (35.5, 41.0)	30.0 (27.4, 32.7)	42.5 (38.9, 46.1)	31.0 (26.8, 35.4)	29.9 (27.1, 32.8)
On billboards	46.2 (43.1, 49.4)	43.2 (39.1, 47.3)	33.8 (29.7, 38.2)	34.3 (29.8, 39.2)	44.9 (40.4, 49.4)
Leaflet/sticker	40.7 (37.5, 43.9)	42.0 (38.5, 45.6)	29.9 (26.3, 33.9)	33.2 (28.8, 38.0)	54.1 (49.4, 58.7)
Internet	9.8 (8.3, 11.5)	5.5 (4.4, 6.8)	5.9 (4.6, 7.6)	5.1 (3.7, 7.0)	8.6 (7.0, 10.6)
Campaign activity	17.9 (15.7, 20.4)	10.1 (7.9, 12.7)	13.9 (11.6, 16.7)	16.0 (12.3, 20.6)	23.2 (19.4, 27.5)
Demonstration board	21.7 (19.1, 24.6)	31.9 (28.3, 35.7)	32.8 (29.1, 36.8)	28.6 (24.7, 32.9)	35.3 (31.0, 39.7)
Somewhere else	2.3 (1.6, 3.2)	1.3 (0.8, 2.1)	0.5 (0.2, 1.1)	0.7 (0.2, 2.7)	0.7 (0.4, 1.2)
Any location	92.2 (91.1, 93.3)	86.7 (84.5, 88.7)	85.7 (82.2, 88.6)	85.5 (82.8, 87.8)	88.4 (85.5, 90.7)
Current smokers[1]					
In newspapers or magazines	40.5 (36.3, 45.0)	27.6 (24.1, 31.5)	16.6 (13.2, 20.7)	14.3 (11.1, 18.3)	24.1 (20.7, 27.9)
On television	77.4 (73.7, 80.6)	67.6 (63.3, 71.7)	69.6 (63.0, 75.5)	70.1 (64.7, 75.0)	78.1 (73.7, 81.9)
On the radio	36.0 (31.5, 40.7)	28.5 (25.0, 32.2)	39.4 (34.2, 45.0)	31.6 (25.7, 38.1)	29.6 (25.2, 34.3)
On billboards	46.8 (42.3, 51.4)	40.3 (35.2, 45.5)	29.7 (24.6, 35.3)	33.2 (27.4, 39.6)	44.1 (38.2, 50.1)
Leaflet/sticker	39.8 (34.9, 45.0)	38.6 (33.5, 44.0)	26.2 (21.6, 31.3)	30.2 (24.4, 36.8)	54.8 (48.6, 60.9)
Internet	5.3 (3.7, 7.5)	1.7 (0.9, 3.1)*	2.4 (1.2, 4.7)*	1.6 (0.9, 2.8)	3.8 (2.2, 6.4)
Campaign activity	15.1 (12.0, 18.9)	6.4 (4.7, 8.6)	9.0 (6.7, 12.0)	12.3 (8.6, 17.5)	20.3 (16.2, 25.1)
Demonstration board	18.7 (15.1, 22.9)	25.8 (21.1, 31.1)	21.4 (17.2, 26.2)	21.6 (16.9, 27.3)	30.6 (25.6, 36.2)
Somewhere else	3.6 (2.3, 5.7)	0.4 (0.2, 0.9)*	0.2 (0.1, 0.7)*	0.4 (0.1, 1.3)*	0.6 (0.3, 1.5)*
Any location	91.6 (89.1, 93.6)	85.0 (81.3, 88.2)	81.2 (74.5, 86.5)	83.7 (79.1, 87.4)	88.6 (85.4, 91.2)
Non-smokers[2]					
In newspapers or magazines	46.9 (43.7, 50.1)	34.0 (31.3, 36.9)	28.9 (25.5, 32.5)	19.6 (16.5, 23.0)	29.7 (25.6, 34.1)
On television	82.4 (80.3, 84.2)	73.2 (70.2, 76.0)	74.3 (69.7, 78.3)	74.2 (70.3, 77.8)	78.3 (74.5, 81.7)
On the radio	38.7 (35.8, 41.7)	30.4 (27.7, 33.3)	43.3 (39.5, 47.2)	30.8 (26.3, 35.6)	30.0 (26.9, 33.3)
On billboards	46.1 (42.7, 49.5)	44.0 (39.9, 48.3)	35.0 (30.7, 39.7)	34.7 (30.1, 39.5)	45.2 (40.6, 49.8)
Leaflet/sticker	40.8 (37.6, 44.2)	43.1 (39.3, 46.9)	31.0 (27.2, 35.2)	34.2 (29.7, 39.0)	53.8 (49.0, 58.5)
Internet	10.9 (9.2, 12.8)	6.7 (5.4, 8.2)	7.0 (5.4, 8.9)	6.2 (4.4, 8.7)	10.6 (8.6, 13.1)
Campaign activity	18.6 (16.2, 21.2)	11.2 (8.7, 14.4)	15.4 (12.7, 18.5)	17.2 (13.1, 22.2)	24.4 (20.3, 29.1)
Demonstration board	22.5 (19.7, 25.5)	33.7 (30.0, 37.7)	36.1 (32.1, 40.4)	30.8 (26.6, 35.4)	37.2 (32.8, 41.9)
Somewhere else	2.0 (1.3, 2.9)	1.5 (0.9, 2.6)	0.6 (0.2, 1.4)*	0.8 (0.2, 3.2)*	0.7 (0.4, 1.4)*
Any location	92.4 (91.1, 93.5)	87.2 (85.0, 89.2)	87.0 (84.0, 89.6)	86.1 (83.2, 88.5)	88.2 (85.0, 90.9)

[1] Includes daily and occasional (less than daily) smokers.
[2] Includes former and never smokers.
* Indicates that estimate is based on sample size of less than 25.

Table 8.1 (continued): Percentage of adults ≥15 years old who noticed anti-cigarette smoking information during the last 30 days in various places, by smoking status and selected demographic characteristics – GATS Thailand, 2009.

Places	Socioeconomic status				
	Lowest	Low	Middle	High	Highest
Overall					
In newspapers or magazines	18.9 (16.7, 21.3)	18.7 (16.6, 21.0)	26.9 (24.6, 29.4)	34.0 (31.6, 36.5)	47.6 (45.2, 50.0)
On television	67.5 (64.7, 70.3)	71.7 (68.7, 74.6)	77.5 (75.1, 79.7)	79.3 (77.1, 81.3)	80.5 (78.4, 82.3)
On the radio	33.1 (29.8, 36.6)	30.1 (27.1, 33.3)	34.6 (32.1, 37.2)	33.4 (31.2, 35.7)	37.8 (35.5, 40.1)
On billboards	28.6 (25.4, 31.9)	33.9 (30.5, 37.3)	40.6 (37.5, 43.8)	46.6 (43.7, 49.6)	53.3 (50.4, 56.1)
Leaflet/sticker	29.3 (26.4, 32.4)	33.5 (30.2, 36.9)	39.7 (36.8, 42.8)	45.7 (42.6, 48.8)	50.1 (47.4, 52.9)
Internet	7.6 (5.9, 9.8)	4.5 (3.4, 6.0)	4.0 (3.1, 5.2)	6.0 (4.8, 7.4)	10.5 (9.2, 11.9)
Campaign activity	13.7 (11.2, 16.7)	12.2 (10.1, 14.6)	15.1 (12.8, 17.8)	16.0 (13.9, 18.4)	22.2 (19.7, 24.9)
Demonstration board	29.0 (25.9, 32.4)	25.7 (23.0, 28.7)	29.0 (26.4, 31.8)	32.0 (29.2, 34.9)	39.4 (36.5, 42.5)
Somewhere else	0.5 (0.3, 1.0)	1.0 (0.4, 2.4)	0.8 (0.5, 1.2)	1.3 (0.8, 2.1)	1.7 (1.1, 2.6)
Any location	81.0 (78.5, 83.2)	85.3 (83.1, 87.3)	88.0 (86.1, 89.6)	91.5 (89.8, 93.0)	92.6 (91.1, 93.8)
Current smokers[1]					
In newspapers or magazines	11.9 (9.4, 14.8)	14.5 (11.6, 18.0)	20.9 (17.6, 24.7)	28.9 (24.8, 33.3)	38.9 (34.7, 43.3)
On television	63.4 (57.5, 68.9)	67.0 (62.3, 71.4)	74.5 (69.8, 78.8)	75.2 (70.4, 79.4)	78.4 (74.2, 82.1)
On the radio	31.0 (25.1, 37.5)	27.6 (23.1, 32.6)	33.4 (29.0, 38.1)	34.1 (30.1, 38.5)	37.5 (33.2, 41.9)
On billboards	23.0 (18.1, 28.8)	29.2 (24.8, 34.0)	40.4 (35.8, 45.3)	47.4 (42.6, 52.3)	50.1 (45.4, 54.9)
Leaflet/sticker	21.1 (16.9, 26.1)	30.3 (25.6, 35.5)	40.7 (35.9, 45.6)	45.5 (40.0, 51.1)	47.0 (42.2, 51.9)
Internet	1.8 (0.7, 4.2)*	1.7 (1.0, 3.0)*	1.3 (0.8, 2.1)*	2.8 (1.4, 5.4)	6.1 (4.3, 8.6)
Campaign activity	8.4 (5.8, 12.2)	7.9 (5.6, 10.8)	11.9 (8.5, 16.6)	15.7 (12.2, 20.0)	18.3 (15.1, 22.1)
Demonstration board	14.1 (11.0, 18.1)	19.4 (15.5, 24.0)	25.2 (21.1, 29.8)	31.3 (26.6, 36.5)	31.4 (27.2, 36.0)
Somewhere else	0.2 (0.0, 0.5)*	0.3 (0.1, 0.7)*	1.1 (0.5, 2.1)*	0.7 (0.4, 1.4)*	1.3 (0.7, 2.4)*
Any location	78.4 (72.9, 83.0)	83.0 (79.0, 86.3)	86.3 (82.4, 89.5)	88.8 (85.3, 91.5)	90.0 (86.4, 92.7)
Non-smokers[2]					
In newspapers or magazines	20.4 (17.9, 23.2)	20.0 (17.6, 22.7)	29.4 (26.8, 32.2)	36.0 (33.2, 39.0)	49.9 (47.3, 52.6)
On television	68.5 (65.4, 71.4)	73.2 (69.8, 76.3)	78.7 (76.2, 81.0)	80.9 (78.6, 83.0)	81.0 (78.8, 83.0)
On the radio	33.6 (30.1, 37.2)	30.9 (27.6, 34.3)	35.1 (32.4, 37.9)	33.1 (30.4, 36.0)	37.8 (35.4, 40.4)
On billboards	29.8 (26.4, 33.3)	35.3 (31.7, 39.1)	40.7 (37.2, 44.3)	46.3 (43.2, 49.5)	54.1 (51.1, 57.1)
Leaflet/sticker	31.1 (27.9, 34.5)	34.5 (31.0, 38.2)	39.4 (36.2, 42.6)	45.8 (42.5, 49.1)	50.9 (47.9, 54.0)
Internet	8.9 (6.8, 11.4)	5.4 (4.0, 7.2)	5.1 (3.8, 6.8)	7.2 (5.8, 9.1)	11.6 (10.2, 13.3)
Campaign activity	14.9 (12.0, 18.3)	13.5 (11.1, 16.4)	16.5 (14.0, 19.3)	16.1 (13.9, 18.7)	23.2 (20.4, 26.3)
Demonstration board	32.3 (28.7, 36.1)	27.7 (24.7, 30.9)	30.6 (27.8, 33.5)	32.2 (29.2, 35.5)	41.6 (38.3, 44.9)
Somewhere else	0.6 (0.3, 1.2)*	1.2 (0.5, 3.1)	0.6 (0.4, 1.1)*	1.5 (0.9, 2.6)	1.8 (1.1, 2.9)
Any location	81.5 (79.0, 83.8)	86.0 (83.6, 88.1)	88.7 (86.7, 90.4)	92.6 (91.0, 94.0)	93.3 (91.9, 94.4)

[1] Includes daily and occasional (less than daily) smokers.
[2] Includes former and never smokers.
* Indicates that estimate is based on sample size of less than 25.

8.2 Noticed health warning label on cigarette packets and thought about quitting

8.2.1 Noticed health warning label on cigarette packets and thought about quitting among current smokers:

Table 8.2 shows that 93% of current smokers noticed health warnings on cigarette packets and 67% of them thought about quitting smoking because of those health warnings. More males thought about quitting smoking than females. Almost 100% of smokers in the 15–24 year age-group and the 25–44 year age-group noticed those health warnings, and 90.7% of current smokers aged between 45 and 49 years noticed those pictures.

Among the age-groups, approximately 71% of current smokers thought about quitting smoking because of the health warnings. However, only 55.1% of current smokers aged 60 years thought about doing the same. There were no differentials observed with respect to residence, wherein almost an equal (67%) proportion of current smokers in both urban and rural areas had thought about quitting smoking. By educational levels, almost 100% of current smokers with a secondary- and university-level education saw the pictures and an approximately equal proportion thought about quitting, but a lower proportion (62.8%) thought the same among those with primary education.

Classified by region, a low proportion (84.6%) of current smokers in the Northern region saw health warnings whereas almost 98% in Bangkok metropolis were exposed to such warnings. Around 70% of current smokers in the Southern region thought about quitting smoking on seeing such warnings whereas for Bangkok metropolis the rate was a little lower at 64.3%. Classified by socioeconomic status, only 82% of current smokers from the lowest SES saw the health warnings while the rate was 97.5% for those in the highest SES category. About 70% of current smokers from the middle to the highest SES level thought about quitting because of the health warning label while only 60% of those from the lowest SES level thought so.

8.2.2 Users of hand-rolled cigarettes and smokeless tobacco products who noticed the health warning labels on raw tobacco packages and thought about quitting:

According to table 8.2a, 21.8% of current hand-rolled-cigarette smokers and smokeless tobacco users noticed health warnings on packets of shredded-tobacco. Among them, 15.1% thought about quitting smoking due to these warnings. 25.8% of males saw the health warnings and 17.8% thought about quitting smoking. In comparison, 8.5% of females were exposed to the health warnings and only 6.2% thought about quitting.

Classified by age-groups, approximately 30% of those smokers aged 15–24 years and 25–44 years noticed those health warnings, and only about 20% thought about quitting smoking. More than 20% of current hand-rolled-cigarette smokers and smokeless tobacco users—both urban and rural—noticed those health warnings, while only 15% of them thought about quitting. By educational level, 32.5% of smokers with a secondary education noticed the health warnings but only 21.9% thought about quitting.

Considering the figures by region, the highest percentage of current hand-rolled-cigarette smokers and smokeless tobacco users who noticed health warning labels were in the Northeastern region (35.3%). However, only 24.8% thought about quitting smoking on seeing these. By socioeconomic status, 29.7 of current smokers with high SES noticed those health warnings while only 22.2% thought about quitting. Among current smokers from the lowest SES category, 16.2% of them noticed the health warnings and only 9.3% thought about quitting.

Table 8.2: Percentage of current smokers ≥15 years old who noticed health warnings on cigarette packages and considered quitting because of the warning label during the last 30 days, by selected demographic characteristics – GATS Thailand, 2009.

Characteristic	Current smokers[1] who...	
	Noticed health warnings on cigarette packets[2]	Thought about quitting because of the warning label[2]
	Percentage (95% CI)	
Overall	93.0 (91.5, 94.2)	67.0 (64.4, 69.5)
Gender		
Male	94.2 (93.1, 95.2)	67.8 (65.1, 70.4)
Female	75.5 (67.1, 82.3)	55.5 (48.2, 62.6)
Age (years)		
15-24	98.7 (97.0, 99.4)	67.3 (59.2, 74.4)
25-44	97.6 (96.1, 98.5)	70.6 (67.3, 73.7)
45-59	90.7 (87.8, 92.9)	66.5 (63.1, 69.7)
60+	73.9 (69.5, 77.9)	55.1 (50.2, 59.8)
Residence		
Urban	96.6 (95.7, 97.3)	67.7 (65.5, 69.8)
Rural	91.6 (89.5, 93.2)	66.7 (63.2, 70.1)
Education level		
Less than primary	82.6 (78.9, 85.7)	62.8 (59.2, 66.4)
Primary	97.6 (96.2, 98.4)	69.7 (64.9, 74.1)
Secondary	99.2 (98.7, 99.5)	69.7 (65.1, 73.8)
University	98.2 (95.9, 99.2)	65.6 (59.4, 71.3)
Region		
Bangkok	97.8 (96.3, 98.7)	64.3 (60.5, 68.0)
Central	94.4 (92.3, 95.9)	65.5 (61.6, 69.3)
North	84.6 (78.0, 89.5)	65.1 (59.3, 70.5)
Northeast	94.2 (92.0, 95.7)	68.1 (61.8, 73.7)
South	95.0 (93.1, 96.4)	70.2 (65.2, 74.7)
Socioeconomic status		
Lowest	82.0 (77.2, 86.0)	59.9 (54.4, 65.2)
Low	91.9 (89.3, 93.9)	61.6 (55.6, 67.4)
Middle	96.3 (94.7, 97.5)	72.4 (68.6, 76.0)
High	97.2 (95.7, 98.1)	71.8 (67.5, 75.8)
Highest	97.5 (95.7, 98.6)	69.0 (64.8, 73.0)

[1] Includes daily and occasional (less than daily) smokers.
[2] During the last 30 days.

Table 8.2a: Percentage of current hand-rolled-cigarette smokers and smokeless tobacco users ≥15 years old who noticed health warnings on raw tobacco packets and thought about quitting because of the health warnings during the last 30 days, by selected demographic characteristics – GATS Thailand, 2009.

Characteristic	Current hand-rolled-cigarette smokers[1] and smokeless tobacco[2] users who...	
	Noticed health warnings on raw tobacco packages[3]	Thought about quitting because of the warning label[3]
	Percentage (95% CI)	
Overall	21.8 (18.1, 26.0)	15.1 (12.5, 18.3)
Gender		
Male	25.8 (21.4, 30.7)	17.8 (14.6, 21.5)
Female	8.5 (5.9, 12.0)	6.2 (4.0, 9.3)
Age (years)		
15-24	30.8 (20.2, 44.0)	22.8 (13.8, 35.3)
25-44	29.7 (23.9, 36.3)	20.1 (15.7, 25.5)
45-59	18.7 (14.8, 23.4)	13.2 (10.0, 17.3)
60+	11.5 (8.4, 15.4)	7.9 (5.7, 10.9)
Residence		
Urban	23.4 (19.7, 27.5)	15.3 (12.4, 18.7)
Rural	21.5 (17.3, 26.5)	15.1 (12.1, 18.7)
Education level		
Less than primary	15.9 (12.8, 19.7)	11.7 (9.3, 14.7)
Primary	28.5 (22.0, 35.9)	18.9 (13.9, 25.0)
Secondary	32.5 (25.0, 41.0)	21.9 (16.0, 29.3)
University	10.6 (5.0, 20.9)*	5.7 (2.2, 14.5)*
Region		
Bangkok	26.2 (18.6, 35.4)	13.9 (9.3, 20.1)
Central	18.2 (13.8, 23.6)	10.9 (7.8, 15.2)
North	14.0 (9.4, 20.3)	11.1 (7.2, 16.8)
Northeast	35.3 (27.4, 44.2)	24.8 (19.1, 31.5)
South	1.9 (0.8, 4.4)*	1.6 (0.6, 3.9)*
Socioeconomic status		
Lowest	16.2 (11.4, 22.5)	9.3 (6.5, 13.1)
Low	22.3 (17.4, 28.1)	16.4 (12.2, 21.7)
Middle	24.8 (18.6, 32.2)	17.6 (12.2, 24.6)
High	29.7 (21.2, 39.9)	22.2 (15.9, 30.0)
Highest	17.6 (11.4, 26.0)	12.7 (7.6, 20.3)

[1] Includes daily and occasional (less than daily) smokers of hand-rolled cigarettes.
[2] Includes daily and occasional (less than daily) smokeless tobacco users.
[3] During the last 30 days.
* Indicates that estimate is based on sample size of less than 25.

8.3 Noticed cigarette marketing in various public places among adults aged 15 years and over

Table 8.3 presents the distribution of adults aged 15 years and above who noticed cigarette marketing in public places and media, such as in stores where cigarettes are sold, on television, radio, billboards, posters, newspapers or magazines, internet and cinemas, pubs/bars/karaoke shops, etc. Due to effective law enforcement, advertisements in various places are quite low and hence figures for noticing these are grouped into two categories: "in stores where cigarettes are sold" and "anywhere else".

The percentage of overall noticed advertisements "in stores where cigarettes are sold" is 6.7% and in stores "anywhere else" is only 2.3%. Figures for advertisements noticed in sport/ music/ fashion/ art events are also very low (1.3%). Noticed cigarette promotion on clothes or items featuring cigarette brands is 6.6% and advertisements in form of sponsorships are noticed by 15.9%. There is no difference by gender for noticing of the form of advertisements. Persons aged 15–24 years noticed more cigarette advertisements, promotions and sponsorships than persons aged 25 years and above.

Classified by residence, people in urban areas noticed all types of cigarette advertisements more than people in rural areas. People with a secondary education (22.6%) and university-level education (27.1%) noticed more advertisements in the form of sponsorships than those with less than primary education (6.5%). Classified by region, people in the Central and Northern regions noticed more cigarette advertisements in stores than those from other regions. Figures for noticing advertisements anywhere else (social events) are high in the Central (3.2%) and Bangkok metropolis (2.9%) region whereas a high rate (13.2%) of noticing cigarette promotion through clothings or items featuring brand names or logos was observed in the Southern region. Advertisement by sponsorship is also found to be high in the Central (19.6%) and Southern regions (18.6%). Classified by socioeconomic status, people from a high SES category noticed all forms of cigarette advertisements more than those from other SES categories.

Table 8.3: Percentage of adults ≥15 years old who noticed cigarette marketing during the last 30 days in various places, by selected demographic characteristics – GATS Thailand, 2009.

Characteristic	*Noticed advertisements*		Noticed sport/ sporting event, or music/theater/ art/fashion event sponsorship	*Noticed cigarette promotions*		Noticed any advertisement, sponsorship or promotion
	In stores where cigarettes are sold[1]	Anywhere else[2]		Clothing/item with brand name or logo	Other promoting cigarettes[3]	
	Percentage (95% CI)					
Overall	6.7 (5.8, 7.7)	2.3 (2.0, 2.7)	1.3 (1.0, 1.7)	6.6 (5.9, 7.4)	1.8 (1.5, 2.2)	15.9 (14.6, 17.2)
Gender						
Male	6.6 (5.5, 7.8)	2.2 (1.7, 2.8)	1.8 (1.4, 2.5)	7.7 (6.7, 8.7)	2.4 (2.0, 3.0)	17.4 (15.8, 19.0)
Female	6.8 (5.8, 8.0)	2.4 (2.0, 2.9)	0.8 (0.5, 1.3)	5.6 (4.7, 6.6)	1.2 (0.9, 1.6)	14.5 (13.0, 16.0)
Age (years)						
15-24	11.6 (9.3, 14.3)	3.4 (2.4, 4.8)	2.0 (1.2, 3.2)	12.8 (10.6, 15.3)	3.0 (2.1, 4.4)	26.6 (23.4, 30.0)
25+	5.5 (4.7, 6.4)	2.0 (1.7, 2.4)	1.1 (0.8, 1.5)	5.1 (4.5, 5.7)	1.5 (1.2, 1.8)	13.2 (12.1, 14.4)
Residence						
Urban	8.0 (6.9, 9.1)	3.2 (2.7, 3.7)	1.6 (1.3, 2.0)	8.6 (7.8, 9.6)	2.3 (1.8, 2.8)	19.6 (18.2, 21.0)
Rural	6.1 (4.9, 7.6)	1.9 (1.4, 2.5)	1.1 (0.7, 1.8)	5.7 (4.8, 6.7)	1.6 (1.2, 2.1)	14.2 (12.5, 16.0)
Education level						
Less than primary	3.6 (2.9, 4.4)	1.1 (0.8, 1.5)	0.6 (0.3, 1.1)	0.9 (0.7, 1.1)	0.8 (0.6, 1.2)	6.5 (5.6, 7.5)
Primary	6.4 (4.9, 8.2)	1.5 (1.0, 2.3)	0.7 (0.4, 1.1)	5.1 (4.1, 6.4)	1.7 (1.1, 2.4)	13.6 (11.7, 15.7)
Secondary	9.6 (8.1, 11.3)	2.8 (2.2, 3.7)	2.0 (1.3, 3.2)	10.4 (9.1, 11.9)	2.5 (1.9, 3.3)	22.6 (20.5, 24.9)
University	8.0 (6.5, 9.7)	5.5 (4.4, 6.9)	2.5 (1.8, 3.4)	14.7 (12.7, 17.0)	2.7 (1.9, 3.8)	27.1 (24.5, 29.9)
Region						
Bangkok	4.6 (3.7, 5.8)	2.9 (2.2, 3.8)	1.8 (1.3, 2.5)	8.6 (7.0, 10.4)	2.0 (1.5, 2.7)	16.4 (14.3, 18.8)
Central	9.4 (7.8, 11.3)	3.2 (2.4, 4.3)	1.0 (0.7, 1.5)	6.7 (5.5, 8.1)	3.0 (2.3, 3.9)	19.6 (17.2, 22.2)
North	7.4 (5.3, 10.1)	2.5 (1.6, 3.9)	1.7 (1.0, 3.2)	5.9 (4.4, 7.8)	1.3 (0.7, 2.4)	15.8 (12.8, 19.4)
Northeast	6.0 (4.3, 8.4)	1.3 (0.9, 1.9)	1.1 (0.5, 2.4)	3.8 (2.7, 5.3)	1.1 (0.7, 2.0)	11.8 (9.5, 14.5)
South	4.2 (2.7, 6.7)	2.2 (1.5, 3.1)	1.2 (0.8, 1.9)	13.2 (11.0, 15.7)	1.7 (1.1, 2.7)	18.6 (16.0, 21.5)
Socioeconomic status						
Lowest	5.9 (4.4, 8.0)	1.7 (1.1, 2.5)	0.7 (0.4, 1.4)	5.0 (3.8, 6.6)	1.7 (1.1, 2.7)	13.1 (10.9, 15.6)
Low	6.0 (4.8, 7.6)	1.7 (1.2, 2.3)	1.1 (0.6, 1.9)	3.8 (3.0, 4.9)	1.0 (0.7, 1.6)	12.5 (10.7, 14.6)
Middle	7.1 (5.7, 8.9)	2.5 (1.8, 3.5)	1.5 (0.9, 2.5)	7.1 (5.8, 8.6)	1.7 (1.2, 2.3)	16.1 (14.2, 18.2)
High	7.9 (6.5, 9.7)	2.7 (1.9, 3.7)	1.9 (1.3, 2.9)	8.5 (7.1, 10.1)	2.8 (2.1, 3.8)	19.2 (17.1, 21.4)
Highest	7.0 (5.9, 8.4)	3.6 (2.9, 4.5)	1.6 (1.2, 2.2)	10.8 (9.4, 12.5)	2.3 (1.7, 3.0)	21.6 (19.4, 24.0)

[1] Means point of sale.
[2] Includes on television, radio, billboards, posters, newspapers or magazines, in cinemas, Internet, public transportation, public walls, etc.
[3] Includes distribution of free samples, sale prices, coupons, free gifts/discounts on other products, mailers promoting cigarettes.

8.4 Noticed cigarette marketing in various places among current smokers

In Table 8.4 the level of noticing cigarette marketing in various places by current smokers was similar to that of the overall population as well as for those classified by demographic characteristics. Similar patterns were also found with regard to noticing social events and activities supported by cigarette companies, cigarette sale promotions and advertisement in the form of sponsorships.

Table 8.4 Percentage of current smokers ≥15 years old who noticed cigarette marketing during the last 30 days in various places, by selected demographic characteristics – GATS Thailand, 2009.

Characteristic	*Noticed advertisements*		Noticed sport/ sporting event, or music/ theater/ art/fashion event sponsorship	*Noticed cigarette promotions*		Noticed any advertisement, sponsorship or promotion
	In stores where cigarettes are sold[1]	Anywhere else[2]		Clothing/item with brand name or logo	Other promoting cigarettes[3]	
			Percentage (95% CI)			
Overall	6.6 (5.2, 8.4)	1.7 (1.2, 2.3)	1.7 (1.2, 2.3)	7.0 (5.9, 8.3)	2.8 (2.1, 3.7)	17.0 (15.0, 19.5)
Gender						
Male	6.6 (5.1, 8.4)	1.6 (1.2, 2.2)	1.7 (1.2, 2.4)	7.1 (6.0, 8.5)	2.9 (2.2, 3.9)	17.2 (15.1, 19.5)
Female	7.7 (4.8, 12.3)	2.6 (1.3, 4.9)*	1.4 (0.5, 3.6)*	4.6 (2.6, 8.0)*	1.1 (0.5, 2.5)*	15.0 (10.8, 20.4)
Age (years)						
15-24	12.1 (7.7, 18.5)	1.8 (0.7, 4.5)*	2.5 (1.1, 5.8)*	13.8 (9.4, 19.7)	4.7 (2.8, 7.8)	28.3 (22.0, 35.7)
25+	5.5 (4.5 6.8)	1.7 (1.2, 2.2)	1.5 (1.0, 2.2)	5.6 (4.8, 6.6)	2.4 (1.7, 3.4)	14.8 (13.2, 16.6)
Residence						
Urban	8.7 (7.1, 10.4)	2.2 (1.6, 3.0)	2.1 (1.5, 2.9)	10.7 (9.2, 12.5)	3.7 (2.7, 4.9)	22.8 (20.5, 25.3)
Rural	5.8 (4.1, 8.2)	1.5 (0.9, 2.3)	1.5 (0.9, 2.5)	5.5 (4.2, 7.3)	2.4 (1.6, 3.7)	14.7 (12.2, 17.6)
Education level						
Less than primary	3.9 (3.0, 5.1)	1.4 (0.8, 2.2)	0.9 (0.4, 2.1)*	1.1 (0.7, 1.8)	1.2 (0.7, 2.1)	8.0 (6.5, 9.7)
Primary	7.0 (4.7, 10.3)	0.8 (0.3, 1.8)*	1.0 (0.5, 1.8)*	6.0 (4.3, 8.2)	2.8 (1.7, 4.5)	16.7 (13.4, 20.5)
Secondary	9.2 (6.6, 12.7)	2.2 (1.4, 3.5)	2.7 (1.5, 4.5)	11.8 (9.5, 14.7)	4.0 (2.7, 5.9)	24.2 (20.5, 28.4)
University	6.7 (4.1, 10.8)	4.1 (2.2, 7.3)*	3.0 (1.5, 6.2)*	16.5 (12.0, 22.2)	4.8 (2.1, 10.4)*	28.9 (23.0, 35.6)
Region						
Bangkok	3.1 (1.9, 4.9)	1.6 (0.9, 2.9)*	2.0 (1.1, 3.8)*	11.1 (8.2, 14.8)	2.2 (1.3, 3.7)*	18.1 (14.5, 22.4)
Central	8.9 (6.7, 11.8)	1.8 (1.1, 3.1)*	1.8 (1.0, 3.2)*	7.9 (5.4, 11.4)	5.1 (3.3, 7.9)	22.3 (18.3, 27.0)
North	8.6 (5.5, 13.1)	2.3 (1.1, 5.0)*	2.5 (1.1, 5.5)*	4.7 (3.0, 7.3)	1.6 (0.8, 3.2)*	14.8 (11.1, 19.6)
Northeast	6.3 (3.5, 11.1)	1.2 (0.7, 2.3)*	1.4 (0.6, 3.0)*	2.6 (1.5, 4.6)	1.8 (0.9, 3.8)*	12.2 (8.5, 17.1)
South	3.7 (2.2, 6.3)	1.7 (0.9, 3.3)	0.9 (0.5, 1.6)*	14.9 (11.2, 19.5)	3.1 (1.6, 5.9)*	20.6 (16.4, 25.4)
Socioeconomic status						
Lowest	5.4 (3.0, 9.4)	1.2 (0.6, 2.4)*	1.2 (0.5, 2.5)*	3.6 (2.1, 6.1)	3.1 (1.5, 6.0)*	13.0 (9.5, 17.6)
Low	6.0 (3.9, 9.0)	1.1 (0.5, 2.3)*	1.1 (0.5, 2.4)*	5.2 (3.1, 8.8)	1.8 (1.0, 3.4)*	14.1 (10.6, 18.6)
Middle	7.8 (5.3, 11.4)	1.4 (0.8, 2.4)*	1.9 (0.9, 4.0)*	6.8 (5.0, 9.1)	2.4 (1.5, 3.7)	17.5 (14.3, 21.3)
High	7.6 (5.5, 10.4)	2.5 (1.3, 5.0)*	2.1 (0.9, 4.6)*	9.3 (6.8, 12.6)	3.9 (2.4, 6.2)	19.7 (16.2, 23.6)
Highest	5.8 (4.1, 8.1)	2.6 (1.5, 4.4)	2.2 (1.3, 3.9)*	11.6 (9.3, 14.6)	3.4 (1.6, 6.9)*	22.5 (18.9, 26.5)

[1] Means point of sale.
[2] Includes on television, radio, billboards, posters, newspapers or magazines, in cinemas, Internet, public transportation, public walls, etc .
[3] Includes distribution of free samples, sale prices, coupons, free gifts/discounts on other products, mailers promoting cigarettes.
* Indicates that estimate is based on sample size of less than 25.

8.5 Noticed cigarette marketing in various places among non-smokers

In Table 8.5, the level of noticing cigarette marketing in various places by non-smokers is similar to that of the overall population and current smokers, as well as for those classified by demographic characteristics. Similar patterns were found in stores where cigarettes are sold, and during social events and activities supported by cigarette companies, cigarette promotion and advertisement in the form of sponsorships.

Table 8.5: Percentage of non-smokers ≥15 years old who noticed cigarette marketing during the last 30 days in various places, by selected demographic characteristics – GATS Thailand, 2009.

Characteristic	*Noticed advertisements*		Noticed sport or sporting event, or music/ theater/art/fashion event sponsorship	*Noticed cigarette promotions*		Noticed any advertisement, sponsorship or promotion
	In stores where cigarettes are sold[1]	Anywhere else[2]		Clothing/item with brand name or logo	Other promoting cigarettes[3]	
	Percentage (95% CI)					
Overall	6.7 (5.8, 7.8)	2.5 (2.1, 3.0)	1.2 (0.8, 1.7)	6.5 (5.7, 7.3)	1.5 (1.2, 1.9)	15.5 (14.2, 16.9)
Gender						
Male	6.6 (5.4, 8.0)	2.7 (2.0, 3.5)	2.0 (1.4, 2.8)	8.1 (6.9, 9.5)	2.0 (1.5, 2.8)	17.5 (15.7, 19.5)
Female	6.8 (5.7, 8.0)	2.4 (2.0, 2.9)	0.8 (0.5, 1.3)	5.6 (4.8, 6.7)	1.2 (0.9, 1.6)	14.5 (13.0, 16.0)
Age (years)						
15-24	11.5 (8.9, 14.6)	3.8 (2.7, 5.4)	1.9 (1.0, 3.3)	12.5 (10.2, 5.3)	2.6 (1.6, 4.2)	26.1 (22.6, 29.9)
25+	5.5 (4.7, 6.8)	2.1 (1.8, 2.6)	1.0 (0.7, 1.4)	4.9 (4.3, 5.6)	1.2 (1.0, 1.5)	12.7 (11.5, 13.9)
Residence						
Urban	7.7 (6.7, 8.9)	3.5 (2.9, 4.0)	1.5 (1.2, 1.9)	8.1 (7.2, 9.1)	1.9 (1.5, 2.4)	18.7 (17.3, 20.2)
Rural	6.2 (5.0, 7.7)	2.0 (1.5, 2.7)	1.0 (0.6, 1.8)	5.7 (4.7, 6.9)	1.3 (0.9, 1.8)	14.0 (12.2, 16.0)
Education level						
Less than primary	3.5 (2.8, 4.5)	1.0 (0.7, 1.4)	0.5 (0.3, 0.8)	0.8 (0.6, 1.1)	0.7 (0.5, 1.1)	6.0 (5.1, 7.1)
Primary	6.1 (4.7, 7.9)	1.8 (1.1, 2.8)	0.6 (0.3, 1.0)*	4.8 (3.6, 6.4)	1.2 (0.7, 2.2)	12.3 (10.4, 14.6)
Secondary	9.7 (8.0, 11.7)	3.0 (2.2, 4.0)	1.8 (1.0, 3.4)	10.0 (8.4, 11.8)	2.1 (1.4, 3.0)	22.2 (19.7, 24.8)
University	8.2 (6.6, 10.1)	5.8 (4.5, 7.4)	2.4 (1.7, 3.4)	14.4 (12.3, 16.8)	2.4 (1.6, 3.4)	26.8 (24.0, 29.8)
Region						
Bangkok	5.0 (3.9, 6.3)	3.2 (2.4, 4.2)	1.7 (1.2, 2.5)	8.0 (6.4, 9.9)	2.0 (1.4, 2.8)	16.0 (13.8, 18.5)
Central	9.5 (7.7,11.7)	3.7 (2.7, 5.0)	0.8 (0.5, 1.2)	6.3 (5.1, 7.7)	2.4 (1.7, 3.3)	18.8 (16.4, 21.4)
North	7.0 (5.1, 9.7)	2.6 (1.7, 3.9)	1.5 (0.8, 2.9)	6.3 (4.5, 8.6)	1.2 (0.6, 2.4)	16.1 (12.9, 19.8)
Northeast	5.9 (4.2, 8.2)	1.3 (0.8, 2.2)	1.0 (0.4, 2.9)*	4.1 (2.8, 6.0)	0.9 (0.5, 1.8)*	11.7 (9.2, 144.6)
South	4.4 (2.6, 7.3)	2.4 (1.5, 3.6)	1.4 (0.8, 2.4)	12.4 (10.2, 15.1)	1.2 (0.7, 1.9)	17.8 (15.0, 21.0)
Socioeconomic status						
Lowest	6.1 (4.4, 8.3)	1.8 (1.1, 2.7)	0.6 (0.3, 1.5)*	5.3 (3.9, 7.2)	1.4 (0.8, 2.6)	13.1 (10.6, 15.9)
Low	6.1 (4.7, 7.7)	1.9 (1.3, 2.7)	1.1 (0.6, 2.2)	3.4 (2.6, 4.5)	0.8 (0.5, 1.4)*	12.0 (10.1, 14.2)
Middle	6.8 (5.2, 8.9)	2.9 (2.0, 4.3)	1.3 (0.6, 2.6)	7.2 (5.6, 9.2)	1.4 (0.9, 2.2)	15.5 (13.3, 18.0)
High	8.1 (6.4, 10.2)	2.7 (1.9, 3.9)	1.9 (1.2, 3.0)	8.2 (6.6, 10.0)	2.4 (1.6, 3.4)	19.0 (16.6, 21.6)
Highest	7.4 (6.1, 8.9)	3.8 (3.0, 4.9)	1.5 (1.1, 2.1)	10.6 (9.0, 12.5)	2.0 (1.4, 2.7)	21.4 (19.1, 23.9)

[1] Means point of sale.
[2] Includes on television, radio, billboards, posters, newspapers or magazines, in cinemas, Internet, public transportation, public walls, etc .
[3] Includes distribution of free samples, sale prices, coupons, free gifts/discounts on other products, mailers promoting cigarettes.
* Indicates that estimate is based on sample size of less than 25.

In short, anti-smoking campaigns through any location or in various places were noticed less by adults with the following characteristics: living in rural areas, are from the Northeastern and Northern regions, and belonging to the lowest SES category. Television is the most accessible media for anti-smoking campaigns for all. However, current smokers are less exposed to anti-smoking campaigns than non-smokers.

Health warnings in colour are a strong medium to communicate health risks and trigger thoughts about quitting among seven in 10 of current smokers. The survey also shows that health warnings with full colour pictures on cigarettes packets are four times more effective in triggering thoughts about quitting than black-and-white pictures that are found on packets of shredded tobacco. The pattern of noticing cigarette marketing in various places among all adults - current smokers as well as non-smokers is similar across all demographic subgroups.

9

Knowledge, attitudes and perceptions

9. Knowledge, attitudes and perceptions

Smoking harms nearly every organ of the body; is the cause of many diseases, and adversely affects the health of both smokers and non-smokers[26]. There are approximately 4 000 chemicals in each cigarette, hundreds of which are toxic. The adverse health effects from cigarette smoking account for an estimated 42 000 deaths, or nearly one out of every ten deaths, annually in Thailand[27]. The effectiveness of widespread public awareness campaigns about cigarette hazards undertaken by several tobacco control partners in Thailand is revealed by the results of the national surveys of 2004 and 2007. These surveys have revealed that 93.3% and 96.7% respectively of Thai adults aged ≥15 years who were smokers at the time of the survey received information on the hazards of tobacco use. This is similar to the proportion of non-smokers who received similar information (95.9% in 2004)[1].

This chapter presents the perceptions and views of the overall population aged 15 years and above about the hazards of smoking and its various dimensions, for example the effects of smoking on health, the adverse health effects caused by exposure to second-hand smoke, and the influence of pictorial health warnings on the desire to quit.

Key findings:

- *98.6% of adults believe that smoking causes serious illnesses.*
- *97.5% of adults believe smoking causes lung cancer while only 65.7% of adults believe smoking causes impotence.*
- *94.9% of adults believe that exposure to SHS causes serious illnesses in non-smokers.*
- *Approximately 90% of adults believe that breathing other people's smoke causes lung cancer in adults and lung illnesses in children. Only 58.5% of adults believe breathing other people's smoke leads to premature births.*
- *39.7% of adults think smoking manufactured cigarettes is more harmful than smoking hand-rolled cigarettes.*

9.1 Beliefs that cigarette smoking causes serious illnesses and specific diseases

9.1.1 Based on overall adults aged 15 years and over:

The GATS survey covers prevalent beliefs on the effects of cigarette smoking on health among the population aged 15 years and above, and features various diseases caused by cigarette smoking. Almost all adults (98.6%) believe that cigarette smoking causes many serious diseases and illnesses. Lung cancer (97.5%), larynx cancer (91.5%), mouth cancer (90.8%) and emphysema (90.3%) are the reported serious diseases caused by smoking. The relation between cigarette smoking and impotence is the least known (65.7%), followed by its relation to heart attacks (75.7%) and strokes (79.6%).

There is no difference between the genders in the perceptions about the effects of cigarette smoking on health, except for the belief that smoking causes impotence (70.5% for males and 61.1% for females). There is also very little difference in such perceptions and beliefs across the age-groups. The age-group of 60 years and older has a lower percentage of those beliefs compared with other age groups, especially the perception about smoking causing impotence. Urban adults have a wider perception of all health effects of smoking than rural adults. The extent is similar among adults having less than primary education, among adults in the Northern region and for adults in the lowest SES group. Perceptions about the relation between smoking and impotence are lower in the Central region and between smoking and emphysema lower in the Northeastern region. When classified by economic status, adults with the highest SES level have a higher percentage of conviction about the overall health effects of tobacco than adults belonging to other SES levels (*Table 9.1*).

9.1.2 Based on smoking status:

Current non-smokers have a higher proportion of belief on all facets of the health impact of cigarette smoking than current smokers. There is considerable difference between smokers and non-smokers over the perception that smoking causes heart attack, with the figures being 76.7% for non-smokers and 72.7% for current smokers (*see Table 9.1a and 9.1b*).

The belief among current smokers that cigarette smoking causes serious illnesses and specific diseases does not differ by demographic characteristics (Table 9.1a). However, females have a lower proportion of the belief on all aspects of tobacco health effects than males, especially that smoking causes mouth cancer (79.3% for females and 90.6% for males), larynx cancer (81.0% and 91.1% respectively), and impotence (43.0% and 67.3% respectively). Among different age-groups, current smokers aged 60 years and above have a lower percentage of those beliefs than other age groups. However, figures for the belief that smoking causing serious illnesses, stroke and heart attacks are not very different across the different categories. Among current smokers in rural areas, a lower percentage of those with an education level of less than primary and those in the lowest SES level believe in the overall health effects of tobacco than current smokers of other groups. Current smokers in the Northern region have a lower percentage of such beliefs than of those in other regions.

Among current non-smokers, the percentage of those who believe in all smoking health effects is similar among different demographic characteristics in comparison with current smokers (Table 9.1b). Current non-smokers who are females and living in rural areas have a lower percentage of belief in all aspects of the health effects of tobacco than the males and those living in urban areas. Current non-smokers aged 60 years and above, with less than primary education, in the Northern region and belonging to the lowest SES level have the lowest percentage of belief in all aspects of the health effects of tobacco (*see Table 9.1b*).

Table 9.1: Percentage of adults ≥ 15 years old who believe that smoking causes serious illnesses, stroke, heart attack, lung cancer, mouth cancer, larynx cancer, impotence or emphysema, by selected demographic characteristics – GATS Thailand, 2009.

Characteristic	Adults who believe that smoking causes...							
	Serious illnesses	Stroke	Heart attack	Lung cancer	Mouth cancer	Larynx cancer	Impotence	Emphysema
	Percentage (95% CI)							
Overall	98.6 (98.2, 98.8)	79.6 (78.2, 80.9)	75.7 (74.4, 77.1)	97.5 (97.1, 97.8)	90.8 (89.9, 91.7)	91.5 (90.6, 92.3)	65.7 (64.1, 67.3)	90.3 (89.2, 91.3)
Gender								
Male	98.2 (97.7, 98.7)	79.8 (78.0, 81.6)	75.3 (73.5, 77.0)	97.4 (97.0, 97.8)	90.8 (89.6, 91.8)	91.7 (90.5, 92.7)	70.5 (68.7, 72.3)	90.9 (89.5, 92.1)
Female	98.9 (98.5, 99.1)	79.4 (77.8, 80.9)	76.2 (74.6, 77.7)	97.5 (97.0, 97.9)	90.8 (89.8, 91.8)	91.3 (90.3, 92.2)	61.1 (59.2, 63.1)	89.8 (88.6, 90.9)
Age (years)								
15-24	99.3 (97.8, 99.7)	77.3 (73.8, 80.3)	73.5 (70.3, 76.5)	99.1 (98.5, 99.4)	93.0 (90.9, 94.7)	91.8 (89.8, 93.5)	68.2 (64.9, 71.4)	90.9 (88.5, 92.8)
25-44	99.1 (98.7, 99.4)	81.8 (80.1, 83.5)	77.1 (75.2, 78.8)	98.3 (97.8, 98.6)	93.9 (92.9, 94.7)	94.3 (93.2, 95.2)	70.4 (68.5, 72.4)	93.7 (92.6, 94.7)
45-59	98.7 (98.1, 99.0)	80.7 (79.0, 82.3)	77.1 (75.5, 78.6)	97.6 (96.9, 98.1)	90.1 (88.9, 91.3)	92.1 (90.9, 93.2)	64.1 (62.2, 65.9)	90.3 (88.9, 91.5)
60+	96.0 (94.9, 96.8)	75.0 (72.9, 77.0)	72.9 (70.7, 75.0)	93.0 (91.7, 94.2)	80.7 (78.5, 82.6)	82.4 (80.3, 84.3)	51.9 (49.5, 54.2)	80.5 (78.3, 82.5)
Residence								
Urban	99.1 (98.9, 99.3)	82.6 (81.6, 83.6)	78.4 (77.2, 79.6)	98.3 (98.0, 98.5)	92.2 (91.4, 92.9)	94.0 (93.3, 94.6)	69.3 (68.1, 70.5)	94.5 (93.8, 95.0)
Rural	98.3 (97.8, 98.7)	78.3 (76.3, 80.1)	74.5 (72.6, 76.4)	97.1 (96.6, 97.5)	90.2 (88.9, 91.3)	90.3 (89.0, 91.5)	64.1 (61.8, 66.3)	88.5 (86.9, 89.9)
Education level								
Less than primary	97.0 (96.3, 97.6)	75.9 (73.9, 77.9)	72.7 (70.7, 74.5)	95.1 (94.2, 95.8)	83.9 (82.0, 85.6)	85.6 (83.7, 87.3)	54.5 (52.3, 56.6)	83.1 (81.2, 84.9)
Primary	99.5 (99.0, 99.7)	78.8 (76.2, 81.1)	74.1 (71.0, 76.9)	98.2 (97.5, 98.7)	93.1 (91.7, 94.2)	92.5 (91.0, 93.8)	64.3 (61.1, 67.3)	90.9 (88.9, 92.5)
Secondary	99.2 (98.4, 99.6)	81.1 (79.0, 83.1)	77.0 (74.9, 79.0)	99.0 (98.5, 99.3)	94.9 (93.8, 95.8)	94.8 (93.7, 95.7)	72.7 (70.5, 74.8)	94.5 (93.0, 95.7)
University	99.6 (99.1, 99.8)	87.3 (85.6, 88.9)	83.7 (81.5, 85.7)	99.1 (98.3, 99.5)	95.3 (94.1, 96.2)	97.0 (95.9, 97.8)	80.5 (78.3, 82.4)	98.1 (97.2, 98.7)
Region								
Bangkok	99.5 (99.1, 99.7)	84.3 (82.5, 85.9)	81.8 (79.9, 83.6)	98.8 (98.2, 99.1)	94.1 (92.8, 95.1)	95.5 (94.4, 96.4)	71.9 (70.0, 73.7)	96.7 (95.9, 97.4)
Central	98.8 (98.1, 99.2)	78.0 (76.1, 79.8)	72.3 (70.3, 74.3)	97.1 (96.4, 97.7)	89.8 (88.3, 91.1)	92.3 (91.0, 93.4)	60.7 (58.3, 63.0)	92.4 (91.1, 93.5)
North	97.9 (96.8, 98.6)	73.4 (68.8, 77.6)	70.1 (65.7, 74.2)	97.4 (96.3, 98.1)	87.2 (84.3, 89.7)	88.6 (85.4, 91.2)	63.3 (59.5, 66.9)	89.7 (86.7, 92.1)
Northeast	98.4 (97.6, 98.9)	80.8 (78.0, 83.3)	77.8 (75.0, 80.3)	97.6 (96.9, 98.1)	91.9 (89.9, 93.5)	90.5 (88.6, 92.0)	66.7 (63.0, 70.3)	87.0 (84.4, 89.2)
South	98.8 (98.2, 99.2)	84.4 (82.0, 86.6)	79.8 (76.8, 82.5)	96.9 (95.9, 97.7)	92.5 (90.8, 93.9)	93.4 (91.8, 94.7)	70.6 (67.5, 73.5)	90.9 (88.7, 92.7)
Socioeconomic status								
Lowest	97.4 (96.6, 98.0)	72.4 (69.2, 75.4)	71.1 (67.9, 74.0)	95.6 (94.6, 96.4)	85.3 (83.0, 87.4)	85.1 (82.8, 87.1)	55.5 (52.3, 58.6)	83.1 (80.6, 85.4)
Low	98.3 (97.4, 98.9)	80.4 (78.3, 82.4)	76.3 (73.9, 78.6)	97.5 (96.8, 98.1)	91.2 (89.8, 92.4)	91.7 (90.2, 93.0)	63.6 (60.9, 66.3)	89.4 (87.6, 90.9)
Middle	99.0 (98.5, 99.4)	80.2 (78.0, 82.2)	75.2 (72.8, 77.4)	98.0 (97.3, 98.5)	92.0 (90.7, 93.2)	92.9 (91.5, 94.1)	68.3 (65.8, 70.7)	91.7 (90.1, 93.1)
High	99.2 (98.7, 99.5)	83.5 (81.6, 85.2)	77.1 (74.9, 79.1)	98.6 (98.0, 99.0)	93.4 (92.2, 94.5)	94.6 (93.5, 95.6)	71.0 (68.9, 73.0)	94.6 (93.4, 95.6)
Highest	99.5 (99.3, 99.7)	84.8 (83.0, 86.5)	81.5 (79.6, 83.2)	98.6 (97.8, 99.0)	94.6 (93.5, 95.5)	96.0 (95.0, 96.8)	75.9 (73.9, 77.9)	96.9 (96.0, 97.6)

Table 9.1a: Percentage of current smokers ≥ 15 years old who believe that smoking causes serious illnesses, stroke, heart attack, lung cancer, mouth cancer, larynx cancer, impotence or emphysema, by selected demographic characteristics – GATS Thailand, 2009.

Characteristic	Adults who believe that smoking causes...							
	Serious illnesses	Stroke	Heart attack	Lung cancer	Mouth cancer	Larynx cancer	Impotence	Emphysema
	Percentage (95% CI)							
Overall	97.3 (96.1, 98.1)	78.0 (75.5, 80.4)	72.7 (70.5, 74.8)	96.2 (95.3, 96.9)	89.9 (88.2, 91.3)	90.4 (88.6, 91.9)	65.7 (63.2, 68.1)	88.6 (86.6, 90.3)
Gender								
Male	97.3 (96.1, 98.1)	78.8 (76.3, 81.1)	73.3 (71.1, 75.4)	96.4 (95.6, 97.1)	90.6 (89.2, 91.9)	91.1 (89.5, 92.4)	67.3 (64.8, 69.7)	89.0 (87.0, 90.7)
Female	96.8 (94.1, 98.3)	67.1 (58.7, 74.6)	64.0 (56.0, 71.4)	93.1 (89.1, 95.7)	79.3 (70.7, 85.9)	81.0 (72.2, 87.5)	43.0 (36.1, 50.2)	83.4 (78.1, 87.7)
Age (years)								
15-24	97.5 (89.6, 99.4)	75.0 (67.9, 81.0)	68.3 (61.0, 74.8)	99.1 (97.6, 99.7)	93.8 (90.6, 95.9)	92.7 (87.5, 95.9)	70.2 (62.9, 76.7)	84.4 (77.3, 89.6)
25-44	98.3 (97.1, 99.1)	81.3 (78.1, 84.2)	75.7 (72.7, 78.4)	97.3 (96.0, 98.2)	93.2 (91.5, 94.6)	93.7 (91.8, 95.2)	68.2 (64.6, 71.5)	93.4 (91.4, 94.9)
45-59	97.4 (95.7, 98.5)	78.3 (74.7, 81.5)	73.9 (70.3, 77.2)	95.3 (93.4, 96.6)	88.4 (85.5, 90.8)	88.9 (85.7, 91.4)	64.4 (60.7, 67.8)	87.9 (84.9, 90.4)
60+	92.9 (90.1, 94.9)	70.2 (65.9, 74.1)	65.9 (61.6, 70.0)	90.4 (87.5, 92.7)	76.1 (71.8, 79.9)	78.7 (74.6, 82.2)	54.0 (49.5, 58.5)	78.5 (74.3, 82.1)
Residence								
Urban	98.2 (97.5, 98.7)	82.6 (80.7, 84.3)	75.5 (73.3, 77.6)	97.2 (96.3, 97.9)	91.3 (89.8, 92.6)	92.7 (91.3, 93.8)	69.0 (66.8, 71.2)	92.5 (91.2, 93.7)
Rural	96.9 (95.2, 98.0)	76.3 (72.8, 79.4)	71.6 (68.6, 74.4)	95.8 (94.6, 96.7)	89.3 (87.0, 91.2)	89.5 (87.0, 91.5)	64.4 (61.1, 67.6)	87.0 (84.4, 89.3)
Education level								
Less than primary	95.0 (93.1, 96.4)	72.9 (68.7, 76.7)	68.3 (64.5, 71.8)	93.3 (91.4, 94.8)	82.1 (78.5, 85.2)	83.2 (79.5, 86.3)	56.9 (53.2, 60.4)	82.4 (79.0, 85.3)
Primary	99.1 (97.2, 99.7)	80.3 (76.2, 83.8)	74.3 (69.9, 78.2)	97.0 (95.1, 98.2)	92.7 (90.2, 94.6)	92.4 (89.8, 94.4)	65.3 (60.4, 69.9)	90.6 (87.1, 93.2)
Secondary	97.9 (94.7, 99.1)	79.8 (75.2, 83.7)	74.0 (70.1, 77.6)	98.4 (97.3, 99.0)	94.4 (92.7, 95.8)	94.9 (92.4, 96.7)	73.0 (68.6, 77.0)	92.0 (88.6, 94.5)
University	98.7 (95.9, 99.6)	86.7 (82.0, 90.4)	82.5 (77.4, 86.6)	97.1 (93.7, 98.7)	96.0 (93.4, 97.6)	97.0 (94.4, 98.4)	76.8 (71.7, 81.3)	95.4 (91.5, 97.6)
Region								
Bangkok	98.9 (97.8, 99.5)	84.1 (80.9, 86.9)	78.3 (74.8, 81.4)	98.2 (96.9, 98.9)	93.2 (90.5, 95.1)	93.6 (91.1, 95.4)	73.0 (69.4, 76.3)	95.4 (93.0, 97.0)
Central	97.8 (96.2, 98.8)	77.7 (73.8, 81.2)	71.0 (67.3, 74.5)	95.9 (94.0, 97.2)	90.8 (88.5, 92.7)	92.9 (90.7, 94.7)	62.5 (58.5, 66.4)	91.0 (88.4, 93.0)
North	96.1 (92.7, 97.9)	66.4 (58.7, 73.3)	61.6 (54.5, 68.3)	95.3 (92.2, 97.2)	81.6 (74.2, 87.2)	83.9 (76.2, 89.4)	59.5 (53.2, 65.6)	85.5 (79.1, 90.2)
Northeast	96.6 (93.3, 98.3)	79.8 (74.2, 84.4)	76.4 (72.2, 80.2)	96.3 (94.6, 97.5)	92.0 (89.6, 94.0)	90.1 (86.9, 92.7)	66.2 (60.7, 71.4)	86.0 (81.5, 89.6)
South	98.2 (96.8, 99.0)	84.5 (80.8, 87.6)	76.6 (72.5, 80.3)	96.3 (94.5, 97.5)	91.3 (88.6, 93.4)	92.6 (90.5, 94.3)	72.0 (68.1, 75.6)	90.2 (87.2, 92.6)
Socioeconomic status								
Lowest	94.8 (92.0, 96.7)	67.9 (61.4, 73.7)	63.0 (56.8, 68.8)	92.7 (89.7, 94.9)	80.3 (75.0, 84.7)	82.0 (76.6, 86.3)	52.5 (46.6, 58.2)	79.2 (73.8, 83.8)
Low	96.6 (92.4, 98.5)	76.0 (71.1, 80.3)	70.8 (65.9, 75.2)	96.0 (94.1, 97.3)	90.1 (87.0, 92.5)	89.4 (85.9, 92.1)	65.1 (59.8, 70.1)	87.2 (83.5, 90.2)
Middle	97.9 (96.2, 98.8)	78.9 (74.5, 82.7)	73.9 (69.6, 77.8)	97.0 (95.5, 98.0)	91.6 (89.3, 93.5)	91.3 (87.9, 93.8)	67.1 (62.7, 71.2)	88.5 (84.2, 91.7)
High	98.3 (97.0, 99.1)	85.0 (81.8, 87.7)	76.9 (73.2, 80.2)	98.2 (96.8, 99.0)	92.5 (90.2, 94.2)	94.5 (92.6, 95.9)	71.5 (67.2, 75.5)	94.2 (92.0, 95.8)
Highest	99.0 (98.1, 99.5)	84.1 (79.8, 87.6)	81.3 (77.7, 84.4)	96.9 (94.4, 98.3)	95.6 (93.9, 96.8)	95.9 (94.3, 97.1)	73.9 (69.7, 77.7)	96.0 (94.3, 97.2)

Table 9.1b: Percentage of non-smokers ≥ 15 years old who believe that smoking causes serious illnesses, stroke, heart attack, lung cancer, mouth cancer, larynx cancer, impotence or emphysema, by selected demographic characteristics – GATS Thailand, 2009.

Characteristic	Adults who believe that smoking causes...							
	Serious illnesses	Stroke	Heart attack	Lung cancer	Mouth cancer	Larynx cancer	Impotence	Emphysema
	Percentage (95% CI)							
Overall	99.0 (98.7, 99.2)	80.1 (78.7, 81.4)	76.7 (75.2, 78.1)	97.9 (97.5, 98.2)	91.1 (90.2, 92.0)	91.8 (90.9, 92.7)	65.7 (64.0, 67.3)	90.9 (89.8, 91.9)
Gender								
Male	99.0 (98.5, 99.4)	80.7 (78.4, 82.8)	76.9 (74.6, 79.1)	98.3 (97.7, 98.7)	90.9 (89.4, 92.2)	92.2 (90.6, 93.5)	73.2 (71.0, 75.3)	92.5 (90.9, 93.9)
Female	98.9 (98.6, 99.2)	79.8 (78.2, 81.3)	76.6 (75.0, 78.1)	97.7 (97.2, 98.0)	91.2 (90.2, 92.1)	91.6 (90.6, 92.5)	61.7 (59.7, 63.7)	90.0 (88.8, 91.2)
Age (years)								
15-24	99.7 (98.8, 99.9)	77.8 (73.9, 81.3)	74.8 (71.2, 78.1)	99.0 (98.4, 99.4)	92.8 (90.3, 94.8)	91.6 (89.2, 93.5)	67.7 (63.9, 71.4)	92.5 (89.9, 94.4)
25-44	99.4 (99.0, 99.6)	82.0 (80.2, 83.8)	77.6 (75.6, 79.5)	98.6 (98.1, 99.0)	94.1 (93.0, 95.0)	94.5 (93.3, 95.4)	71.3 (69.2, 73.3)	93.9 (92.6, 94.9)
45-59	99.0 (98.6, 99.3)	81.4 (79.6, 83.2)	78.1 (76.4, 79.7)	98.3 (97.8, 98.7)	90.7 (89.4, 91.8)	93.2 (92.0, 94.2)	64.0 (62.0, 66.0)	91.0 (89.6, 92.3)
60+	96.8 (95.7, 97.6)	76.3 (74.1, 78.4)	74.7 (72.4, 76.9)	93.7 (92.3, 94.9)	81.9 (79.7, 83.9)	83.4 (81.2, 85.3)	51.3 (48.8, 53.8)	81.0 (78.7, 83.1)
Residence								
Urban	99.3 (99.1, 99.5)	82.6 (81.5, 83.8)	79.2 (77.9, 80.4)	98.6 (98.3, 98.8)	92.5 (91.6, 93.3)	94.4 (93.6, 95.0)	69.4 (68.1, 70.7)	95.0 (94.3, 95.6)
Rural	98.8 (98.4, 99.1)	78.9 (76.9, 80.8)	75.5 (73.4, 77.4)	97.5 (97.1, 97.9)	90.5 (89.1, 91.7)	90.6 (89.3, 91.8)	63.9 (61.5, 66.3)	88.9 (87.3, 90.4)
Education level								
Less than primary	97.7 (97.0, 98.2)	76.9 (75.0, 78.7)	74.1 (72.2, 75.8)	95.6 (94.8, 96.3)	84.5 (82.6, 86.1)	86.4 (84.5, 88.0)	53.7 (51.4, 56.0)	83.4 (81.5, 85.1)
Primary	99.6 (99.3, 99.8)	78.2 (75.2, 80.9)	74.0 (70.5, 77.2)	98.6 (97.9, 99.1)	93.2 (91.4, 94.6)	92.6 (90.7, 94.1)	63.8 (60.3, 67.3)	91.0 (88.7, 92.8)
Secondary	99.6 (99.1, 99.8)	81.5 (79.2, 83.7)	78.0 (75.5, 80.2)	99.1 (98.7, 99.5)	95.0 (93.7, 96.0)	94.7 (93.4, 95.8)	72.6 (70.1, 74.9)	95.3 (93.5, 96.6)
University	99.7 (99.3, 99.9)	87.5 (85.6, 89.1)	83.9 (81.4, 86.1)	99.4 (98.9, 99.7)	95.1 (93.8, 96.2)	97.0 (95.8, 97.8)	81.1 (78.7, 83.2)	98.6 (97.8, 99.1)
Region								
Bangkok	99.6 (99.2, 99.8)	84.3 (82.3, 86.1)	82.7 (80.6, 84.5)	98.9 (98.3, 99.3)	94.3 (92.9, 95.4)	95.9 (94.7, 96.9)	71.6 (69.4, 73.8)	97.0 (96.1, 97.7)
Central	99.0 (98.5, 99.4)	78.1 (76.0, 80.1)	72.7 (70.3, 75.1)	97.5 (96.7, 98.1)	89.5 (87.7, 91.0)	92.1 (90.6, 93.3)	60.1 (57.6, 62.7)	92.8 (91.5, 93.9)
North	98.4 (97.5, 99.0)	75.5 (71.2, 79.4)	72.6 (68.4, 76.4)	98.0 (97.2, 98.5)	88.9 (86.7, 90.8)	90.0 (87.4, 92.1)	64.4 (60.6, 68.0)	90.9 (88.4, 92.9)
Northeast	99.0 (98.5, 99.3)	81.1 (78.1, 83.8)	78.2 (75.2, 80.9)	98.0 (97.3, 98.5)	91.8 (89.5, 93.6)	90.6 (88.4, 92.4)	66.9 (62.9, 70.6)	87.3 (84.5, 89.7)
South	99.1 (98.4, 99.5)	84.4 (81.8, 86.7)	81.2 (78.0, 84.0)	97.2 (96.1, 98.0)	93.0 (91.0, 94.5)	93.8 (91.8, 95.3)	70.0 (66.2, 73.5)	91.2 (88.8, 93.1)
Socioeconomic status								
Lowest	97.9 (97.3, 98.5)	73.4 (70.1, 76.6)	72.8 (69.6, 75.8)	96.2 (95.3, 97.0)	86.4 (83.9, 88.6)	85.8 (83.3, 87.9)	56.2 (52.7, 59.6)	84.0 (81.4, 86.3)
Low	98.9 (98.2, 99.3)	81.8 (79.6, 83.8)	78.1 (75.3, 80.6)	98.0 (97.3, 98.5)	91.5 (90.1, 92.8)	92.5 (91.0, 93.7)	63.2 (60.2, 66.0)	90.0 (88.2, 91.6)
Middle	99.5 (99.0, 99.7)	80.8 (78.4, 83.0)	75.7 (73.1, 78.2)	98.4 (97.6, 98.9)	92.2 (90.6, 93.6)	93.5 (92.0, 94.8)	68.7 (66.0, 71.4)	93.1 (91.6, 94.3)
High	99.5 (99.0, 99.7)	82.9 (80.6, 84.9)	77.2 (74.5, 79.6)	98.8 (98.0, 99.2)	93.8 (92.3, 95.0)	94.7 (93.2, 95.9)	70.8 (68.3, 73.1)	94.8 (93.3, 95.9)
Highest	99.7 (99.4, 99.8)	85.0 (83.0, 86.7)	81.5 (79.4, 83.5)	99.0 (98.5, 99.3)	94.3 (93.0, 95.4)	96.0 (94.8, 96.9)	76.5 (74.1, 78.7)	97.1 (96.2, 97.9)

9.2 Beliefs about second-hand smoke (SHS) causing serious illness and specific diseases

Table 9.2 shows that 94.9% of adults aged 15 years and above believe that breathing second-hand smoke (SHS) by non-smokers can cause serious illnesses to them. More adults believe that SHS causes lung cancer in adults (90.7%), lung disease in children (90%) and emphysema (82.4%) than low birth weight (69.2%) , heart disease in adults (64.9%) and premature birth (58.5%).

When viewed by gender, males and females equally believed in the adverse effects of SHS on all aspects of health, except on premature birth and low birth weight where males reported in lesser proportion than females that exposure to SHS causes low birth weight (64.3% and 73.9% respectively) and premature birth (53.3% and 63.5% respectively) in non-smokers. Young adults aged 15-24 years have reported in greater numbers that SHS causes serious illnesses (97.5%) when compared against adults aged 60 years and above (86.8%).

Rural adults believed less in the health impact of SHS than urban adults (94.4% and 96.1%). Adults with less than primary education have the least belief in the health impact of SHS in all diseases, specifically on premature birth (52.0%) and low birth weight (59.7%). Adults in Bangkok metropolis had a higher belief in the health impact of SHS on nearly all specific diseases than adults in other regions, especially regarding the belief that exposure to SHS causes lung cancer (94.0%) and heart disease (71.5%) in adults. Among the different socioeconomic status categories, the lowest SES have the lowest proportion of beliefs about health impacts of SHS in all specific diseases/conditions, especially the impact of SHS on premature birth (49.7%), low birth weight (59.5%) and heart disease in adults (56.6%).

Classified by smoking status, current non-smokers have a higher prevalence of the belief that breathing SHS can cause many serious illnesses and specific diseases than current smokers. The greatest differences are with regard to beliefs in the health impact of SHS on low birth weight (71.6% for non-smokers and 61.7% for smokers) and premature birth (61.0% and 50.5% respectively) (*see Table 9.2a, 9.2b*).

Among current smokers, males clearly have higher beliefs than females on the adverse effects of SHS on all aspects of health. At the same time, persons aged 60 years and over have low levels of belief on the health impact of SHS on all diseases. Current smokers in urban areas have higher level of belief in the health impact of SHS on all diseases than those in rural areas, except for lung illness in adults and premature birth. When categorized by educational levels, smokers with an education of less than primary level have a less degree of belief in the health impact of SHS on all diseases as compared with those with other levels of education. Current smokers in the Northern region have lower levels of belief about the health impact of SHS on all specific diseases than other regions, specifically premature birth (43.7%). By socioeconomic status, the smokers from the lowest SES category have the lowest proportion of belief about the health impact of SHS on all specific diseases, specifically premature birth (38.9%) and low birth weight (47.2%) (*see detail in Table 9.2a*).

Among current non-smokers, males and females have identical beliefs regarding SHS being the cause of heart disease in adults, lung illnesses in children, lung cancer in adults and emphysema in adults. However, more females than males believe that SHS is responsible for low birth weight and premature births. Current non-smokers in urban areas have a higher level of belief on the health impact of SHS on all diseases. Classified by educational level, non-smokers with education up to less than primary level have low prevalence of belief in the health impact of SHS on all diseases when compared with those with other levels of education. Classified by region, the lowest degree of belief in the health impact of SHS on each specific disease are different. By socioeconomic status, the smokers from the lowest SES have the lowest proportion of belief about the health impact of SHS on all specific diseases, specifically premature birth (52.0%), and heart disease in adults (56.9%) (*see detail in Table 9.2b*).

9.3 Pictorial health warnings (PHWs) encourage cessation among smokers

Table 9.3 provides information about the impact of PHWs on the desire to quit among current smokers of manufactured cigarettes or cigars aged 15 years and above. Among the nine PHWs depicted below, the survey found that the three PHWs that have the strongest impact on the desire to quit are: Picture 8 (Smoking causes laryngeal cancer (30.3%)), Picture 7 (Smoking causes oral cancer (24.1%)) and Picture 4 (Cigarette smoke causes lung cancer (17.6%)). Classified by demographic characteristics, all groups of current smokers have reported that these three PHWs have had the strongest impact on their desire or inclination to quit.

Picture1	Picture2	Picture3	Picture 4	Picture5
Cigarette smoke harms people nearby	Smoking causes your breath to smell	Smoking causes fatal emphysema	Cigarette smoke causes lung cancer	Cigarette smoke causes fatal heart failure

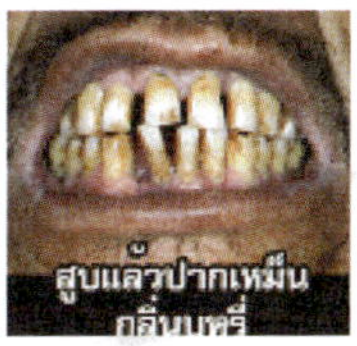

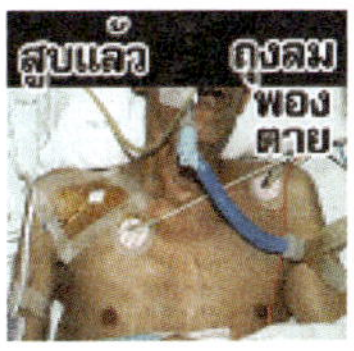

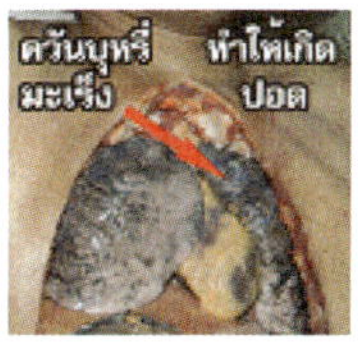

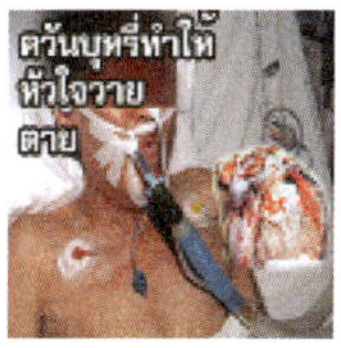

Picture 6	Picture 7	Picture 8	Picture 9
Cigarette smoke leads your life to death	Smoking causes oral cancer	Smoking causes laryngeal cancer	Cigarette smoke causes haemorrhagic stroke

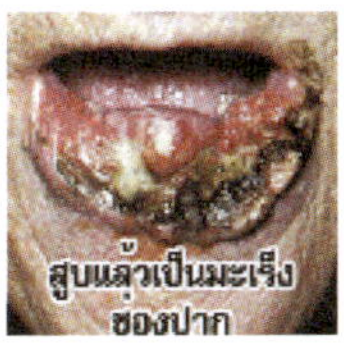

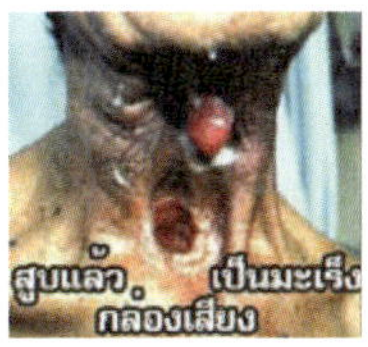

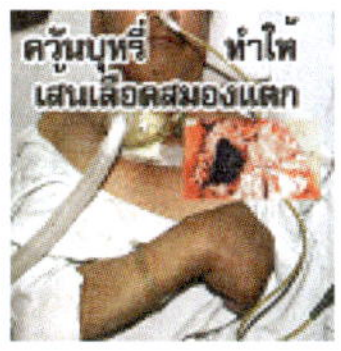

9.4 Pictorial health warnings that encourage continuing abstinence among non-smokers

Table 9.4 shows the impact of PHWs that influence the intention to continue abstinence from smoking among non-smokers aged 15 years and above. Three types of PHWs that have the highest influence on continued abstinence among non-smokers are: Picture 7 (Smoking causes oral cancer (34.4%)), Picture 8 (Smoking causes laryngeal cancer (28.2%)) and Picture 4 (Cigarette smoke causes lung cancer (16.1%)). When viewed according to demographic characteristics, all groups of non-smokers have reported that these three pictures have had the highest influence on their intention to continue their abstinence from smoking.

It should also be noted that current manufactured-cigarette and cigar smokers and non-smokers have all reported that these three PHWs are the most effective.

Table 9.2: Percentage of adults ≥15 years of age who believe that second-hand smoke causes serious illnesses and specific diseases in non-smokers, by selected demographic characteristics – GATS Thailand, 2009.

Characteristic	Belief that breathing second-hand smoke causes the following in non-smokers:						
	Serious illnesses	Heart disease in adults	Lung illness in children	Lung cancer in adults	Emphysema	Low birth weight[1]	Premature birth[2]
	Percentage (95% CI)						
Overall	94.9 (94.3, 95.5)	64.9 (63.5, 66.4)	90.0 (89.2, 90.9)	90.7 (89.9, 91.5)	82.4 (81.2, 83.6)	69.2 (67.8, 70.6)	58.5 (57.0, 60.1)
Gender							
Male	94.6 (93.9, 95.3)	65.8 (63.8, 67.6)	90.0 (89.0, 90.9)	90.7 (89.7, 91.6)	83.3 (81.9, 84.6)	64.3 (62.3, 66.2)	53.3 (51.2, 55.3)
Female	95.2 (94.5, 95.8)	64.1 (62.3, 65.9)	90.1 (89.0, 91.1)	90.7 (89.8, 91.6)	81.6 (79.9, 83.1)	73.9 (72.4, 75.4)	63.5 (61.7, 65.3)
Age (years)							
15-24	97.5 (96.4, 98.2)	58.0 (54.8, 61.2)	92.8 (90.8, 94.4)	94.1 (92.5, 95.4)	82.8 (80.0, 85.3)	67.8 (64.2, 71.3)	54.4 (50.5, 58.3)
25-44	97.0 (96.3, 97.5)	67.3 (65.3, 69.2)	93.1 (92.1, 94.0)	93.8 (92.9, 94.6)	86.6 (85.2, 87.9)	74.8 (73.0, 76.6)	63.3 (61.4, 65.3)
45-59	94.5 (93.6, 95.2)	68.8 (67.0, 70.6)	89.7 (88.5, 90.8)	90.1 (88.8, 91.2)	82.9 (81.4, 84.4)	70.9 (69.1, 72.6)	61.5 (59.6, 63.4)
60+	86.8 (84.9, 88.4)	61.7 (59.4, 64.0)	78.6 (76.3, 80.7)	78.9 (76.5, 81.0)	69.8 (67.2, 72.4)	53.3 (50.8, 55.8)	46.3 (43.9, 48.7)
Residence							
Urban	96.1 (95.6, 96.5)	67.7 (66.3, 69.0)	91.3 (90.5, 92.0)	92.9 (92.2, 93.4)	85.6 (84.6, 86.6)	71.0 (69.8, 72.2)	59.4 (58.0, 60.9)
Rural	94.4 (93.6, 95.1)	63.7 (61.7, 65.7)	89.5 (88.2, 90.6)	89.8 (88.6, 90.8)	81.0 (79.2, 82.6)	68.5 (66.5, 70.4)	58.1 (55.9, 60.3)
Education level							
Less than primary	89.6 (88.4, 90.8)	62.0 (59.9, 64.1)	82.7 (81.0, 84.2)	83.4 (81.7, 84.9)	74.0 (72.0, 76.0)	59.7 (57.5, 61.8)	52.0 (49.9, 54.1)
Primary	96.5 (95.4, 97.3)	64.3 (61.6, 67.0)	91.6 (89.9, 93.0)	92.3 (90.7, 93.6)	84.2 (82.2, 86.1)	71.1 (68.3, 73.8)	58.8 (55.7, 61.9)
Secondary	97.9 (97.3, 98.4)	64.7 (62.6, 66.8)	94.2 (93.2, 95.1)	95.1 (94.1, 95.9)	86.0 (84.4, 87.6)	73.0 (70.8, 75.0)	60.4 (58.1, 62.6)
University	98.9 (98.4, 99.2)	74.5 (72.2, 76.7)	96.6 (95.6, 97.4)	96.7 (95.8, 97.4)	92.9 (91.2, 94.3)	82.6 (80.6, 84.5)	71.4 (69.0, 73.8)
Region							
Bangkok	96.5 (95.7, 97.2)	71.5 (69.4, 73.6)	92.2 (90.9, 93.3)	94.0 (92.9, 94.9)	88.7 (87.1, 90.1)	70.3 (68.2, 72.4)	60.1 (57.8, 62.4)
Central	94.8 (93.8, 95.6)	61.4 (59.2, 63.5)	88.8 (87.5, 90.1)	89.8 (88.5, 91.0)	83.0 (81.2, 84.7)	68.7 (66.1, 71.2)	55.4 (52.7, 58.1)
North	93.5 (91.6, 95.1)	60.8 (56.7, 64.8)	89.7 (87.4, 91.7)	90.7 (88.7, 92.4)	83.3 (80.3, 86.0)	66.3 (62.5, 69.9)	57.2 (53.5, 60.9)
Northeast	95.4 (94.3, 96.4)	66.2 (63.0, 69.2)	90.0 (88.0, 91.6)	90.9 (89.0, 92.4)	79.0 (76.1, 81.7)	70.6 (67.7, 73.4)	61.2 (57.7, 64.5)
South	94.6 (93.0, 95.9)	68.8 (66.1, 71.4)	91.2 (88.9, 93.0)	89.5 (87.1, 91.5)	83.5 (80.7, 86.0)	70.0 (66.9, 72.9)	58.1 (54.4, 61.7)
Socioeconomic status							
Lowest	91.0 (89.4, 92.4)	56.6 (53.5, 59.7)	83.8 (81.2, 86.0)	85.5 (83.4, 87.5)	74.0 (71.1, 76.7)	59.5 (56.5, 62.4)	49.7 (46.4, 52.9)
Low	95.5 (94.4, 96.3)	64.7 (62.1, 67.3)	90.5 (89.0, 91.8)	91.4 (89.9, 92.7)	82.8 (80.4, 84.9)	68.7 (66.1, 71.1)	59.9 (57.3, 62.5)
Middle	95.6 (94.6, 96.4)	66.6 (64.4, 68.8)	91.1 (89.7, 92.3)	91.9 (90.6, 93.0)	82.6 (80.5, 84.5)	71.5 (69.3, 73.7)	59.8 (57.3, 62.4)
High	97.0 (96.2, 97.7)	68.9 (66.5, 71.3)	94.0 (93.0, 94.9)	93.5 (92.3, 94.6)	87.5 (85.8, 88.9)	75.6 (73.5, 77.6)	62.2 (59.7, 64.6)
Highest	97.2 (96.5, 97.9)	72.0 (69.8, 74.0)	93.9 (92.8, 94.8)	93.5 (92.4, 94.4)	89.7 (88.3, 90.9)	75.9 (73.8, 77.8)	64.8 (62.3, 67.2)

[1] Defined as a birth weight with <2500 grams.
[2] Defined as a birth during 28-34 weeks of gestation.

Table 9.2a: Percentage of current smokers ≥ 15 years of age who believe that breathing second-hand smoke causes serious illnesses and specific diseases in non-smokers, by selected demographic characteristics – GATS Thailand, 2009.

Characteristic	Belief that breathing second-hand smoke causes the following in non-smokers:						
	Serious illnesses	Heart disease in adults	Lung illness in children	Lung cancer in adults	Emphysema	Low birth weight[1]	Premature birth[2]
	Percentage (95% CI)						
Overall	93.1 (91.9, 94.2)	64.3 (61.8, 66.7)	87.5 (86.0, 88.9)	88.7 (87.3, 90.0)	81.1 (78.9, 83.0)	61.7 (59.1, 64.3)	50.5 (47.8, 53.2)
Gender							
Male	93.5 (92.4, 94.5)	64.9 (62.4, 67.4)	88.0 (86.6, 89.3)	89.1 (87.8, 90.4)	81.5 (79.4, 83.4)	62.2 (59.6, 64.8)	50.9 (48.1, 53.6)
Female	88.1 (81.0, 92.8)	56.2 (48.2, 63.9)	80.8 (73.6, 86.4)	83.2 (76.5, 88.3)	74.9 (68.2, 80.6)	54.8 (47.0, 62.3)	46.0 (38.7, 53.4)
Age (years)							
15-24	96.4 (92.9, 98.2)	59.5 (51.9, 66.7)	89.7 (84.7, 93.2)	93.7 (89.4, 96.4)	80.3 (73.6, 85.6)	59.0 (51.3, 66.2)	46.2 (38.6, 53.9)
25-44	95.6 (94.1, 96.8)	67.2 (63.9, 70.4)	91.0 (89.1, 92.7)	91.9 (90.1, 93.3)	86.0 (83.1, 88.5)	66.6 (63.2, 69.9)	53.7 (50.1, 57.4)
45-59	90.6 (88.3, 92.5)	66.3 (62.6, 69.7)	85.9 (83.3, 88.2)	86.0 (83.3, 88.2)	79.0 (75.7, 81.8)	61.0 (57.4, 64.4)	52.3 (48.6, 56.0)
60+	84.9 (81.8, 87.6)	56.9 (52.7, 61.0)	75.6 (71.7, 79.2)	76.8 (73.0, 80.3)	68.6 (64.3, 72.6)	49.5 (44.8, 54.1)	41.7 (37.2, 46.4)
Residence							
Urban	93.7 (92.6, 94.7)	66.4 (64.0, 68.8)	87.1 (85.3, 88.6)	89.6 (88.1, 90.9)	82.6 (80.7, 84.4)	62.6 (60.2, 64.9)	48.6 (46.2, 51.0)
Rural	92.9 (91.2, 94.3)	63.5 (60.2, 66.7)	87.7 (85.6, 89.5)	88.4 (86.5, 90.1)	80.4 (77.6, 83.0)	61.4 (57.9, 64.8)	51.3 (47.7, 54.9)
Education level							
less than primary	87.2 (84.5, 89.5)	59.9 (56.2, 63.5)	80.3 (77.3, 83.0)	81.5 (78.6, 84.0)	72.9 (69.4, 76.2)	54.1 (50.3, 58.0)	46.4 (42.5, 50.3)
Primary	96.1 (94.2, 97.4)	66.0 (61.9, 70.0)	90.6 (87.9, 92.7)	92.0 (89.5, 94.0)	85.5 (81.9, 88.5)	63.0 (58.2, 67.6)	50.8 (45.8, 55.8)
Secondary	96.3 (94.6, 97.5)	64.2 (59.7, 68.5)	91.4 (88.9, 93.4)	93.1 (90.9, 94.9)	84.0 (80.2, 87.2)	66.2 (61.6, 70.5)	52.5 (47.8, 57.2)
University	96.8 (94.1, 98.3)	79.1 (74.0, 83.5)	93.5 (90.1, 95.8)	92.3 (88.5, 94.9)	90.6 (86.5, 93.6)	73.5 (67.5, 78.8)	60.5 (53.7, 66.8)
Region							
Bangkok	93.3 (91.2, 94.9)	69.8 (65.9, 73.4)	87.6 (84.6, 90.0)	89.3 (86.7, 91.5)	84.1 (80.9, 86.9)	62.2 (58.2, 66.0)	48.7 (44.6, 52.7)
Central	93.6 (91.6, 95.2)	63.4 (59.5, 67.2)	87.1 (84.7, 89.2)	89.1 (86.6, 91.2)	83.6 (80.8, 86.1)	63.8 (59.1, 68.3)	48.2 (43.2, 53.3)
North	89.7 (84.8, 93.2)	56.3 (49.7, 62.7)	84.1 (78.7, 88.3)	86.5 (81.6, 90.2)	79.4 (72.8, 84.7)	54.3 (47.3, 61.1)	43.7 (37.4, 50.1)
Northeast	93.9 (91.6, 95.6)	65.8 (60.3, 70.9)	87.9 (84.8, 90.5)	89.3 (86.5, 91.6)	77.9 (73.1, 82.0)	63.7 (58.4, 68.8)	55.9 (50.3, 61.5)
South	94.4 (92.6, 95.8)	68.3 (64.2, 72.1)	90.9 (88.4, 93.0)	89.2 (86.3, 91.6)	84.1 (80.4, 87.2)	62.4 (57.6, 66.9)	51.0 (46.0, 56.1)
Socioeconomic status							
Lowest	86.5 (82.0, 90.0)	55.0 (48.8, 61.0)	76.9 (72.0, 81.1)	81.5 (76.9, 85.3)	69.3 (63.0, 75.0)	47.2 (41.0, 53.4)	38.9 (32.9, 45.4)
Low	93.6 (91.4, 95.3)	62.3 (57.2, 67.1)	87.4 (84.4, 89.9)	89.2 (86.2, 91.6)	81.4 (77.1, 85.0)	57.5 (52.3, 62.7)	47.6 (42.1, 53.1)
Middle	94.5 (92.6, 96.0)	65.1 (60.8, 69.2)	89.3 (86.3, 91.7)	90.5 (88.0, 92.4)	80.8 (76.9, 84.2)	66.1 (61.6, 70.4)	54.9 (50.2, 59.4)
High	95.9 (94.3, 97.0)	68.7 (64.1, 72.9)	91.9 (89.7, 93.6)	91.0 (88.5, 93.0)	87.3 (84.4, 89.7)	71.3 (67.5, 74.9)	56.6 (51.9, 61.3)
Highest	94.9 (92.9, 96.3)	72.9 (68.3, 77.0)	92.7 (90.5, 94.4)	91.4 (88.9, 93.4)	88.1 (84.8, 90.7)	67.1 (62.7, 71.1)	54.7 (49.8, 59.5)

[1] Defined as a birth weight with <2500 grams.
[2] Defined as a birth during 28-34 weeks of gestation.

Table 9.2b: Percentage of non-smokers ≥ 15 years of age who believe that breathing second-hand smoke causes serious illnesses and specific diseases in non-smokers, by selected demographic characteristics – GATS Thailand, 2009.

Characteristic	Belief that breathing other people's smoke causes the following in non-smokers:						
	Serious illnesses	Heart disease in adults	Lung illness in children	Lung cancer in adults	Emphysema	Low birth weight[1]	Premature birth[2]
	Percentage (95% CI)						
Overall	95.5 (94.9, 96.0)	65.1 (63.6, 66.6)	90.8 (89.9, 91.7)	91.3 (90.5, 92.2)	82.8 (81.5, 84.1)	71.6 (70.2, 72.9)	61.0 (59.5, 62.6)
Gender							
Male	95.6 (94.7, 96.4)	66.5 (64.1, 68.8)	91.6 (90.3, 92.8)	92.0 (90.7, 93.2)	84.8 (83.1, 86.4)	66.0 (63.7, 68.3)	55.3 (52.8, 57.8)
Female	95.4 (94.8, 96.0)	64.4 (62.6, 66.2)	90.4 (89.3, 91.4)	91.0 (90.0, 91.9)	81.8 (80.2, 83.3)	74.5 (73.0, 76.0)	64.1 (62.3, 65.8)
Age (years)							
15-24	97.7 (96.5, 98.5)	57.7 (54.1, 61.2)	93.5 (91.2, 95.3)	94.2 (92.4, 95.6)	83.4 (80.1, 86.3)	70.0 (65.8, 73.9)	56.5 (52.1, 60.8)
25-44	97.4 (96.8, 98.0)	67.3 (65.1, 69.4)	93.9 (92.9, 94.8)	94.5 (93.6, 95.4)	86.8 (85.3, 88.1)	77.8 (76.0, 79.5)	66.8 (64.8, 68.8)
45-59	95.7 (94.8, 96.4)	69.6 (67.7, 71.5)	90.9 (89.6, 92.1)	91.4 (90.0, 92.6)	84.2 (82.5, 85.8)	74.0 (72.2, 75.7)	64.4 (62.3, 66.5)
60+	87.2 (85.2, 89.0)	63.0 (60.5, 65.4)	79.3 (76.9, 81.6)	79.4 (76.9, 81.7)	70.2 (67.4, 72.8)	54.4 (51.8, 57.0)	47.5 (44.9, 50.0)
Residence							
Urban	96.7 (96.2, 97.1)	68.0 (66.5, 69.5)	92.4 (91.6, 93.2)	93.8 (93.1, 94.4)	86.5 (85.4, 87.5)	73.3 (72.0, 74.6)	62.4 (60.8, 64.0)
Rural	94.9 (94.1, 95.6)	63.8 (61.7, 65.8)	90.1 (88.7, 91.3)	90.2 (88.9, 91.4)	81.2 (79.2, 83.0)	70.8 (68.8, 72.7)	60.4 (58.2, 62.6)
Education level							
Less than primary	90.4 (89.2, 91.5)	62.7 (60.6, 64.8)	83.4 (81.7, 85.0)	84.0 (82.2, 85.6)	74.4 (72.3, 76.4)	61.4 (59.4, 63.5)	53.8 (51.8, 55.8)
Primary	96.6 (95.4, 97.5)	63.6 (60.3, 66.7)	92.0 (89.9, 93.7)	92.4 (90.4, 94.0)	83.7 (81.3, 85.9)	74.4 (71.3, 77.4)	62.1 (58.6, 65.5)
Secondary	98.4 (97.7, 98.9)	64.9 (62.4, 67.3)	95.1 (93.9, 96.0)	95.7 (94.6, 96.6)	86.7 (84.7, 88.4)	75.0 (72.5, 77.3)	62.7 (60.0, 65.4)
University	99.2 (98.7, 99.5)	73.8 (71.1, 76.3)	97.1 (96.1, 97.9)	97.4 (96.5, 98.2)	93.3 (91.4, 94.8)	84.1 (82.0, 86.0)	73.3 (70.6, 75.8)
Region							
Bangkok	97.3 (96.4, 98.0)	71.9 (69.6, 74.2)	93.2 (91.9, 94.4)	95.1 (94.0, 96.0)	89.8 (88.0, 91.3)	72.2 (69.9, 74.4)	62.8 (60.3, 65.3)
Central	95.1 (94.1, 96.0)	60.8 (58.3, 63.1)	89.4 (87.8, 90.8)	90.0 (88.5, 91.3)	82.8 (80.7, 84.8)	70.2 (67.8, 72.6)	57.6 (54.9, 60.3)
North	94.7 (93.2, 95.8)	62.1 (58.0, 66.0)	91.4 (89.4, 93.0)	92.0 (90.3, 93.4)	84.5 (81.9, 86.8)	69.8 (66.6, 72.8)	61.2 (57.9, 64.4)
Northeast	95.9 (94.7, 96.8)	66.3 (63.1, 69.3)	90.6 (88.4, 92.4)	91.3 (89.2, 93.1)	79.4 (76.0, 82.4)	72.8 (69.7, 75.7)	62.8 (59.2, 66.3)
South	94.7 (92.7, 96.2)	69.1 (65.8, 72.1)	91.3 (88.6, 93.4)	89.6 (86.9, 91.8)	83.3 (80.3, 85.9)	73.2 (70.1, 76.1)	61.1 (57.3, 64.7)
Socioeconomic status							
Lowest	92.0 (90.5, 93.3)	56.9 (53.6, 60.2)	85.3 (82.5, 87.6)	86.4 (84.1, 88.5)	75.1 (72.0, 77.9)	62.1 (59.0, 65.2)	52.0 (48.6, 55.3)
Low	96.0 (95.0, 96.9)	65.5 (62.6, 68.2)	91.4 (89.9, 92.8)	92.0 (90.5, 93.4)	83.2 (80.5, 85.6)	72.1 (69.6, 74.4)	63.8 (61.2, 66.3)
Middle	96.0 (94.9, 97.0)	67.3 (64.7, 69.8)	91.8 (90.2, 93.1)	92.4 (90.9, 93.7)	83.3 (81.1, 85.3)	73.8 (71.1, 76.2)	61.9 (59.1, 64.6)
High	97.5 (96.5, 98.2)	69.0 (66.3, 71.6)	94.8 (93.6, 95.8)	94.5 (93.0, 95.8)	87.5 (85.5, 89.3)	77.3 (75.0, 79.5)	64.3 (61.5, 67.1)
Highest	97.9 (97.0, 98.5)	71.7 (69.3, 74.0)	94.2 (92.9, 95.3)	94.0 (92.8, 95.1)	90.1 (88.4, 91.5)	78.2 (76.0, 80.2)	67.4 (64.8, 70.0)

[1] Defined as a birth weight with <2500 grams.
[2] Defined as a birth during 28-34 weeks of gestation.

Table 9.3: Percentage of adults ≥ 15 years of age who are current manufactured-cigarette or cigar smokers who feel a particular PHW makes them want to quit, by selected demographic characteristics – GATS Thailand, 2009.

Characteristic	The PHW[1] which makes a current smoker[2] want to quit										
	1	2	3	4	5	6	7	8	9	None of them	Total
	Percentage (95% CI)										
Overall	6.7 (5.6, 8.2)	2.7 (2.0, 3.6)	3.7 (3.0, 4.6)	17.6 (15.6, 19.8)	4.6 (3.5, 5.9)	4.4 (3.5, 5.5)	24.1 (21.5, 26.8)	30.3 (27.6, 33.1)	1.6 (0.9, 2.5)	4.4 (3.4, 5.7)	100
Gender											
Male	6.8 (5.6, 8.3)	2.6 (1.9, 3.5)	3.7 (3.0, 4.6)	17.7 (15.6, 19.9)	4.5 (3.4, 5.9)	4.4 (3.5, 5.5)	24.0 (21.4, 26.9)	30.3 (27.5, 33.2)	1.5 (0.9, 2.5)	4.5 (3.5, 5.8)	100
Female	5.1 (2.8, 9.1)*	5.9 (2.4, 13.8)*	2.4 (1.0, 5.6)*	15.5 (10.5, 22.2)	6.6 (3.2, 12.9)*	3.9 (1.8, 8.2)*	25.1 (17.0, 35.3)	31.1 (22.9, 40.7)	2.5 (0.7, 8.1)*	1.9 (0.7, 5.0)*	100
Age (years)											
15-24	4.4 (2.1, 9.0)*	2.4 (1.0, 5.7)*	0.8 (0.3, 2.3)*	15.1 (11.0, 20.4)	5.3 (2.6, 10.7)*	4.8 (2.8, 8.2)	32.7 (25.1, 41.3)	30.1 (23.2, 38.0)	2.7 (0.9, 7.7)*	1.6 (0.5, 5.1)*	100
25-44	8.4 (6.7, 10.5)	1.8 (1.2, 2.9)	2.4 (1.7, 3.5)	18.3 (15.7, 21.2)	4.0 (2.9, 5.6)	4.7 (3.5, 6.2)	21.2 (18.3, 24.4)	33.6 (30.4, 37.0)	1.4 (0.9, 2.2)*	4.2 (2.8, 6.1)	100
45-59	5.7 (4.1, 7.8)	4.8 (3.1, 7.3)	8.2 (5.9, 11.3)	19.5 (16.1, 23.5)	4.3 (3.0, 6.1)	3.7 (2.4, 5.6)	21.1 (17.7, 24.8)	24.0 (20.6, 27.8)	0.8 (0.4, 1.5)*	7.9 (5.7, 10.9)	100
60+	4.5 (2.2, 9.0)*	5.2 (3.1, 8.8)*	12.8 (8.3, 19.1)	14.8 (10.3, 20.9)	7.1 (3.8, 12.8)*	1.5 (0.6, 4.0)*	24.3 (18.5, 31.3)	21.5 (15.5, 29.0)	0.8 (0.2, 2.7)*	7.5 (4.9, 11.4)	100
Residence											
Urban	6.9 (5.7, 8.3)	2.7 (1.9, 3.6)	3.5 (2.7, 4.5)	19.5 (17.5, 21.7)	4.3 (3.4, 5.6)	4.4 (3.4, 5.7)	21.6 (19.5, 23.9)	29.9 (27.3, 32.6)	1.4 (0.8, 2.2)	5.8 (4.6, 7.3)	100
Rural	6.7 (5.0, 8.9)	2.7 (1.8, 4.2)	3.8 (2.8, 5.1)	16.5 (13.7, 19.7)	4.7 (3.2, 6.8)	4.3 (3.1, 6.0)	25.4 (21.7, 29.7)	30.6 (26.6, 34.8)	1.7 (0.8, 3.3)*	3.6 (2.4, 5.6)	100
Education level											
Less than primary	3.4 (2.2, 5.3)	4.5 (2.6, 7.6)	7.4 (5.3, 10.4)	18.5 (15.0, 22.6)	6.5 (4.2, 9.8)	2.9 (1.7, 5.1)*	26.0 (21.7, 30.8)	24.0 (20.0, 28.5)	0.5 (0.2, 1.3)*	6.3 (4.4, 8.9)	100
Primary	6.9 (4.9, 9.7)	2.0 (1.0, 3.9)*	3.4 (2.1, 5.4)	18.8 (15.1, 23.1)	5.7 (3.2, 9.8)	3.3 (2.0, 5.2)	21.8 (17.3, 27.1)	32.7 (28.2, 37.5)	2.1 (1.2, 3.8)*	3.3 (1.8, 6.0)	100
Secondary	5.9 (4.2, 8.3)	1.9 (1.1, 3.1)	1.9 (1.3, 2.9)	16.4 (13.7, 19.5)	3.6 (2.5, 5.2)	5.2 (3.7, 7.3)	25.4 (20.9, 30.4)	34.1 (29.6, 39.0)	1.4 (0.5, 4.0)**	4.2 (2.7, 6.5)	100
University	15.2 (10.0, 22.3)	4.8 (2.1, 10.7)*	5.3 (2.9, 9.6)*	18.2 (13.3, 24.5)	2.6 (1.4, 4.9)*	5.8 (3.2, 10.3)*	21.1 (15.5, 28.0)	19.8 (15.5, 25.0)	2.4 (1.2, 4.8)*	4.8 (2.9, 7.8)	100
Region											
Bangkok	7.3 (5.5, 9.6)	2.5 (1.6, 4.1)*	4.5 (2.9, 6.8)	17.5 (14.6, 20.9)	4.0 (2.5, 6.3)	5.4 (3.8, 7.7)	18.2 (15.2, 21.5)	28.5 (24.4, 32.9)	1.8 (0.9, 3.6)*	10.3 (7.5, 14.1)	100
Central	6.3 (4.4, 8.8)	2.2 (1.2, 4.1)*	5.1 (3.5, 7.4)	17.4 (13.8, 21.5)	5.8 (4.1, 8.3)	7.0 (4.7, 10.3)	21.4 (17.0, 26.6)	29.4 (24.9, 34.3)	1.5 (0.7, 3.1)*	3.9 (2.4, 6.3)	100
North	3.6 (2.3, 5.7)	2.5 (1.2, 5.1)*	3.3 (2.1, 5.2)	16.5 (12.1, 22.0)	3.7 (2.0, 6.7)*	4.5 (2.1, 9.4)*	29.7 (23.4, 37.0)	33.8 (27.0, 41.4)	0.5 (0.1, 1.8)*	1.9 (1.0, 3.6)*	100
Northeast	8.3 (5.6, 12.0)	3.2 (1.9, 5.4)*	2.6 (1.6, 4.3)*	16.1 (12.1, 21.2)	3.3 (1.5, 7.3)*	1.3 (0.6, 2.5)*	28.8 (22.8, 35.5)	30.3 (24.2, 37.3)	1.9 (0.6, 5.7)*	4.3 (2.3, 7.7)	100
South	6.7 (4.0, 11.0)	2.9 (1.2, 6.5)*	3.4 (2.0, 5.7)	21.7 (17.3, 26.8)	6.1 (3.7, 10.0)	5.2 (3.4, 8.1)	18.9 (15.0, 23.5)	30.1 (25.7, 34.9)	1.8 (1.0, 3.3)*	3.2 (1.6, 6.3)	100
Socioeconomic status											
Lowest	6.4 (3.5, 11.1)*	3.6 (1.4, 9.1)*	3.8 (2.1, 6.7)*	19.4 (12.7, 28.5)	5.1 (1.5, 16.0)*	3.3 (1.4, 7.4)*	17.3 (12.4, 23.5)	37.3 (29.6, 45.7)	1.0 (0.2, 4.7)*	2.8 (1.6, 4.9)*	100
Low	5.8 (3.6, 9.1)	1.7 (0.7, 3.9)*	2.9 (1.5, 5.6)*	14.6 (11.0, 19.1)	5.7 (3.4, 9.5)	2.6 (1.5, 4.5)*	32.2 (25.0, 40.3)	31.4 (24.7, 39.0)	1.3 (0.5, 3.1)*	1.8 (1.0, 3.2)*	100
Middle	6.3 (3.9, 9.9)	2.6 (1.4, 5.0)*	2.5 (1.5, 4.1)	16.7 (13.7, 20.3)	3.5 (2.0, 6.0)	3.5 (2.3, 5.3)	24.6 (20.0, 29.8)	32.9 (28.1, 38.1)	2.2 (0.7, 6.2)*	5.2 (3.0, 8.8)	100
High	6.7 (4.6, 9.7)	2.6 (1.6, 4.1)*	3.7 (2.5, 5.5)	20.4 (16.3, 25.3)	4.1 (2.7, 6.3)	5.9 (3.8, 9.1)	24.4 (19.1, 30.6)	27.4 (23.1, 32.2)	1.3 (0.7, 2.6)*	3.5 (2.3, 5.2)	100
Highest	8.8 (6.3, 12.0)	3.4 (2.1, 5.5)	6.3 (4.3, 9.2)	17.3 (14.1, 21.0)	5.2 (3.6, 7.5)	6.4 (4.2, 9.7)	18.9 (15.3, 23.2)	24.1 (20.1, 28.7)	1.5 (0.7, 3.1)*	8.1 (5.5, 11.7)	100

[1] PHW: Pictorial health warning text and pictures can be found in Appendix E; [2] Includes current smokers of manufactured cigarettes or cigars.

* Indicates that estimate is based on sample size of less than 25.

Remark: No. of PHWs 1=Cigarette smoke harms people nearby, 2=Smoking causes your breath to smell, 3=Smoking caused emphysema, 4=Cigarette smoke causes lung cancer, 5= Cigarette smoke causes fatal heart failure, 6= Cigarette smoke leads your life to death, 7= Smoking causes oral cancer, 8=Smoking causes laryngeal cancer, 9=Cigarette smoke caused haemorrhagic stroke

Table 9.4: Percentage of adults ≥ 15 years of age who are non-smokers who are motivated by a particular PHW to not smoke, by selected demographic characteristics – GATS Thailand, 2009.

Characteristic	The PHW[1] which makes non-smokers[2] not want to smoke										Total
	1	2	3	4	5	6	7	8	9	None of them	
	Percentage (95% CI)										
Overall	7.1 (6.3, 7.9)	2.7 (2.3, 3.1)	2.7 (2.3, 3.2)	16.1 (14.9, 17.3)	3.8 (3.3, 4.3)	3.2 (2.7, 3.8)	34.4 (32.8, 36.0)	28.2 (26.8, 29.8)	1.7 (1.1, 2.6)	0.1 (0.1, 0.3)	100
Gender											
Male	8.4 (6.9, 10.2)	2.6 (1.8, 3.7)	2.7 (1.9, 3.8)	16.1 (14.0, 18.5)	3.4 (2.6, 4.3)	4.0 (2.9, 5.4)	31.3 (28.3, 34.5)	29.1 (26.1, 32.3)	2.2 (0.8, 6.2)	0.2 (0.1, 0.5)*	100
Female	6.6 (5.8, 7.5)	2.7 (2.3, 3.2)	2.7 (2.3, 3.3)	16.1 (14.8, 17.4)	3.9 (3.4, 4.6)	3.0 (2.5, 3.6)	35.4 (33.7, 37.2)	28.0 (26.4, 29.6)	1.5 (1.2, 2.0)	0.1 (0.0, 0.2)*	100
Age (years)											
15-24	4.8 (3.4, 6.7)	1.4 (0.7, 2.8)*	1.2 (0.5, 2.8)*	14.8 (12.2, 17.8)	3.2 (2.3, 4.5)	4.3 (2.8, 6.4)	39.2 (35.1, 43.4)	29.5 (26.2, 33.0)	1.6 (0.4, 6.8)*	0.0 (0.0, 0.2)*	100
25-44	8.9 (7.7, 10.2)	2.2 (1.7, 3.0)	2.1 (1.6, 2.7)	16.3 (14.7, 18.0)	3.4 (2.7, 4.2)	3.5 (2.8, 4.2)	30.7 (28.7, 32.9)	31.2 (29.1, 33.4)	1.6 (1.1, 2.3)	0.1 (0.0, 0.4)*	100
45-59	6.6 (5.5, 7.8)	3.0 (2.4, 3.8)	4.4 (3.6, 5.3)	16.3 (14.6, 18.2)	3.7 (3.0, 4.6)	1.8 (1.3, 2.5)	37.4 (35.0, 39.9)	25.0 (23.1, 27.0)	1.6 (1.1, 2.4)	0.2 (0.1, 0.4)*	100
60+	5.8 (4.6, 7.4)	7.2 (5.7, 9.1)	5.9 (4.6, 7.7)	17.5 (15.2, 20.2)	7.0 (5.6, 8.7)	2.9 (1.9, 4.3)	31.3 (28.7, 34.0)	19.4 (16.9, 22.2)	2.7 (1.8, 3.9)	0.3 (0.1, 0.6)*	100
Residence											
Urban	7.2 (6.4, 8.0)	2.4 (2.1, 2.9)	2.9 (2.5, 3.3)	16.4 (15.3, 17.5)	3.8 (3.2, 4.4)	3.1 (2.6, 3.8)	33.1 (31.7, 34.6)	29.6 (28.3, 31.0)	1.3 (1.0, 1.6)	0.2 (0.1, 0.4)*	100
Rural	7.0 (6.0, 8.2)	2.8 (2.3, 3.4)	2.6 (2.1, 3.3)	15.9 (14.2, 17.7)	3.8 (3.1, 4.5)	3.3 (2.6, 4.2)	35.0 (32.7, 37.4)	27.6 (25.4, 29.8)	1.9 (1.1, 3.3)	0.1 (0.0, 0.3)*	100
Education level											
Less than primary	5.6 (4.7, 6.7)	5.1 (4.3, 6.1)	4.6 (3.8, 5.5)	16.6 (14.8, 18.6)	5.2 (4.3, 6.1)	2.2 (1.7, 2.8)	35.3 (33.1, 37.4)	23.2 (21.3, 25.2)	2.0 (1.5, 2.7)	0.2 (0.1, 0.5)*	100
Primary	7.6 (6.0, 9.6)	1.5 (1.0, 2.2)	1.8 (1.1, 3.0)	15.6 (13.3, 18.3)	3.0 (2.0, 4.3)	3.9 (2.9, 5.4)	34.8 (31.1, 38.7)	30.4 (27.2, 33.8)	1.4 (0.8, 2.5)	0.0 (0.0, 0.0)*	100
Secondary	6.6 (5.4, 8.0)	1.9 (1.3, 3.0)	2.0 (1.3, 3.0)	15.7 (13.9, 17.7)	3.3 (2.6, 4.2)	3.6 (2.6, 5.0)	34.9 (31.9, 37.9)	30.0 (27.5, 32.7)	1.9 (0.8, 4.5)	0.1 (0.0, 0.3)*	100
University	10.0 (8.2, 12.2)	1.8 (1.2, 2.8)	2.5 (1.8, 3.5)	16.6 (14.1, 19.3)	3.4 (2.4, 4.9)	3.3 (2.3, 4.6)	31.1 (28.3, 34.1)	29.9 (27.1, 32.8)	1.3 (0.8, 2.1)	0.1 (0.0, 0.3)*	100
Region											
Bangkok	7.2 (5.9, 8.7)	2.0 (1.5, 2.6)	2.8 (2.2, 3.4)	18.3 (16.3, 20.5)	3.6 (2.7, 4.8)	2.9 (2.1, 4.1)	31.0 (28.6, 33.4)	30.0 (27.8, 32.4)	1.9 (1.3, 2.7)	0.3 (0.1, 0.8)*	100
Central	6.4 (5.4, 7.6)	2.2 (1.7, 2.9)	3.1 (2.5, 3.8)	14.9 (13.2, 16.8)	3.9 (3.0, 5.2)	4.6 (3.6, 5.9)	33.3 (31.0, 35.8)	30.8 (28.3, 33.4)	0.7 (0.5, 1.2)	0.1 (0.0, 0.2)*	100
North	6.3 (4.9, 8.2)	2.3 (1.6, 3.3)	3.4 (2.6, 4.6)	18.7 (15.5, 22.4)	3.6 (2.6, 4 9)	2.2 (1.5, 3.3)	31.9 (28.7, 35.2)	30.0 (25.9, 34.4)	1.6 (1.1, 2.4)	0.0 (0.0, 0.0)*	100
Northeast	7.6 (5.9, 9.8)	3.6 (2.6, 4.8)	2.2 (1.4, 3.4)	14.7 (12.3, 17.4)	2.8 (2.1, 3 8)	2.8 (1.8, 4.3)	41.7 (37.8, 45.8)	22.3 (19.3, 25.6)	2.3 (1.0, 5.6)	0.0 (0.0, 0.1)*	100
South	7.8 (6.2, 9.7)	2.6 (2.0, 3.5)	2.5 (1.8, 3.5)	16.0 (13.5, 18.9)	6.3 (4.8, 8.2)	3.5 (2.6, 4.9)	24.6 (22.2, 27.1)	34.2 (31.0, 37.7)	2.0 (1.3, 3.2)	0.5 (0.1, 1.6)*	100
Socioeconomic status											
Lowest	5.2 (3.9, 6.9)	2.5 (1.8, 3.5)	2.7 (1.9, 3.8)	15.6 (13.4, 18.2)	4.3 (3.3, 5.6)	3.6 (2.3, 5.7)	38.0 (34.1, 42.1)	26.5 (23.2, 30.0)	1.6 (0.9, 2.7)	0.0 (0.0, 0.1)*	100
Low	7.1 (5.5, 9.1)	3.4 (2.4, 4.8)	2.2 (1.6, 2.9)	16.8 (14.5, 19.4)	4.3 (3.3, 5.6)	3.6 (2.7, 4.9)	34.3 (31.1, 37.6)	26.2 (23.5, 29.0)	2.1 (0.9, 4.9)	0.0 (0.0, 0.2)*	100
Middle	6.7 (5.5, 8.1)	3.1 (2.3, 4.2)	2.9 (2.1, 4.0)	15.0 (13.0, 17.3)	4.1 (3.2, 5.3)	2.9 (2.1, 3.9)	34.2 (31.0, 37.6)	29.6 (26.8, 32.7)	1.3 (0.8, 2.1)	0.2 (0.0, 0.8)*	100
High	8.7 (7.0, 10.7)	1.7 (1.2, 2.5)	3.1 (1.8, 5.3)	16.1 (13.9, 18.5)	2.7 (1.9, 3.7)	2.9 (2.1, 4.0)	31.1 (28.4, 34.0)	32.3 (29.0, 35.7)	1.2 (0.8, 1.9)	0.2 (0.1, 0.6)*	100
Highest	8.9 (7.1, 11.1)	2.2 (1.6, 3.2)	3.2 (2.4, 4.1)	16.9 (14.9, 19.2)	2.7 (2.0, 3.6)	2.8 (2.1, 3.9)	32.1 (29.5, 34.7)	28.9 (26.4, 31.4)	2.1 (1.3, 3.4)	0.2 (0.1, 0.5)*	100

1 PHWs are in Appendix E.
2 Includes former and never smokers.
* Indicates that estimate is based on sample size of less than 25.
Remark: No. of PHWs 1=Cigarette smoke harms people nearby, 2=Smoking causes your breath to smell, 3=Smoking caused emphysema, 4=Cigarette smoke causes lung cancer,
5= Cigarette smoke causes fatal heart failure, 6= Cigarette smoke leads your life to death, 7= Smoking causes oral cancer, 8=Smoking causes laryngeal cancer, 9=Cigarette smoke caused haemorrhagic stroke

9.5 Beliefs on the harmful effects of manufactured cigarettes

Table 9.5 provides information about the beliefs regarding the harmful effects of manufactured cigarettes among three groups of people: adults aged 15 years and above, current smokers, and non-smokers. Among adults aged 15 years and above, 39.7% believe that manufactured cigarettes are more harmful than hand-rolled cigarettes. More female adults believe that "manufactured cigarettes are more harmful than hand-rolled cigarettes" compared to male adults (42.2% against 37.1%). Classified by age groups, adults aged 60 years have the highest rate of belief that "manufactured cigarettes are more harmful than hand-rolled cigarettes" (50.7%), while the lowest degree of such a belief is found in adults aged 25–44 years.

Adults living in rural areas (42.7%) have a higher prevalence of the belief that "manufactured cigarettes are more harmful than hand-rolled cigarettes" than those living in urban areas (33.0%). Compared according to education levels, the available data reveals that adults with a higher level of education (university-level) reported lesser proportions (29.4%) of belief that "manufactured cigarettes are more harmful than hand-rolled cigarettes" compared to adults with lower education (less than primary (48.0%) and primary (39.6%)) levels.

Classified by regions, adults living in the Southern region have reported a higher rate (62.7%) of belief that "manufactured cigarettes are more harmful than hand-rolled cigarettes". The lowest figures for this belief came from Bangkok metropolis (29.5%). Viewed according to socioeconomic status, the results indicated that persons with higher SES levels have less prevalence of the belief that "manufactured cigarettes are more harmful than hand-rolled cigarettes". The lowest SES category has the highest rate of belief that "manufactured cigarettes are more harmful than hand-rolled cigarettes" (45.2%), and the lowest prevalence of this belief (29.7%) is found among those belonging to the highest SES level of the population.

Among current smokers aged 15 years and above, the findings showed results similar in comparison with overall adults, with 41.2% believing that "manufactured cigarettes are more harmful than hand-rolled cigarettes". More female smokers tend to believe that "manufactured cigarettes are more harmful than hand-rolled cigarettes" than male smokers (60.5% against 39.9%). Classified by age groups, smokers aged 60 years and above have the highest prevalence of the belief that "manufactured cigarettes are more harmful than hand-rolled cigarettes" (61.2%) while the lowest prevalence (28.7%) of this belief is found among smokers of the age-group of 15–24 years.

Smokers living in rural areas have a higher prevalence of the belief that "manufactured cigarettes are more harmful than hand-rolled cigarettes" than those living in urban areas (45.3% in rural and 30.7% in urban). Classified by education levels, smokers having less than primary education have the highest prevalence of the belief that "manufactured cigarettes are more harmful than hand-rolled cigarettes" (56.9%) and the lowest prevalence of this belief is found among smokers with an education of university level (20.8%).

Categorized by region, smokers living in the Southern region had the highest prevalence of the belief that "manufactured cigarettes are more harmful than hand-rolled cigarettes" (62.5%) and the lowest figures for the same (25.1%) emerged from Bangkok metropolis. By socioeconomic status, smokers with the lowest SES had the highest prevalence of the belief that "manufactured cigarettes are more harmful than hand-rolled cigarettes" (50.0%) and the lowest prevalence (32.2%) was among people from the highest SES level.

Among non-smokers aged 15 years and above, a similar pattern was observed with respect to the prevalence of this belief and this is consistent with that among overall adults and current smokers—39.2% believed that "manufactured cigarettes are more harmful than hand-rolled cigarettes". Among non-smokers, females aged 60 years and above, living in rural areas, having less than primary education level, living in the Southern region, and belonging to the lowest SES had a high proportion of prevalence of the belief that "manufactured cigarettes are more harmful than hand-rolled cigarettes".

Table 9.5: Percentage of adults ≥15 years of age who believe manufactured cigarettes are more harmful than hand-rolled cigarettes, by smoking status and selected demographic characteristics – GATS Thailand, 2009.

Characteristic	Manufactured cigarettes more harmful than hand–rolled cigarettes		
	Adults ≥15 years old	Current smokers	Non-smokers
		Percentage (95% CI)	
Overall	39.7 (38.0, 41.4)	41.2 (38.8, 43.7)	39.2 (37.4, 41.1)
Gender			
Male	37.1 (35.3, 39.0)	39.9 (37.5, 42.4)	34.7 (32.4, 37.1)
Female	42.2 (40.0, 44.4)	60.5 (52.7, 67.8)	41.6 (39.5, 43.8)
Age (years)			
15-24	40.5 (37.0, 44.0)	28.7 (22.9, 35.2)	43.4 (39.3, 47.5)
25-44	35.7 (33.7, 37.7)	36.3 (33.2, 39.5)	35.5 (33.3, 37.8)
45-59	39.4 (37.3, 41.5)	48.8 (45.4, 52.2)	36.3 (34.0, 38.7)
60+	50.7 (48.2, 53.2)	61.2 (56.2, 66.0)	47.8 (45.1, 50.6)
Residence			
Urban	33.0 (31.6, 34.3)	30.7 (28.4, 33.1)	33.6 (32.1, 35.1)
Rural	42.7 (40.3, 45.1)	45.3 (42.1, 48.6)	41.8 (39.2, 44.5)
Education level			
Less than primary	48.0 (45.7, 50.2)	56.9 (53.4, 60.3)	45.0 (42.6, 47.4)
Primary	39.6 (36.6, 42.7)	42.5 (37.8, 47.3)	38.4 (34.8, 42.1)
Secondary	35.5 (33.2, 37.9)	28.5 (25.0, 32.4)	37.6 (34.8, 40.5)
University	29.4 (26.9, 31.9)	20.8 (15.9, 26.7)	30.8 (28.1, 33.7)
Region			
Bangkok	29.5 (27.5, 31.6)	25.1 (21.6, 29.0)	30.6 (28.2, 33.1)
Central	41.0 (37.8, 44.3)	42.8 (38.3, 47.4)	40.5 (37.1, 43.9)
North	43.6 (39.2, 48.1)	48.4 (42.1, 54.8)	42.1 (37.6, 46.8)
Northeast	30.5 (27.3, 33.9)	29.9 (25.8, 34.4)	30.7 (26.8, 34.8)
South	62.7 (59.5, 65.8)	62.5 (57.6, 67.1)	62.8 (59.5, 66.0)
Socioeconomic status			
Lowest	45.2 (41.9, 48.6)	50.0 (43.5, 56.5)	44.2 (40.7, 47.7)
Low	41.7 (38.7, 44.7)	46.6 (41.8, 51.4)	40.1 (36.7, 43.7)
Middle	41.3 (38.9, 43.8)	38.5 (34.3, 43.0)	42.5 (39.6, 45.4)
High	36.1 (33.8, 38.5)	36.3 (32.1, 40.7)	36.0 (33.4, 38.8)
Highest	29.7 (27.3, 32.3)	32.2 (27.7, 37.1)	29.1 (26.6, 31.7)

In short, most Thai adults believe that smoking cigarettes and exposure to tobacco smoke causes serious illnesses. More people attribute smoking to be the cause of heart and lung diseases than of impotence, premature birth and low birth weight. Adults aged 60 years and above, living in rural areas, with an education level of less than primary, and belonging to the lowest SES level have the least knowledge of the specific health effects of tobacco use. Pictorial warnings on cigarette packets were found to be more effective to communicate the harmful effects of tobacco on health than pictorial warnings on packets of shredded tobacco used for hand-rolled cigarettes.

10

Conclusion and Recommendations

10. Conclusion and Recommendations

10.1 Conclusion

The Global Adult Tobacco Survey (GATS) is a globally standard tool for systematically monitoring adult tobacco use and for tracking key tobacco control indicators which can be utilized by policy-makers to strengthen tobacco control in Thailand. In addition, it allows international comparability and the opportunity to learn valuable lessons from tobacco control in Thailand.

GATS uses standard protocol that ensures international comparability. It features the highest level of quality control and standardization. Thailand has taken several measures on quality control during the implementation process to produce most reliable results. The findings of this survey on the prevalence of tobacco smoking, both current and on a daily basis, among the study population and also among males and females are quite consistent with the findings of the Health Welfare Survey (HWS) which was conducted around the same time by the National Statistical Office (NSO).

However, GATS provides far more detailed information related to the provisions of the WHO Framework Convention that will be very useful for monitoring and planning the national tobacco control programme.

Based on the experiences of this survey it can be concluded that reliable survey results depend on the following;

1. Good sampling design and use of the correct available data to estimate sample size: For this survey, the non-response rates were found to be much higher than anticipated and sample size had to be recalculated and additional data collected to obtain the minimum required responses.
2. The correct selection of and effective training for the survey team: The training should be conducted in such a way that it allows maximum interaction and sufficient hands-on learning opportunity. This survey has the advantage of having deployed experienced surveyors and field supervisors and having used hand-held PCs.
3. Good supervisory management and quality control: There should be an established mechanism that can detect errors or mistakes early and take immediate corrective action.
4. Good logistical support to the survey team, for example, timely replacement of batteries or non-functional hand-held PCs in the field.
5. Good system for data transfer from the field to the project manager.

The survey team gains considerable knowledge, particularly on survey methodology, interview techniques, data weighting, data analysis and report-writing. These are found very useful for improving the quality and effectiveness of future national surveys and these will ensure the sustainability of tobacco surveillance activities.

10.2 Recommendations

The results obtained from GATS provided updated or recent information on the use of both smoked and smokeless tobacco and the degree of exposure to second-hand smoke (SHS) by demographic patterns and the same were presented to key persons and stakeholders. Some policy recommendations have emerged in accordance with WHO Framework Convention provisions and the MPOWER guidelines. These recommendations include the followings:

M: Monitor

Key strategies should be implemented for effective monitoring of tobacco use, including:

a) Periodic implementation of surveys under the global tobacco surveillance system (GTSS).
b) Reorganization of the national tobacco control unit with defined roles and responsibilities to monitor activities within the government set-up to sustain the tobacco surveillance system.
c) Increase collaboration among tobacco control experts from various institutes and also among tobacco control stakeholders to strengthen the tobacco surveillance system.
d) Establish communication with national and international agencies for technical and financial support to administer surveys regularly under GTSS.
e) Strengthen the channel of coordination between local networks and nationwide tobacco control surveillance.
f) Apply information technology to establish systematically the tobacco surveillance system.
g) Develop a monitoring plan to respond to indicators and Framework Convention guidelines.

P: Protect

The community as a whole should be protected from tobacco smoke by:

a) Advocacy of the 100% smoke-free laws to include more public places to protect the public from exposure to tobacco smoke pollution.
b) Enforce smoke-free laws actively and effectively.
c) The conduct of public communication campaigns through different media to increase social awareness on the harmful effects of tobacco use and the exposure to tobacco smoke.
d) Increasing public awareness levels on the right of non-smokers to be free from exposure to second-hand smoke, especially in public places that are totally or partially smoke-free areas by the Non-Smoker's Health Protection Act, 1992.
e) Train youth to advocate for enforcing smoke-free law.
f) Formulate both formal and informal education curricula to enhance knowledge and develop the right attitudes and perceptions about the harms caused by tobacco use and exposure to tobacco smoke.

O: Offer help

Users of either smoking or smokeless tobacco products should be offered help to quit by:

a) Expansion and sustained tobacco cessation services with appropriate cessation methods.
b) Widespread publicity campaigns to increase quit rates, especially through the quit-on-your-own mode and through counseling or psycho-behavioural therapy.
c) Building capacity for health-care providers on tobacco cessation services: ask, advice, assess, assist, arrange and use at least 2A (ask and advice) in routine activities.
d) Advocate with the National Security Office to include new drugs in the national drugs lists to be made available adequately to help tobacco users quit tobacco.
e) Increase capacity of quit-lines to serve the maximum number of people who desire to quit.
f) Establish health promotion activities, including tobacco cessation, in private and public health-care facilities.
g) Integrate tobacco cessation services in primary health care (PHC) settings.
h) Provide formal training to health professional students.
i) Establish community cessation services.

W: Warn

Effective and optimum warnings about the dangers of tobacco use should be distributed equally to all across geographical and socioeconomic barriers. This will be achieved through the following strategies:

a) Formulate effective pictorial health warnings to be used with shredded tobacco products used for hand-rolled cigarettes and chewing tobacco.
b) Disseminate information on health concerns and the economic impact of smoking and the harmful effects of exposure to second-hand smoke through media campaigns.
c) Formulate policies to ban smuggling/import of tobacco products without health warnings.

E: Enforce

Bans on tobacco advertising, promotion and sponsorship should be enforced through:

a) Raising social awareness on tobacco's harms and exposing the motives of tobacco industries in their tobacco promotion activities.
b) Coordinate with government and nongovernmental organizations for tobacco control at every level, and especially in remote areas, for the systematic monitoring of advertising by the tobacco industry.
c) Enforce laws and regulations rigorously to eliminate advertising by the tobacco industry.
d) Increase capacity of call centres dealing with complaints on violation of tobacco control law and provide an effective examination and investigation system.

R: Raise taxes on tobacco

Increasing the excise tax on tobacco products has been viewed as one of the most effective ways to discourage youth from taking to tobacco and to reduce tobacco use and thereby save lives. Based on the findings of GATS Thailand, the following measures are recommended:

a) Advocacy for raising tax on shredded tobacco products used for hand-rolled cigarettes and chewing tobacco.
b) Strengthening the community monitoring of local grocery stores where cigarettes are sold to ensure that persons less than 18 years of age cannot have access to the same.
c) Increasing the level of public concern about illicit cigarettes which often do not carry the mandatory pictorial health warning.
d) Enhancing the level of political commitment to regularly revise and increase taxes on tobacco, including on shredded tobacco and imported cigarettes.

Thailand is committed to implement the WHO Framework Convention and the MPOWER policy package. Monitoring tobacco use through periodic surveys is a critical component of tobacco control, as envisaged in the Framework Convention and MPOWER policy package, and needs to be integrated into the National Plan of Action.

Reference

1. Tobacco control research and knowledge management center. *Thailand's tobacco use situation, 1991-2007*. Bangkok: Charoendee Munkong Printing, 2008.

2. National Statistical Office. *Survey of smoking behavior in Thai population 2007*. Bangkok: National Statistic Office, 2007.

3. Wanchai W. *Determining the cost of treatment for smoking-related heart and lung disease*. Bangkok: Office for Tobacco Consumption Control, 1991.

4. Theera L. *Cigarettes smoking-lung cancer: life and economic loss*. Bangkok: Faculty of Medicine, Siriraj Hospital; 1994.

5. Jayanton P. *Expenditure and quality of life lost due to disease caused by smoking: research submitted to the Health System Research Institute*. Bangkok: Health System Research Institute, 2001.

6. Sarntisart I. *An economic analysis of tobacco control in Thailand*. HNP Discussion Paper: Economics of Tobacco Control Paper No.15. Washington D.C: World Bank, October 2003. http://www1.worldbank.org/tobacco/pdf/Sarntisart-An%20Economic_Thailand_new.pdf – accessed 27 October 2009.

7. Leartsakulpanitch J, Nganthavee W, Salole E. The economic burden of smoking – related disease in Thailand: a prevalence – based analysis. *Journal of the Medical Association of Thailand*. 2007 Sep; 90(9): 1925-9.

8. Kunaluck K. *Economic loss assessment of lung cancer caused by smoking: research report submitted to the Faculty of Economics*. Bangkok: Thammasat University, 1996.

9. Ministry of Public Health Thailand, Bureau of Policy and Strategy, Health Information Development. *Number of deaths and death rates per 100 000 population by leading causing of death 2003 – 2007 [table]*. Nonthaburi. http://bps.ops.moph.go.th/webenglish/Death.html - accessed 27 October 2009.

10. Sirikunya L. *Cigarette smoking and laryngeal cancer: research report submitted to the Office for Tobacco Consumption Control*. Bangkok, 1999.

11. Jategaonkar N. *Civil society monitoring of the framework conventional on tobacco control: 2007 status report of the framework convention alliance*. Geneva: Framework Convention Alliance, 2007.

12. Supawongse C. *Two decades of tobacco - consumption control in Thailand: successes and challenges*. Bangkok: USA Printing, 2007.

13. Group of Tobacco and Alcohol Consumption Control. *Tobacco products control act B.E. 2535 (1992) (Certified on 29th day of March B.E. 2535) and non-smoker's health protection act B.E. 2535 (1992) (Certified on 30th day of March B.E. 2535).* Nonthaburi : Department of Disease Control, Ministry of Public Health, 2007.

14. Termsirikulchai L, Benjakul S, Kengganpanich M, Theskayan N, Nakju S. *Thailand tobacco control country profile.* Bangkok: World Health Organization, Country Office for Thailand, 2008.

15. Global Tobacco Surveillance System (GTSS), *Global Adult Tobacco Survey (GATS): Core Questionnaire with Optional Questions.* 2008.

16. Office of the National Economic and Social Development Board (NESDB). *Population Projection for Thailand 2000 – 2030.* http://www.nesdb.go.th - accessed 2 November 2009.

17. Thananithisakdi C, Nimpitakpong P, Bunditanukul K. *Current data of cessation clinics in Thailand*: the proceeding of the 5th national conference on Tobacco or Health, May 4-6 2005. Bangkok: Charoendee-munkong Printing, 2005.

18. Wongwiwatananukij S. Pharmacotherapy in Smoking Cessation. In: Wattanasirichaikul S, ed. *Tobacco control for health professional.* Bangkok, 2007. pp 465 - 90.

19. Kengganpanich M, Termsirikulchai L, Nakju S. Global Health Professional survey (GHPS): Thailand, 2006. In: Wattanasirichaikul S, ed. *Tobacco control consumption for health professional.* Bangkok, 2007. pp 307 – 40.

20. Visarutvong C. *Cigarettes excise tax for cigarettes smoking Control.* Bangkok: Charoendee Mungkong Printing, 2007.

21. Sirirassamee B. *Report of tobacco control policy evaluation in Thailand: national smoker survey round 2 (2006).* Bangkok: Institute for Population and Social Research, Mahidol University, 2007.

22. Macroeconomic Strategy and Planning Office. *Economic outlook: Thai economic performance in Q2 and outlook for 2009.* Office of the National Economic and Social Development Board (NESDB). http://www.nesdb.go.th/Portals/0/eco_datas/economic/eco_state/2_52/Press%20Thai%20Q2-2009.pdf - accessed 27 October 2009.

23. Ministry of Public Health. *Tobacco Products Control Act B.E.2535 (A.D. 1992).* Bangkok. http://www.searo.who.int/LinkFiles/Legislation_and_Policy_Thai_legislation.pdf – accessed 27 October 2009.

24. Ministry of Public Health. Notification of the Ministry of Public Health (No. 11) B.E.2549 (A.D. 2006). Re: criteria, procedures and conditions for displaying pictures and statements relating to warning on harm; date, month and year of manufacture; manufacturing source and sale only in the kingdom of Thailand on labels of cigarettes and cigars. Issued under the tobacco products control act. B.E. 2535. Bangkok: Ministry of Public Health, 29th September 2006. http://thaiantitobacco.com/eng/files/tc/announce_moph11_eng.pdf-accessed 27 October 2009.

25. Ministry of Public Health. Notification of the Ministry of Public Health (No. 14) B.E.2550 (A.D. 2007). Re: criteria, procedures and conditions for displaying pictorial labels and statements of warning on harm of tobacco. Issued under the tobacco products control action B.E. 2535 (A.D. 1992). Bangkok: Ministry of Public Health, 30th May 2007. http://thaiantitobacco.com/eng/files/tc/announce_moph_eng_tobacco.pdf - 1 November 2009.

26. U.S. Department of Health and Human Services. *The Health consequences of smoking: a report of the surgeon general.* Centers for Disease Control and Prevention, National Center for Chronic Disease Prevention and Health Promotion, Office on Smoking and Health, 2004. http://www.cdc.gov/tobacco/data_statistics/fact_sheets/health_effects/effects_cig_smoking - accessed 09 October 2009.

27. ASH Thailand. *Warning! smoking can kill you [web site in Thai]. http://www.ashthailand.or.th/th/content_image/informationcenter/288.pdf* - accessed 2 November 2009.

28. SAS/STAT 9.1 User's Guide (2004). SAS Institute Inc, Gary NC, USA.

29. SPSS Statistics 17.0 Command Syntax Reference (2008). SPSS Inc, Chicago IL. USA.

Appendix

Appendix A: Questionnaire

GLOBAL ADULT TOBACCO SURVEY (GATS)

Optional Questionnaire of Thailand
Specific Questionnaire of Thailand

SECTION A. BACKGROUND CHARACTERISTICS

AA5_1. (Ask both employee and unemployee) How much do you get average income monthly?

(a) Total In-cash income .... ☐☐☐☐☐☐ THB/month

If "has not", record "0"

- (a1) Wages/ Salaries .... ☐☐☐☐☐☐ THB/month
- (a2) OT .... ☐☐☐☐☐☐ THB/month
- (a3) Income from pensions .... ☐☐☐☐☐☐ THB/month
- (a4) Net profit from business/ farming .... ☐☐☐☐☐☐ THB/month
- (a5) Income from other people outside household .... ☐☐☐☐☐☐ THB/month
- (a6) Income from government or other organization for elderly and disability .... ☐☐☐☐☐☐ THB/month
- (a7) Income from rent of accommodation, land or other Properties .... ☐☐☐☐☐☐ THB/month
- (a8) Others (e.g. lottery winnings, commission, gambling, or saving interests etc) .... ☐☐☐☐☐☐ THB/month

(b) Total In-kind income .... ☐☐☐☐☐☐ THB/month

If "has not", record "0"

- (b1) Rental estimated of free-occupied house (include own house) .... ☐☐☐☐☐☐ THB/month
- (b2) Unpaid of goods and services .... ☐☐☐☐☐☐ THB/month
- (b3) Unpaid of food and beverages .... ☐☐☐☐☐☐ THB/month

A11. What is your marital status? Would you say

- Single .... ☐ 1
- Married .... ☐ 2
- Separated .... ☐ 3
- Divorced .... ☐ 4
- Widowed .... ☐ 5

SECTION B. TOBACCO SMOKING

BB19. What was the most important factor which pushed you quit smoking successfully?
(Please read item by item and select only one choice)

Cigarette price... ☐ 1
Health Problem .... ☐ 2
Family asked for quitting............................. ☐ 3
Campaign for not smoking .... ☐ 4
Others .... ☐ 5

SECTION C. SMOKELESS TOBACCO

NONE

SECTION D1. CESSATION – TOBACCO SMOKING

NONE

SECTION D2. CESSATION – SMOKELESS TOBACCO

NONE

SECTION E. SECONDHAND SMOKE

EE3_1. [IF B1=1 OR 2, ADMINISTER. ELSE, SKIP TO E4]

Do you think that not being allowed to smoke in your home would make quitting easier?

YES .... ☐ 1
NO .... ☐ 2
DON'T KNOW .... ☐ 7

E18. Based on what you know or believe, does breathing smoke from other people's cigarettes cause any of the following?

READ EACH ITEM:	YES	NO	DON'T KNOW
a. Heart disease in adults?	☐ 1	☐ 2	☐ 7
b. Lung illness in children?	☐ 1	☐ 2	☐ 7
c. Lung cancer in adults?	☐ 1	☐ 2	☐ 7
d. Emphysema?	☐ 1	☐ 2	☐ 7
e. Low birth weight (< 2.5 kilograms)?	☐ 1	☐ 2	☐ 7
f. Premature birth (28 - 34 weeks)?	☐ 1	☐ 2	☐ 7

E19. During the past 30 days, did you visit any schools?

YES .... ☐ 1
NO .... ☐ 2 → SKIP TO E21
DON'T KNOW .... ☐ 7 → SKIP TO E21

E20. Did anyone smoke inside of any schools that you visited in the past 30 days?

YES .... ☐ 1
NO .... ☐ 2
DON'T KNOW .... ☐ 7

E21. During the past 30 days, did you visit any universities?

YES .... ☐ 1
NO .... ☐ 2 → SKIP TO E25
DON'T KNOW .... ☐ 7 → SKIP TO E25

E22. Did anyone smoke inside of any universities that you visited in the past 30 days?

YES .... ☐ 1
NO .... ☐ 2
DON'T KNOW .... ☐ 7

E25. During the past 30 days, did you visit any bars or night clubs?

YES.............................. ☐ 1
NO .... ☐ 2 → SKIP TO EE26_1
DON'T KNOW .... ☐ 7 → SKIP TO EE26_1

E26. Did anyone smoke inside of any bars or night clubs that you visited in the past 30 days?

YES.............................. ☐ 1
NO .... ☐ 2
DON'T KNOW .... ☐ 7

EE26_1. During the past 30 days, did you visit any outside market?

YES.............................. ☐ 1
NO .... ☐ 2 → SKIP TO E29b
DON'T KNOW .... ☐ 7 → SKIP TO E29b

EE26_2. Did anyone smoke in any outside market you visited in the past 30 days?

YES.............................. ☐ 1
NO .... ☐ 2
DON'T KNOW .... ☐ 7

E29b. Do you support the law that prohibits smoking inside of private workplaces which do not have air-conditioning?

YES.......................... ☐ 1
NO .... ☐ 2
DON'T KNOW .... ☐ 7

E29g. Do you support the law that prohibits smoking absolutely (100%) in universities?

YES.......................... ☐ 1
NO .... ☐ 2
DON'T KNOW .... ☐ 7

E29h. Do you support the law that prohibits smoking absolutely (100%) in of religious places?

YES.......................... ☐ 1
NO .... ☐ 2
DON'T KNOW .... ☐ 7

SECTION F. ECONOMICS – MANUFACTURED CIGARETTES

F5. Were these cigarettes filtered or non-filtered?

FILTERED................................☐ 1
NON-FILTERED.....................☐ 2
DON'T KNOW ....☐ 7

F6. Were these cigarettes labeled as light, mild, or low tar?

LIGHT....................................☐ 1
MILD.....................................☐ 2
LOW TAR ....☐ 3
NONE OF THE ABOVE..........☐ 4
DON'T KNOW ....☐ 7

FF7. The last time you purchased cigarettes for yourself, did the cigarette package have a pictorial health warning?

YES ....☐ 1
NO ....☐ 2
DON'T KNOW ....☐ 7

FF8. Which of the following statements comes closest to your opinion on cigarette prices:

Cigarettes are too expensive and I cannot afford to buy as many as I would like..............☐ 1
Cigarettes are expensive, but I can still buy as many as I like...☐ 2
Cigarettes are a reasonable price ....☐ 3
Cigarettes are very cheap...☐ 4
Cigarettes are so cheap I smoke more than I should ....☐ 5

SECTION G. MEDIA

STRUCTURE #1 – ASKING ABOUT ONLY ONE PRODUCT (E.G., CIGARETTES)

GG3_1 [ADMINISTER IF B1 = 1 OR 2. ELSE GO TO G4]

Did the health warnings make you concerned or think about the dangers of cigarettes on health?

YES .... ☐ 1
NO .... ☐ 2
DON'T KNOW .... ☐ 7

GG3_2 Do the health warnings on cigarette packages make you more likely to try to quit smoking? Would you say yes a lot, yes a little, or not at all?

YES A LOT .... ☐ 1
YES A LITTLE.................................... ☐ 2
NOT AT ALL...................................... ☐ 3

GG3_3 In your opinion, should the cigarette packet have a quit line number, that is a number people can call to get advice on quitting smoking?

YES .... ☐ 1
NO .... ☐ 2
DON'T KNOW .... ☐ 7

GG5. In the last 30 days, have you noticed any music, theatre, art, or fashion events that are associated with cigarette brands or cigarette companies?

YES......................... ☐ 1
NO .... ☐ 2
DON'T KNOW .... ☐ 7

GG5_1. In the last 30 days, did you see a live program of sport racing from abroad which had brands or symbol cigarette companies?

YES......................... ☐ 1
NO .... ☐ 2
DON'T KNOW .... ☐ 7

SECTION H. KNOWLEDGE, ATTITUDES & PERCEPTIONS

H2_3. Do you believe cigarettes are addictive?

- YES.................................... ☐ 1
- NO .... ☐ 2
- DON'T KNOW .... ☐ 7

HH4. According to your knowledge or beliefs, does tobacco product which specifies low nicotine or mild/light, less harmful, more harmful or about the same as general tobacco products?

- LESS HARMFUL................. ☐ 1
- MORE HARMFUL............. ☐ 2
- ABOUT THE SAME .... ☐ 3
- DON'T KNOW .... ☐ 7

SECTION I. PICTORIAL

TAKE OUT THE FOLLOWING PICTURES AND SHOW THEM TO THE RESPONDENT:

[NOTE: THE INTERVIEWERS WILL HAVE HARD COPIES OF THESE PICTURES TO SHOW TO THE RESPONDENTS]

Picture1	Picture2	Picture3	Picture 4	Picture5	Picture6
Cigarette Smoke Harms People Nearby	Smoking Causes Your Breath to Smell	Smoking Causes Fatal Emphysema	Cigarette Smoke Causes Lung Cancer	Cigarette Smoke Causes Fatal Heart Failure	Cigarette Smoke Leads Your Life to Death

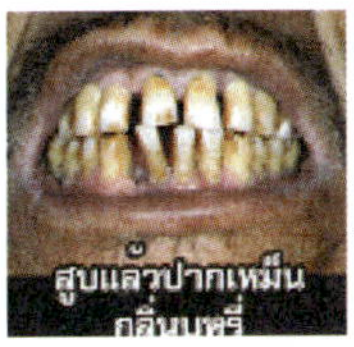

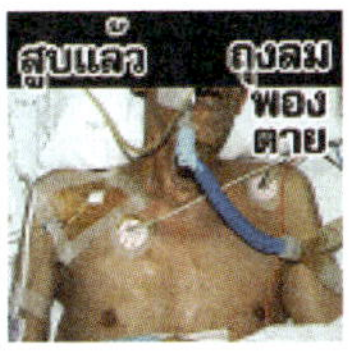

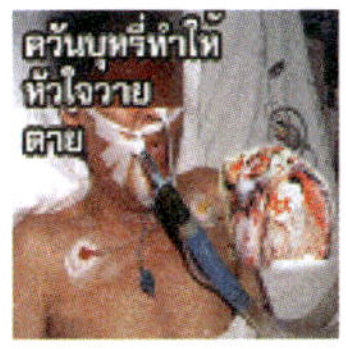

Picture 7	Picture 8	Picture 9
Smoking Causes Oral Cancer	Smoking Causes Laryngeal Cancer	Cigarette Smoke Causes Hemorrhagic Stroke

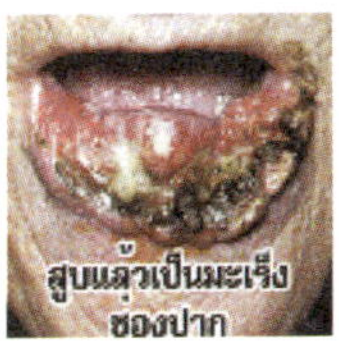

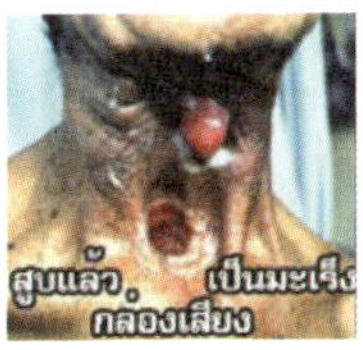

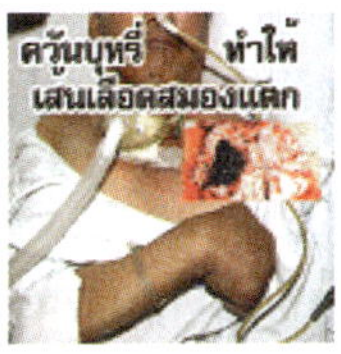

I1.[IF (B1 = 1 OR 2) AND (B6a> 0 OR B10a>0) AND (B6e >0 OR B10e >0] , ADMINISTER. ELSE, SKIP TO I2.]

Of these pictorial health warnings, which one makes you want to quit smoking the most?

PICTURE 1 CIGARETTE SMOKE HARMS PEOPLE NEARBY .... ☐ 1
PICTURE 2 SMOKING CAUSES YOUR BREATH TO SMELL .... ☐ 2
PICTURE 3 SMOKING CAUSES FATAL EMPHYSEMA .... ☐ 3
PICTURE 4 CIGARETTE SMOKE CAUSES LUNG CANCER .... ☐ 4
PICTURE 5 CIGARETTE SMOKE CAUSES FATAL HEART FAILURE .... ☐ 5
PICTURE 6 CIGARETTE SMOKE LEADS YOUR LIFE TO DEATH .... ☐ 6
PICTURE 7 SMOKING CAUSES ORAL CANCER .... ☐ 7
PICTURE 8 SMOKING CAUSES LARYNGEAL CANCER .... ☐ 8
PICTURE 9 CIGARETTE SMOKE CAUSES HEMORRHAGIC STROKE .... ☐ 9

NONE OF THEM .... ☐ 10
DON'T KNOW .... ☐ 77

I2. [IF B3 = 3 and C3 = 3, ADMINISTER. ELSE, SKIP TO I3.]

Of these pictorial health warnings, which one makes you not want to smoke cigarettes the most?

PICTURE 1 CIGARETTE SMOKE HARMS PEOPLE NEARBY .... ☐ 1
PICTURE 2 SMOKING CAUSES YOUR BREATH TO SMELL.................... ☐ 2
PICTURE 3 SMOKING CAUSES FATAL EMPHYSEMA .... ☐ 3
PICTURE 4 CIGARETTE SMOKE CAUSES LUNG CANCER.................... ☐ 4
PICTURE 5 CIGARETTE SMOKE CAUSES FATAL HEART FAILURE.................... ☐ 5
PICTURE 6 CIGARETTE SMOKE LEADS YOUR LIFE TO DEATH .... ☐ 6
PICTURE 7 SMOKING CAUSES ORAL CANCER.................... ☐ 7
PICTURE 8 SMOKING CAUSES LARYNGEAL CANCER.................... ☐ 8
PICTURE 9 CIGARETTE SMOKE CAUSES HEMORRHAGIC STROKE .... ☐ 9

NONE OF THEM.................... ☐ 10
DON'T KNOW .... ☐ 77

I3. [IF (B1 = 1 OR 2) AND (B6 ≠ (a)/(e) OR B10 ≠ (a)/(e)), OR (C1 = 1 OR 2), THEN ADMINISTER. ELSE, SKIP TO I7]

In the past 30 days, did you notice any pictorial health warnings on raw tobacco packs?

YES..................... ☐ 1
NO .... ☐ 2 → SKIP TO I7
DID NOT SEE ANY RAW TOBACCO PACKS .... ☐ 3 → SKIP TO I7

I4 In the past 30 days, have the pictorial warning on the raw tobacco pack make you concern or think about the danger of raw tobacco on health?

YES .... ☐ 1
NO .... ☐ 2
DON'T KNOW ..... ☐ 7

I5. In the past 30 days, have the pictorial health warnings on raw tobacco packs led you to think about quitting?

YES..................... ☐ 1
NO .... ☐ 2
DON'T KNOW ..... ☐ 7

I6. Do the pictorial warning on raw tobacco packages effect on your try to quit using raw tobacco?

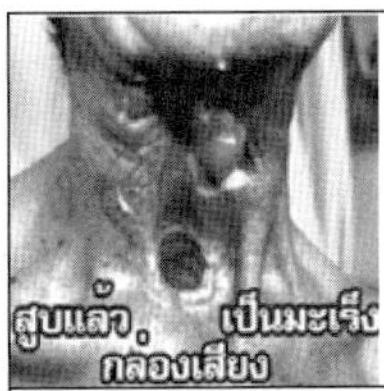	I6_a Picture 1 Smoking causes laryngeal cancer	YES A LOT .... ☐ 1 YES A LITTLE .... ☐ 2 NOT AT ALL .... ☐ 3
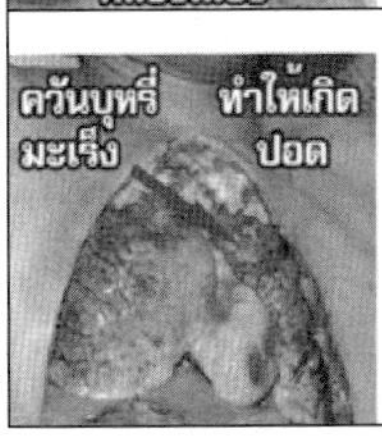	I6_b Picture 2 cigarette smoke causes lung cancer	YES A LOT .... ☐ 1 YES A LITTLE .... ☐ 2 NOT AT ALL .... ☐ 3

I7. As far as you know, which of the following do you think is true: manufactured cigarettes are more harmful than hand-rolled tobacco, hand-rolled tobacco is more harmful than manufactured cigarettes, or they are equally harmful?

MANUFACTURED MORE HARMFUL .... ☐ 1
HAND-ROLLED MORE HARMFUL.......... ☐ 2
EQUALLY HARMFUL .... ☐ 3
DON'T KNOW .... ☐ 7

Appendix B: Sample Design

B.1 Sample Design

The Global Adults Tobacco Survey in Thailand (GATS-Thailand) used a three-stage stratified cluster sampling design. The design is described in this section.

The target population was stratified into 4 regions (North, Northeast, Central, and South) and Bangkok metropolis. Each of the 4 regions was further stratified into urban and rural area, making 9 strata in total (Bangkok metropolis has only urban area).

Sample size of 2,000 individuals was needed to meet the desired precision for a specific estimate of each interested stratum of region by urban/rural and gender. For each of 5 regions, 2,000 males and 2,000 females were sampled. These numbers were equally allocated in both rural and urban areas, except for Bangkok metropolis that all areas were considered as urban (Table B1).

Table B1 Sample size allocation before non-response rate is taken into consideration

Region	Urban		Rural		Total
	Male	Female	Male	Female	
Bangkok	2,000	2,000	-	-	4,000
Central	1,000	1,000	1,000	1,000	4,000
North	1,000	1,000	1,000	1,000	4,000
Northeast	1,000	1,000	1,000	1,000	4,000
South	1,000	1,000	1,000	1,000	4,000
Total	**6,000**	**6,000**	**4,000**	**4,000**	**20,000**

Based on previous surveys conducted by NSO, the non-response rate was assumed to be 5% for urban area and 2.5% for rural area. This would result in final sample size of 20,960 persons (Table B2) after taking the non-response rates into account.

Table B2 Number of sample size (eligible persons) by region and urban/rural after non-response rate is taken into consideration

Region	Number of sample size		
	Total	Urban	Rural
Bangkok	4,224	4,224	-
Central	4,184	2,112	2,072
North	4,184	2,112	2,072
Northeast	4,184	2,112	2,072
South	4,184	2,112	2,072
Total	**20,960**	**12,672**	**8,288**

A three-stage stratified cluster sampling was adopted for this survey. At stage 1, blocks in the urban and villages in the rural were taken as primary sampling units (PSUs). PSUs were selected systematically by probability proportional to size (PPS) method. The total number of blocks and villages and the sample size (blocks/villages) for the systematic sampling are shown in Table B3 and B4.

The number of households in each block/village was used as the measure of size (MOS). The selection probability of ith block/village was given by;

$$P_{hi} = \frac{\alpha_h M_{hi}}{M_h}$$

Where M_{hi} is number of households of ith block/village in h[th] stratum

M_h is number of households in h[th] stratum

α_h is the number of blocks/villages selected in h[th] stratum

$i = 1,2,...,m_h$, $h = 1,2,...,9$

Table B3 Total number of blocks/villages, by region and urban/rural

Region	Number of blocks/villages		
	Total	Urban	Rural
Bangkok	16,717	16,717	-
Central	26,477	11,636	14,841
North	19,541	4,912	14,629
Northeast	35,325	5,654	29,671
South	11,906	3,674	8,232
Whole Kingdom	**109,966**	**42,593**	**67,373**

Table B4 Number of sampled blocks/villages, by region and urban/rural

Region	Number of blocks/villages		
	Total	Urban	Rural
Bangkok	264	264	
Central	206	132	74
North	206	132	74
Northeast	206	132	74
South	206	132	74
Whole Kingdom	**1,088**	**792**	**296**

At the second stage, a fixed number of households (16 for urban and 28 for rural) were selected from each sample PSU in every stratum, using systematic random sampling. The selection probability at stage 2 was given by

$$P_{hij} = \frac{n_{hi}}{N_{hi}}$$

Where n_{hi} is number of households were selected of ith block/village in h[th] stratum

N_{hi} is number of households were counted from the listing of ith block/village in h[th] stratum

$$i = 1,2,...,m_h \ , \ h = 1,2,...,9$$

One half of the selected households were randomly assigned as "male" households, where only males would be interviewed, and another half as "female" households, where only females would be interviewed. Within the selected household, one eligible person was randomly selected at the last stage. Its selection probability is given by

$$P_{hijk} = \frac{1}{R_{hij}}$$

Where R_{hij} is number of eligible persons were selected of jth household, i[th] block/village in h[th] stratum.

After three months of field implementation, a sample of 20,960 households was obtained. However, only 18,756 individuals aged 15 years and over completed the survey (with an overall response rate of 93.6%) which was less than the minimal requirement of 20,000. Even though Thailand strived to achieve the highest response rate possible, some PSUs had response rates less than 90% and therefore, more samples were required. A simple random sampling method was used to identify additional households. There were an additional 186 PSUs in 30 provinces identified for sampling. Ultimately, the final sample included 22,768 households where 20,566 individuals completed the survey, resulting in an overall response rate of 94.2%

B.2 Sample Weighting

The weighting process for the GATS included three main steps: (1) the base weight or design weight, calculated from all steps of random selection in the sample design, (2) an adjustment for non-response by sample households and samples individuals eligible for the survey and (3) a post-stratification calibration adjustment of sample totals to projection of population 15 years old and above by region, area, gender and age group.

1) Base weight

Base weights equal to the reciprocal of the probability of selection assigned to each sample person. The probability of selection is the product of the probabilities of selection: (1) the primary sampling unit (PSU); (2) the household within the PSU; and (3) the eligible sample person within the household.

2) Adjustment for unit non-response

The base weights were adjusted for non-response on two factors: household level non-response adjustments, and person level non-response adjustments. Household level non-response adjustments were made within PSU. The corresponding household level weighting class adjustment were computed as one divided by the weighted household response rate for each sample PSUs. The person level response rate was computed within strategically formed subgroups: region, urban/rural, gender, age group and smoking status. This produced non-response adjusted base weights for sample persons who responded.

3) Post-Stratification calibration adjustment

Population projections of persons 15 years by region, urban/rural residence, gender and age group were used for a post-Stratification calibration adjustment.

The final weights assigned to each responding unit were computed as the product of the base weights, the non-response adjustment and post-stratification calibration adjustment. The final weights were used in all analysis to produce estimates of population parameters.

Appendix C: Estimation of Sampling Errors

The estimates from a sample survey are affected by two types of error: (1) non-sampling errors, and(2) sampling errors. ***Non-sampling errors*** are the results of mistakes made in implementing data collection and data processing, such as errors in coverage, response errors, non-response errors, faulty questionnaires, interviewer recording errors, processing errors, etc. Although numerous efforts were made during the implementation of the GATS to minimize those errors, non-sampling errors are impossible to avoid and difficult to evaluate statistically.

The sample of respondents selected in the GATS is only one of the samples that could have been selected from the same population, using the same design and sample size. Each of these samples would yield results that differ somewhat from the results of the actual sample selected. ***Sampling errors*** are a measure of the variability between all possible samples. The extent of variability is not known exactly, but can be estimated statistically from the survey results.

The following sampling error measures are presented for each of the selected indicator:

- *Standard error (se):* Sampling errors are usually measured in terms of standard errors for particular indicators. Standard error of an estimate is thus simply the square root of the variance of that estimate, and is computed in the same units as the estimate $\hat{\theta}$.
- *Design effect (deft)* is the ratio of the actual variance of an indicator, under the sampling method used in the survey, to the variance calculated under the assumption of simple random sampling. The square root of the design effect (deft) is used to show the efficiency of the sample design. A deft value of 1.0 indicates that the sample design is as efficient as a simple random sample, while a deft value above 1.0 indicates the increase in the standard error due to the use of a more complex sample design. In general, for a well designed study, the deft usually ranges from 1 to 3. It is common, however, for the deft to be much larger, up to 7 or 8.
- *Relative standard error (rse)* is the ratio of the standard error to the value of the indicator
- *Confidence limits* are calculated to show the interval within which the true value for the population can be reasonably assumed to fall. For any given statistic calculated from the survey, the value of that statistics will fall within a range of plus or minus two times the standard error of the statistic in 95 percent of all possible samples of identical size and design.

For the calculation of sampling errors from GATS data, SPSS Version 17.0 with the complexity of sample design (CSPLAN module) has been used. The results are shown in the tables that follow. In addition to the sampling error measures described above, the tables also include un-weighted and weighted counts of denominators for each indicator (Table C1 – C5).

Table C1: Sampling Errors of key indicator for overall adults ≥ 15 years and over

Indicator	Estimate	Standard Error	Un-weighted Count	Weighted count in 1000s	Design Effect	Relative Error	Lower Limit	Upper Limit
Current Tobacco Smokers	23.74	0.48	4,907	12,492.3	2.67	0.02	22.79	24.69
Current Smokeless Users	3.89	0.24	741	2,047.6	3.23	0.06	3.42	4.37
Current Cigarette Smokers	23.53	0.48	4,866	12,381.6	2.63	0.02	22.59	24.47
Current Manufactured Cigarette Smokers	14.96	0.40	3,198	7,873.0	2.55	0.03	14.18	15.74
Current Hand-rolled Cigarette Smokers	14.07	0.48	2,548	7,401.3	3.90	0.03	13.13	15.00
Current Smoker of Other Tobacco Products	0.28	0.09	57	144.7	5.78	0.32	0.10	0.45
Daily Tobacco Smoker	20.32	0.47	4,273	10,691.1	2.77	0.02	19.40	21.23
Number of Manufactured Cigarettes Smoked per Day	10.30	0.21	2,581	6.0	2.26	0.02	9.89	10.71
Number of Hand-rolled Cigarettes Smoked	10.97	0.27	2,252	6.5	2.76	0.02	10.44	11.50
Age at Daily Smoking Initiation in 4 Categories	18.54	0.10	6,763	16.2	2.44	0.01	18.34	18.75
Former Daily Tobacco Smokers Among All Adults	8.86	0.31	2,185	4,663.7	2.48	0.04	8.25	9.47
Former Tobacco Smokers Among Ever Daily Smokers	28.84	0.94	2,185	4,663.7	2.92	0.03	27.00	30.69
Time Since Quitting Smoking in Years	12.54	0.30	2,848	6.3	2.09	0.02	11.95	13.12
First Daily Use of Tobacco Within 5 Minutes of Waking	24.36	1.27	1,061	2,603.7	3.75	0.05	21.87	26.85
Current Tobacco Users	27.24	0.56	5,569	14,336.2	3.21	0.02	26.15	28.33
Uses Only Smoked Tobacco	85.72	0.77	4,827	12,288.0	2.71	0.01	84.21	87.23
Smoking Quit Attempt in the Past 12 Months	49.75	1.38	2,478	6,438.8	3.86	0.03	47.04	52.46
Visited a Health Care Provider in the Past 12 Months	34.85	1.13	1,872	4,510.7	2.85	0.03	32.63	37.07
Health Care Provider Asked about Smoking	60.24	1.76	1,199	2,717.7	2.42	0.03	56.79	63.69
Health Care Provider Advised Quitting Smoking	51.93	1.79	1,028	2,343.0	2.40	0.03	48.43	55.44
Use of Pharmacotherapy for Smoking Cessation	10.59	1.07	284	681.9	3.02	0.10	8.48	12.70
Use of Counseling/Advice or Quit Lines for Smoking Cessation	5.79	0.75	145	372.5	2.58	0.13	4.31	7.26
Quit on Your Own	88.92	1.29	2,191	5,725.7	4.20	0.01	86.39	91.46
Use of Other Methods for Smoking Cessation	2.87	0.44	94	183.7	1.71	0.15	2.01	3.73
Plans to Quit Smoking Some Day but not in next 12 Months	36.04	1.23	1,751	4,501.4	3.25	0.03	33.62	38.46
Exposure to SHS at Work	27.23	1.21	1,376	3,303.4	3.91	0.04	24.85	29.61
Exposure to SHS at Home	39.13	0.96	7,277	20,498.0	7.85	0.02	37.26	41.00
Exposure to SHS in Government Buildings/Offices	3.94	0.27	871	2,046.5	4.06	0.07	3.40	4.48

Table C1 (continued): Sampling Errors of key indicator for overall adults ≥ 15 years and over

Indicator	Estimate	Standard Error	Un-weighted Count	Weighted count in 1000s	Design Effect	Relative Error	Lower Limit	Upper Limit
Exposure to SHS in Health Care Facilities	2.05	0.16	510	1,064.8	2.55	0.08	1.74	2.36
Exposure to SHS in Restaurants	8.98	0.39	2,163	4,677.1	3.80	0.04	8.22	9.75
Exposure to SHS on Public Transportation	6.33	0.37	1,382	3,288.4	4.61	0.06	5.61	7.05
Exposure to SHS at Outside Market	53.53	0.77	11,109	28,072.2	4.83	0.01	52.03	55.04
Last Brand of Cigarette Purchased - Krongthip	51.09	1.61	1,411	3,828.2	3.18	0.03	47.93	54.24
Last Cigarette Purchase at Grocery	91.15	0.61	2,663	6,830.4	1.41	0.01	89.96	92.35
Total Monthly Expenditures on Manufactured Cigarettes	575.75	13.40	3,055	7.5	2.20	0.02	549.49	602.00
Last pack purchased had pictorial warning	97.38	0.64	1,718	3,748.8	2.88	0.01	96.12	98.64
Noticed Anti-Smoking Information in Newspapers or in Magazines	27.37	0.73	6,270	14,401.1	5.50	0.03	25.95	28.80
Noticed Anti-Smoking Information on Local TV	74.44	0.82	15,530	39,158.5	7.27	0.01	72.84	76.05
Noticed Anti-Smoking Information on Radio	33.49	0.90	6,909	17,616.9	7.47	0.03	31.73	35.25
Noticed Anti-Smoking Information on Billboards	39.01	1.09	8,202	20,521.1	10.24	0.03	36.88	41.14
Noticed Anti-Smoking Information on Leaflet or Sticker	38.29	1.03	8,088	20,142.8	9.26	0.03	36.27	40.32
Noticed Anti-Smoking Information on Internet	6.31	0.38	1,160	3,319.9	4.93	0.06	5.58	7.05
Noticed Anti-Smoking Information in Public Campaign Activity	15.35	0.86	3,170	8,071.1	11.59	0.06	13.67	17.03
Noticed Anti-Smoking Information Demonstration Board	30.35	0.97	5,834	15,958.3	9.17	0.03	28.44	32.25
Noticed Anti-Smoking Information Somewhere Else	0.99	0.19	206	509.3	7.36	0.19	0.62	1.36
Noticed Health Warning Labels on Cigarette Packages	80.98	0.57	16,342	42,594.6	4.35	0.01	79.86	82.10
Thinking of Quitting Because of Health Warning Labels on Cigarette Packages	66.98	1.30	3,291	8,357.8	3.78	0.02	64.42	69.54
Noticed Health Warning Labels on Raw Tobacco Packages	21.63	2.01	526	1,988.3	7.56	0.09	17.69	25.57
Thinking of Quitting Because of Health Warning Labels on Raw Tobacco Packages	15.05	1.46	367	1,383.3	5.28	0.10	12.19	17.91
Noticed Cigarette Advertisements in Stores	6.69	0.49	1,245	3,518.8	7.91	0.07	5.73	7.65
Noticed Cigarette Advertisements Anywhere Else	2.30	0.19	477	1,182.8	3.36	0.08	1.92	2.68
Noticed Sponsorship of Sport or Arts Event	1.30	0.19	256	684.3	5.59	0.14	0.93	1.67
Noticed Cigarette Promotions - Clothing/item with brand name or logo	6.61	0.37	1,406	3,475.6	4.44	0.06	5.89	7.32

Table C1 (continued): Sampling Errors of key indicator for overall adults ≥ 15 years and over

Indicator	Estimate	Standard Error	Un-weighted Count	Weighted count in 1000s	Design Effect	Relative Error	Lower Limit	Upper Limit
Noticed Other Promotion	1.80	0.17	335	947.7	3.51	0.10	1.46	2.14
Believes that Tobacco Smoking Causes Serious Illness	98.56	0.16	20,273	51,846.3	3.57	0.00	98.25	98.87
Believes that Tobacco Smoking Causes Strokes	79.62	0.68	16,658	41,873.6	5.91	0.01	78.28	80.96
Believes that Tobacco Smoking Causes Heart Attacks	75.74	0.69	15,820	39,834.6	5.35	0.01	74.39	77.10
Believes that Tobacco Smoking Causes Lung Cancer	97.47	0.17	20,051	51,266.1	2.44	0.00	97.14	97.81
Believes that Tobacco Smoking Causes Mouth Cancer	90.82	0.45	18,668	47,764.7	4.93	0.00	89.94	91.69
Believes that Tobacco Smoking Causes Larynx Cancer	91.48	0.44	18,972	48,113.2	5.17	0.00	90.61	92.35
Believes that Tobacco Smoking Causes Impotence	65.69	0.81	13,668	34,545.2	5.93	0.01	64.11	67.28
Believes that Tobacco Smoking Causes Emphysema	90.33	0.53	18,867	47,510.3	6.60	0.01	89.30	91.37
Believes that SHS Causes Serious Illness in Non-Smokers	94.93	0.28	19,443	49,932.4	3.44	0.00	94.37	95.48
Believes that SHS Causes Heart Disease	64.94	0.73	13,827	34,156.6	4.85	0.01	63.50	66.37
Believes that SHS Causes Lung Illness in Children	90.04	0.43	18,472	47,364.6	4.27	0.00	89.20	90.89
Believes that SHS Causes Lung Cancer in Adults	90.73	0.41	18,616	47,722.2	4.04	0.00	89.93	91.53
Believes that SHS Causes Emphysema	82.42	0.62	17,159	43,344.9	5.48	0.01	81.21	83.64
Believes that SHS Causes Low Birth Weight	69.24	0.72	14,193	36,410.2	4.97	0.01	67.84	70.65
Believes that SHS Causes Premature Birth	58.54	0.80	12,081	30,787.0	5.42	0.01	56.97	60.11
Pictorial Warning #8 Most Makes Smokers Want to Quit	30.31	1.40	916	2,372.2	2.97	0.05	27.56	33.06
Pictorial Warning #7 Most Influences Non-Smokers to Not Smoke	34.37	0.82	3,821	10,845.8	3.57	0.02	32.77	35.98
Believes Manufactured Cigarettes are More Harmful	39.70	0.86	7,877	20,046.8	6.07	0.02	38.01	41.38
Daily Manufactured Cigarette Smoker	11.33	0.34	2,581	5,959.4	2.35	0.03	10.66	11.99
Daily Hand-rolled Cigarette Smoker	12.39	0.46	2,252	6,520.2	3.94	0.04	11.50	13.28
Daily Smokeless Tobacco User	3.42	0.23	630	1,797.1	3.44	0.07	2.96	3.88
Average Price per Pack of Manufactured Cigarettes	44.69	0.37	3,055	63.3	3.90	0.01	43.96	45.42

Table C2: Sampling Errors of key indicator for male adults ≥ 15 years and over

Indicator	Estimate	Standard Error	Un-weighted Count	Weighted count in 1000s	Design Effect	Relative Error	Lower Limit	Upper Limit
Current Tobacco Smokers	45.56	0.92	4,475	11,652.0	3.44	0.02	43.75	47.36
Current Smokeless Users	1.33	0.15	172	339.3	1.84	0.12	1.02	1.63
Current Cigarette Smokers	45.41	0.92	4,461	11,615.5	3.45	0.02	43.61	47.22
Current Manufactured Cigarette Smokers	29.58	0.78	2,997	7,565.0	2.97	0.03	28.04	31.11
Current Hand-rolled Cigarette Smokers	27.00	0.93	2,321	6,905.9	4.37	0.03	25.19	28.82
Current Smoker of Other Tobacco Products	0.25	0.08	27	64.6	2.83	0.33	0.09	0.42
Daily Tobacco Smoker	39.24	0.90	3,938	10,035.2	3.43	0.02	37.47	41.00
Number of Manufactured Cigarettes Smoked per Day	10.35	0.22	2,428	5.7	2.35	0.02	9.92	10.78
Number of Hand-rolled Cigarettes Smoked	11.17	0.27	2,077	6.1	2.61	0.02	10.65	11.70
Age at Daily Smoking Initiation in 4 Categories	18.24	0.10	6,204	15.1	2.49	0.01	18.05	18.44
Former Daily Tobacco Smokers Among All Adults	16.75	0.63	2,004	4,282.9	2.86	0.04	15.51	17.98
Former Tobacco Smokers Among Ever Daily Smokers	28.43	0.97	2,004	4,282.9	2.85	0.03	26.54	30.33
Time Since Quitting Smoking in Years	12.22	0.29	2,525	5.7	1.91	0.02	11.65	12.79
First Daily Use of Tobacco Within 5 Minutes of Waking	24.70	1.32	990	2,478.0	3.70	0.05	22.11	27.29
Current Tobacco Users	46.40	0.93	4,597	11,868.4	3.46	0.02	44.59	48.22
Uses Only Smoked Tobacco	97.14	0.33	4,424	11,528.4	1.77	0.00	96.50	97.78
Smoking Quit Attempt in the Past 12 Months	49.93	1.44	2,252	6,020.4	3.79	0.03	47.11	52.74
Visited a Health Care Provider in the Past 12 Months	33.94	1.17	1,655	4,092.9	2.83	0.03	31.64	36.24
Health Care Provider Asked about Smoking	59.87	1.88	1,061	2,450.8	2.44	0.03	56.18	63.55
Health Care Provider Advised Quitting Smoking	52.26	1.90	920	2,139.6	2.39	0.04	48.55	55.98
Use of Pharmacotherapy for Smoking Cessation	10.59	1.15	252	637.8	3.12	0.11	8.35	12.84
Use of Counseling/Advice or Quit Lines for Smoking Cessation	5.56	0.78	127	334.9	2.62	0.14	4.03	7.10
Quit on Your Own	89.03	1.36	1,999	5,360.1	4.24	0.02	86.37	91.69
Use of Other Methods for Smoking Cessation	2.78	0.46	82	165.9	1.74	0.17	1.88	3.67
Plans to Quit Smoking Some Day but not in next 12 Months	36.77	1.28	1,617	4,284.3	3.16	0.03	34.26	39.28
Exposure to SHS at Work	34.94	1.94	871	2,199.2	4.50	0.06	31.15	38.74
Exposure to SHS at Home	43.37	1.16	3,967	11,036.6	5.51	0.03	41.09	45.65
Exposure to SHS in Government Buildings/Offices	4.82	0.40	535	1,218.1	3.47	0.08	4.04	5.60

Table C2 (continued): Sampling Errors of key indicator for male adults ≥ 15 years and over

Indicator	Estimate	Standard Error	Un-weighted Count	Weighted count in 1000s	Design Effect	Relative Error	Lower Limit	Upper Limit
Exposure to SHS in Health Care Facilities	2.03	0.25	236	513.2	3.09	0.12	1.54	2.52
Exposure to SHS in Restaurants	10.85	0.55	1,262	2,750.5	3.14	0.05	9.77	11.93
Exposure to SHS on Public Transportation	5.07	0.35	588	1,280.1	2.55	0.07	4.38	5.76
Exposure to SHS at Outside Market	54.44	0.95	5,513	1,3874.2	3.61	0.02	52.59	56.29
Last Brand of Cigarette Purchased - Krongthip	51.96	1.66	1,359	3,741.5	3.18	0.03	48.70	55.22
Last Cigarette Purchase at Grocery	91.52	0.61	2,508	6,589.9	1.39	0.01	90.32	92.72
Total Monthly Expenditures on Manufactured Cigarettes	579.24	14.09	2,867	7.2	2.33	0.02	551.62	606.85
Last pack purchased had pictorial warning	97.40	0.66	1,609	3,570.9	2.82	0.01	96.11	98.68
Noticed Anti-Smoking Information in Newspapers or in Magazines	29.14	0.90	3,342	7,450.1	3.97	0.03	27.37	30.91
Noticed Anti-Smoking Information on Local TV	73.93	0.94	7,597	18,893.7	4.65	0.01	72.08	75.78
Noticed Anti-Smoking Information on Radio	34.94	1.13	3,513	8,932.0	5.63	0.03	32.73	37.15
Noticed Anti-Smoking Information on Billboards	39.82	1.23	4,110	10,177.8	6.35	0.03	37.40	42.23
Noticed Anti-Smoking Information on Leaflet or Sticker	39.11	1.27	4,072	9,997.8	6.79	0.03	36.62	41.60
Noticed Anti-Smoking Information on Internet	5.45	0.46	563	1,393.1	4.08	0.08	4.55	6.35
Noticed Anti-Smoking Information in Public Campaign Activity	14.98	0.89	1,568	3,829.9	6.22	0.06	13.24	16.72
Noticed Anti-Smoking Information Demonstration Board	30.23	1.09	2,889	7,727.8	5.69	0.04	28.09	32.38
Noticed Anti-Smoking Information Somewhere Else	0.94	0.15	111	235.7	2.53	0.16	0.64	1.24
Noticed Health Warning Labels on Cigarette Packages	89.24	0.49	8,689	22,812.0	2.49	0.01	88.29	90.20
Thinking of Quitting Because of Health Warning Labels on Cigarette Packages	67.81	1.34	3,036	7,891.3	3.68	0.02	65.19	70.44
Noticed Health Warning Labels on Raw Tobacco Packages	25.66	2.36	459	1,810.5	6.96	0.09	21.04	30.27
Thinking of Quitting Because of Health Warning Labels on Raw Tobacco Packages	17.77	1.73	319	1,253.8	4.92	0.10	14.37	21.16
Noticed Cigarette Advertisements in Stores	6.56	0.58	639	1,676.3	5.45	0.09	5.43	7.69
Noticed Cigarette Advertisements Anywhere Else	2.19	0.25	241	547.1	2.99	0.12	1.69	2.69
Noticed Sponsorship of Sport or Arts Event	1.84	0.27	181	471.4	4.01	0.15	1.32	2.37
Noticed Cigarette Promotions - Clothing/item with brand name or logo	7.67	0.51	846	1,959.9	3.63	0.07	6.68	8.66

Table C2 (continued): Sampling Errors of key indicator for male adults ≥ 15 years and over

Indicator	Estimate	Standard Error	Un-weighted Count	Weighted count in 1000s	Design Effect	Relative Error	Lower Limit	Upper Limit
Noticed Other Promotion	2.44	0.26	223	623.1	2.85	0.11	1.93	2.95
Believes that Tobacco Smoking Causes Serious Illness	98.24	0.25	9,888	25,111.3	3.75	0.00	97.74	98.73
Believes that Tobacco Smoking Causes Heart Attacks	75.28	0.89	7,734	19,239.0	4.23	0.01	73.54	77.01
Believes that Tobacco Smoking Causes Lung Cancer	97.42	0.22	9,779	24,896.9	1.86	0.00	97.00	97.84
Believes that Tobacco Smoking Causes Mouth Cancer	90.79	0.55	9,115	23,202.4	3.67	0.01	89.71	91.87
Believes that Tobacco Smoking Causes Larynx Cancer	91.67	0.57	9,298	23,426.8	4.21	0.01	90.56	92.78
Believes that Tobacco Smoking Causes Impotence	70.52	0.91	7,194	18,020.1	4.04	0.01	68.73	72.31
Believes that Tobacco Smoking Causes Emphysema	90.88	0.64	9,300	23,224.9	5.03	0.01	89.62	92.15
Believes that SHS Causes Serious Illness in Non-Smokers	94.65	0.36	9,456	24,191.7	2.51	0.00	93.95	95.34
Believes that SHS Causes Heart Disease	65.77	0.97	6,849	16,810.4	4.18	0.01	63.87	67.66
Believes that SHS Causes Lung Illness in Children	89.99	0.51	8,987	23,001.5	2.85	0.01	89.00	90.98
Believes that SHS Causes Lung Cancer in Adults	90.71	0.49	9,055	23,184.4	2.84	0.01	89.76	91.67
Believes that SHS Causes Emphysema	83.31	0.71	8,439	21,282.6	3.62	0.01	81.92	84.69
Believes that SHS Causes Low Birth Weight	64.29	0.98	6,489	16,428.7	4.19	0.02	62.37	66.21
Believes that SHS Causes Premature Birth	53.29	1.05	5,413	13,618.3	4.47	0.02	51.22	55.35
Pictorial Warning #8 Most Makes Smokers Want to Quit	30.28	1.45	855	2,276.4	2.97	0.05	27.43	33.12
Pictorial Warning #7 Most Influences Non-Smokers to Not Smoke	31.34	1.59	858	2,536.9	3.48	0.05	28.22	34.45
Believes Manufactured Cigarettes are More Harmful	37.10	0.95	3,648	9,201.7	3.78	0.03	35.23	38.97
Daily Manufactured Cigarette Smoker	22.42	0.69	2,428	5,735.3	2.72	0.03	21.08	23.77
Daily Hand-rolled Cigarette Smoker	23.96	0.89	2,077	6,129.0	4.41	0.04	22.21	25.72
Daily Smokeless Tobacco User	0.91	0.13	118	233.7	1.82	0.14	0.66	1.16
Average Price per Pack of Manufactured Cigarettes	44.66	0.38	2,867	61.2	3.98	0.01	43.91	45.41

Table C3: Sampling Errors of key indicator for female adults ≥ 15 years and over

Indicator	Estimate	Standard Error	Un-weighted Count	Weighted count in 1000s	Design Effect	Relative Error	Lower Limit	Upper Limit
Current Tobacco Smokers	3.11	0.25	432	840.3	2.12	0.08	2.62	3.59
Current Smokeless Users	6.32	0.43	569	1,708.3	3.29	0.07	5.47	7.16
Current Cigarette Smokers	2.83	0.21	405	766.0	1.68	0.07	2.42	3.24
Current Manufactured Cigarette Smokers	1.14	0.11	201	308.0	1.09	0.09	0.93	1.35
Current Hand-rolled Cigarette Smokers	1.83	0.19	227	495.3	2.03	0.10	1.47	2.20
Current Smoker of Other Tobacco Products	0.30	0.13	30	80.1	6.11	0.44	0.04	0.55
Daily Tobacco Smoker	2.43	0.22	335	655.9	2.18	0.09	1.99	2.86
Number of Manufactured Cigarettes Smoked per Day	8.94	0.57	153	0.2	0.75	0.06	7.83	10.05
Number of Hand-rolled Cigarettes Smoked	7.78	0.94	175	0.4	1.85	0.12	5.94	9.61
Age at Daily Smoking Initiation in 4 Categories	22.60	0.58	559	1.1	1.65	0.03	21.46	23.74
Former Daily Tobacco Smokers Among All Adults	1.41	0.15	181	380.8	1.78	0.11	1.11	1.71
Former Tobacco Smokers Among Ever Daily Smokers	34.43	2.90	181	380.8	2.08	0.08	28.74	40.11
Time Since Quitting Smoking in Years	15.16	1.06	323	0.7	1.95	0.07	13.09	17.24
First Daily Use of Tobacco Within 5 Minutes of Waking	19.18	2.54	71	125.8	1.39	0.13	14.20	24.15
Current Tobacco Users	9.13	0.50	972	2,467.9	3.21	0.06	8.14	10.11
Uses Only Smoked Tobacco	30.78	2.04	403	759.5	1.89	0.07	26.78	34.77
Smoking Quit Attempt in the Past 12 Months	47.39	3.56	226	418.4	2.31	0.08	40.41	54.37
Visited a Health Care Provider in the Past 12 Months	47.32	3.28	217	417.8	1.96	0.07	40.90	53.75
Health Care Provider Asked about Smoking	63.88	4.18	138	266.9	1.64	0.07	55.68	72.08
Health Care Provider Advised Quitting Smoking	48.70	4.44	108	203.5	1.70	0.09	40.00	57.40
Use of Pharmacotherapy for Smoking Cessation	10.53	2.55	32	44.1	1.55	0.24	5.53	15.52
Quit on Your Own	87.38	2.52	192	365.6	1.30	0.03	82.44	92.32
Plans to Quit Smoking Some Day but not in next 12 Months	25.84	2.61	134	217.1	1.53	0.10	20.72	30.96
Exposure to SHS at Work	18.92	1.11	505	1,104.3	2.02	0.06	16.75	21.09
Exposure to SHS at Home	35.13	1.07	3310	9,461.4	5.28	0.03	33.03	37.23
Exposure to SHS in Government Buildings/Offices	3.10	0.35	336	828.4	4.18	0.11	2.42	3.78

Table C3 (continued): Sampling Errors of key indicator for female adults ≥ 15 years and over

Indicator	Estimate	Standard Error	Un-weighted Count	Weighted count in 1000s	Design Effect	Relative Error	Lower Limit	Upper Limit
Exposure to SHS in Health Care Facilities	2.06	0.19	274	551.6	1.81	0.09	1.70	2.43
Exposure to SHS in Restaurants	7.21	0.42	901	1,926.6	2.79	0.06	6.38	8.04
Exposure to SHS on Public Transportation	7.52	0.56	794	2,008.3	4.62	0.07	6.44	8.61
Exposure to SHS at Outside Market	52.68	0.98	5,596	14,198.0	4.03	0.02	50.76	54.60
Last Brand of Cigarette Purchased – Krongthip	29.62	4.54	52	86.7	1.86	0.15	20.73	38.51
Last Cigarette Purchase at Grocery	82.20	3.31	155	240.5	1.41	0.04	75.70	88.69
Total Monthly Expenditures on Manufactured Cigarettes	489.91	42.88	188	0.3	1.03	0.09	405.87	573.96
Last pack purchased had pictorial warning	97.14	1.85	109	178.0	1.37	0.02	93.52	100.75
Noticed Anti-Smoking Information in Newspapers or in Magazines	25.70	0.80	2,928	6,951.0	3.50	0.03	24.14	27.27
Noticed Anti-Smoking Information on Local TV	74.93	0.93	7,933	20,264.8	4.87	0.01	73.11	76.76
Noticed Anti-Smoking Information on Radio	32.12	0.91	3,396	8,684.9	3.95	0.03	30.34	33.89
Noticed Anti-Smoking Information on Billboards	38.25	1.11	4,092	10,343.3	5.52	0.03	36.07	40.43
Noticed Anti-Smoking Information on Leaflet or Sticker	37.52	1.08	4,016	10,145.1	5.19	0.03	35.42	39.63
Noticed Anti-Smoking Information on Internet	7.13	0.51	597	1,926.8	4.10	0.07	6.13	8.12
Noticed Anti-Smoking Information in Public Campaign Activity	15.70	0.98	1,602	4,241.2	7.70	0.06	13.77	17.63
Noticed Anti-Smoking Information Demonstration Board	30.45	1.09	2,945	8,230.6	5.95	0.04	28.31	32.60
Noticed Anti-Smoking Information Somewhere Else	1.03	0.26	95	273.6	6.65	0.25	0.53	1.53
Noticed Health Warning Labels on Cigarette Packages	73.17	0.89	7,653	19,782.7	4.24	0.01	71.42	74.91
Thinking of Quitting Because of Health Warning Labels on Cigarette Packages	55.51	3.72	255	466.5	2.41	0.07	48.23	62.80
Noticed Health Warning Labels on Raw Tobacco Packages	8.33	1.50	67	177.8	2.27	0.18	5.39	11.26
Thinking of Quitting Because of Health Warning Labels on Raw Tobacco Packages	6.07	1.29	48	129.5	2.26	0.21	3.53	8.60
Noticed Cigarette Advertisements in Stores	6.81	0.58	606	1,842.5	5.61	0.09	5.67	7.96
Noticed Cigarette Advertisements Anywhere Else	2.41	0.24	236	635.7	2.58	0.10	1.93	2.88
Noticed Sponsorship of Sport or Arts Event	0.79	0.20	75	212.9	5.25	0.25	0.40	1.17
Noticed Cigarette Promotions - Clothing/item with brand name or logo	5.61	0.47	560	1,515.7	4.46	0.08	4.68	6.54

Table C3 (continued): Sampling Errors of key indicator for female adults ≥ 15 years and over

Indicator	Estimate	Standard Error	Un-weighted Count	Weighted count in 1000s	Design Effect	Relative Error	Lower Limit	Upper Limit
Noticed Other Promotion	1.20	0.18	112	324.6	2.93	0.15	0.84	1.56
Believes that Tobacco Smoking Causes Serious Illness	98.86	0.14	10,385	26,735.0	1.95	0.00	98.58	99.15
Believes that Tobacco Smoking Causes Strokes	79.40	0.80	8,449	21,468.3	4.10	0.01	77.84	80.97
Believes that Tobacco Smoking Causes Heart Attacks	76.18	0.79	8,086	20,595.5	3.62	0.01	74.63	77.73
Believes that Tobacco Smoking Causes Lung Cancer	97.52	0.22	10,272	26,369.2	2.10	0.00	97.09	97.95
Believes that Tobacco Smoking Causes Mouth Cancer	90.84	0.51	9,553	24,562.3	3.35	0.01	89.83	91.85
Believes that Tobacco Smoking Causes Larynx Cancer	91.30	0.50	9,674	24,686.3	3.31	0.01	90.32	92.28
Believes that Tobacco Smoking Causes Impotence	61.13	0.99	6,474	16,525.1	4.31	0.02	59.20	63.07
Believes that Tobacco Smoking Causes Emphysema	89.82	0.61	9,567	24,285.4	4.25	0.01	88.62	91.01
Believes that SHS Causes Serious Illness in Non-Smokers	95.19	0.33	9,987	25,740.6	2.50	0.00	94.55	95.84
Believes that SHS Causes Heart Disease	64.15	0.93	6,978	17,346.2	3.93	0.01	62.33	65.97
Believes that SHS Causes Lung Illness in Children	90.10	0.55	9,485	24,363.2	3.55	0.01	89.02	91.17
Believes that SHS Causes Lung Cancer in Adults	90.74	0.47	9,561	24,537.9	2.79	0.01	89.82	91.67
Believes that SHS Causes Emphysema	81.59	0.81	8,720	22,062.4	4.59	0.01	80.00	83.18
Believes that SHS Causes Low Birth Weight	73.93	0.78	7,704	19,981.5	3.36	0.01	72.39	75.47
Believes that SHS Causes Premature Birth	63.51	0.90	6,668	17,168.8	3.66	0.01	61.75	65.27
Pictorial Warning #8 Most Makes Smokers Want to Quit	31.12	4.55	61	95.8	1.94	0.15	22.19	40.05
Pictorial Warning #7 Most Influences Non-Smokers to Not Smoke	35.42	0.90	2,963	8,308.9	3.16	0.03	33.67	37.18
Believes Manufactured Cigarettes are More Harmful	42.20	1.11	4,229	10,845.1	5.03	0.03	40.03	44.38
Daily Manufactured Cigarette Smoker	0.83	0.08	153	224.2	0.90	0.10	0.66	0.99
Daily Hand-rolled Cigarette Smoker	1.45	0.16	175	391.1	1.86	0.11	1.14	1.76
Daily Smokeless Tobacco User	5.78	0.42	512	1,563.4	3.43	0.07	4.95	6.61
Average Price per Pack of Manufactured Cigarettes	45.49	1.10	188	2.1	0.83	0.02	43.33	47.64

Table C4: Sampling Errors of key indicator for adults ≥ 15 years and over living in urban areas

Indicator	Estimate	Standard Error	Un-weighted Count	Weighted count in 1000s	Design Effect	Relative Error	Lower Limit	Upper Limit
Current Tobacco Smokers	21.50	0.48	2,701	3,513.7	1.66	0.02	20.56	22.43
Current Smokeless Users	1.54	0.16	209	252.1	1.96	0.10	1.24	1.85
Current Cigarette Smokers	21.44	0.48	2,692	3,504.7	1.66	0.02	20.51	22.37
Current Manufactured Cigarette Smokers	17.70	0.43	2,153	2,892.9	1.55	0.02	16.86	18.54
Current Hand-rolled Cigarette Smokers	6.45	0.31	892	1,053.6	1.94	0.05	5.84	7.05
Daily Tobacco Smoker	18.46	0.44	2,339	3,017.2	1.58	0.02	17.60	19.32
Number of Manufactured Cigarettes Smoked per Day	11.22	0.20	1,813	2.4	0.81	0.02	10.84	11.60
Number of Hand-rolled Cigarettes Smoked	9.93	0.32	777	0.9	0.67	0.03	9.30	10.57
Age at Daily Smoking Initiation in 4 Categories	18.77	0.10	3,782	4.6	0.71	0.01	18.57	18.97
Former Daily Tobacco Smokers Among All Adults	8.33	0.28	1,262	1,361.1	1.31	0.03	7.77	8.88
Former Tobacco Smokers Among Ever Daily Smokers	29.43	0.93	1,262	1,361.1	1.57	0.03	27.61	31.25
Time Since Quitting Smoking in Years	12.84	0.36	1,659	1.9	0.86	0.03	12.13	13.54
First Daily Use of Tobacco Within 5 Minutes of Waking	27.97	1.28	629	843.4	1.90	0.05	25.46	30.48
Current Tobacco Users	22.86	0.50	2,885	3,736.9	1.79	0.02	21.87	23.85
Uses Only Smoked Tobacco	93.25	0.64	2,675	3,484.2	1.90	0.01	91.99	94.52
Smoking Quit Attempt in the Past 12 Months	51.72	1.29	1,401	1,863.1	1.85	0.02	49.19	54.25
Visited a Health Care Provider in the Past 12 Months	35.85	1.16	978	1,292.6	1.62	0.03	33.58	38.12
Health Care Provider Asked about Smoking	59.21	2.01	621	765.4	1.64	0.03	55.27	63.15
Health Care Provider Advised Quitting Smoking	48.80	2.03	523	630.8	1.62	0.04	44.81	52.79
Use of Pharmacotherapy for Smoking Cessation	14.77	1.28	200	275.2	1.82	0.09	12.26	17.28
Use of Counseling/Advice or Quit Lines for Smoking Cessation	6.35	0.85	87	118.2	1.69	0.13	4.69	8.00
Quit on Your Own	89.02	1.20	1,234	1,658.5	2.08	0.01	86.66	91.38
Use of Other Methods for Smoking Cessation	3.74	0.69	60	69.3	1.83	0.18	2.39	5.09
Plans to Quit Smoking Some Day but not in next 12 Months	33.66	1.36	964	1,182.4	2.23	0.04	30.99	36.32
Exposure to SHS at Work	23.68	0.92	972	1,290.2	1.83	0.04	21.89	25.48
Exposure to SHS at Home	29.11	0.69	3,539	4,742.3	2.84	0.02	27.76	30.46
Exposure to SHS in Government Buildings/Offices	4.48	0.25	588	716.4	1.83	0.06	3.98	4.98

Table C4 (continued): Sampling Errors of key indicator for adults ≥ 15 years and over living in urban areas

Indicator	Estimate	Standard Error	Un-weighted Count	Weighted count in 1000s	Design Effect	Relative Error	Lower Limit	Upper Limit
Exposure to SHS in Health Care Facilities	2.44	0.19	328	391.0	1.80	0.08	2.07	2.81
Exposure to SHS in Restaurants	12.57	0.49	1,590	2,020.8	2.71	0.04	11.60	13.54
Exposure to SHS on Public Transportation	9.47	0.50	1,067	1,515.7	3.54	0.05	8.49	10.45
Exposure to SHS at Outside Market	57.39	0.71	6,988	9,335.9	2.51	0.01	56.01	58.78
Last Brand of Cigarette Purchased – Krongthip	44.83	1.42	893	1,268.7	1.71	0.03	42.05	47.61
Last Cigarette Purchase at Grocery	83.23	1.06	1,739	2,354.9	1.69	0.01	81.14	85.31
Total Monthly Expenditures on Manufactured Cigarettes	682.81	14.82	2,086	2.8	0.88	0.02	653.76	711.85
Last pack purchased had pictorial warning	97.98	0.55	1,243	1,658.9	1.98	0.01	96.89	99.07
Noticed Anti-Smoking Information in Newspapers or in Magazines	38.17	0.76	4,552	6,238.4	3.04	0.02	36.67	39.66
Noticed Anti-Smoking Information on Local TV	77.76	0.65	9,560	12,709.3	3.06	0.01	76.48	79.04
Noticed Anti-Smoking Information on Radio	32.92	0.73	4,124	5,378.9	2.96	0.02	31.49	34.34
Noticed Anti-Smoking Information on Billboards	46.24	0.92	5,464	7,556.5	4.16	0.02	44.45	48.03
Noticed Anti-Smoking Information on Leaflet or Sticker	43.62	0.93	5,267	7,128.2	4.31	0.02	41.81	45.44
Noticed Anti-Smoking Information on Internet	9.02	0.43	930	1,474.2	2.78	0.05	8.18	9.86
Noticed Anti-Smoking Information in Public Campaign Activity	17.36	0.67	2,186	2,836.8	3.83	0.04	16.05	18.67
Noticed Anti-Smoking Information Demonstration Board	30.36	0.82	3,663	4,961.4	3.93	0.03	28.76	31.97
Noticed Anti-Smoking Information Somewhere Else	1.33	0.18	149	216.9	2.95	0.13	0.98	1.68
Noticed Health Warning Labels on Cigarette Packages	82.49	0.52	10,002	13,481.8	2.30	0.01	81.48	83.51
Thinking of Quitting Because of Health Warning Labels on Cigarette Packages	67.69	1.09	1,836	2,376.9	1.48	0.02	65.54	69.83
Noticed Health Warning Labels on Raw Tobacco Packages	23.33	2.00	214	296.4	2.39	0.09	19.40	27.26
Thinking of Quitting Because of Health Warning Labels on Raw Tobacco Packages	15.39	1.59	143	195.6	2.08	0.10	12.27	18.52
Noticed Cigarette Advertisements in Stores	7.95	0.56	841	1,299.3	5.28	0.07	6.86	9.05
Noticed Cigarette Advertisements Anywhere Else	3.18	0.24	338	516.0	2.33	0.08	2.71	3.66
Noticed Sponsorship of Sport or Arts Event	1.64	0.17	185	267.7	2.20	0.10	1.31	1.97
Noticed Cigarette Promotions - Clothing/item with brand name or logo	8.65	0.45	1,045	1,413.2	3.21	0.05	7.76	9.54

Table C4 (continued): Sampling Errors of key indicator for adults ≥ 15 years and over living in urban areas

Indicator	Estimate	Standard Error	Un-weighted Count	Weighted count in 1000s	Design Effect	Relative Error	Lower Limit	Upper Limit
Noticed Other Promotion	2.27	0.24	226	371.3	3.18	0.11	1.80	2.74
Believes that Tobacco Smoking Causes Serious Illness	99.09	0.10	12,209	16,192.9	1.30	0.00	98.90	99.28
Believes that Tobacco Smoking Causes Strokes	82.64	0.51	10,242	13,501.0	2.27	0.01	81.63	83.64
Believes that Tobacco Smoking Causes Heart Attacks	78.41	0.60	9,756	12,810.1	2.60	0.01	77.24	79.58
Believes that Tobacco Smoking Causes Lung Cancer	98.28	0.15	12,118	16,055.7	1.60	0.00	97.99	98.57
Believes that Tobacco Smoking Causes Mouth Cancer	92.22	0.38	11,373	15,066.8	2.48	0.00	91.48	92.97
Believes that Tobacco Smoking Causes Larynx Cancer	94.01	0.33	11,608	15,358.8	2.40	0.00	93.36	94.66
Believes that Tobacco Smoking Causes Impotence	69.34	0.60	8,555	11,322.7	2.10	0.01	68.16	70.52
Believes that Tobacco Smoking Causes Emphysema	94.45	0.30	11,641	15,431.0	2.06	0.00	93.87	95.03
Believes that Secondhand Smoke Causes Serious Illness in Non-Smokers	96.07	0.22	11,804	15,699.2	1.60	0.00	95.64	96.51
Believes that Secondhand Smoke Causes Heart Disease	67.68	0.71	8,542	11,059.7	2.81	0.01	66.30	69.06
Believes that Secondhand Smoke Causes Lung Illness in Children	91.28	0.38	11,244	14,916.2	2.29	0.00	90.53	92.03
Believes that Secondhand Smoke Causes Lung Cancer in Adults	92.85	0.30	11,384	15,170.4	1.73	0.00	92.26	93.45
Believes that Secondhand Smoke Causes Emphysema	85.64	0.49	10,576	13,992.9	2.46	0.01	84.67	86.61
Believes that Secondhand Smoke Causes Low Birth Weight	70.99	0.62	8,703	11,595.8	2.32	0.01	69.77	72.21
Believes that Secondhand Smoke Causes Premature Birth	59.44	0.72	7,375	9,708.6	2.68	0.01	58.02	60.86
Pictorial Warning #8 Most Makes Smokers Want to Quit	29.89	1.35	612	860.6	1.87	0.05	27.24	32.54
Pictorial Warning #7 Most Influences Non-Smokers to Not Smoke	33.12	0.74	2,445	3,503.6	1.88	0.02	31.67	34.56
Believes Manufactured Cigarettes are More Harmful	32.95	0.69	4,036	5,124.7	2.51	0.02	31.61	34.29
Daily Manufactured Cigarette Smoker	14.84	0.39	1,813	2,426.1	1.52	0.03	14.07	15.61
Daily Hand-rolled Cigarette Smoker	5.60	0.28	777	915.4	1.86	0.05	5.05	6.15
Daily Smokeless Tobacco User	1.25	0.15	166	205.1	2.13	0.12	0.97	1.54
Average Price per Pack of Manufactured Cigarettes	45.49	0.46	2,086	27.8	2.10	0.01	44.59	46.38

Table C5: Sampling Errors of key indicator for adults ≥ 15 years and over living in rural areas

Indicator	Estimate	Standard Error	Un-weighted Count	Weighted count in 1000s	Design Effect	Relative Error	Lower Limit	Upper Limit
Current Tobacco Smokers	24.75	0.67	2,206	8,978.6	2.00	0.03	23.43	26.07
Current Smokeless Users	4.95	0.35	532	1,795.5	2.10	0.07	4.27	5.63
Current Cigarette Smokers	24.47	0.67	2,174	8,876.9	1.97	0.03	23.17	25.77
Current Manufactured Cigarette Smokers	13.73	0.54	1,045	4,980.1	2.05	0.04	12.66	14.79
Current Hand-rolled Cigarette Smokers	17.50	0.69	1,656	6,347.6	2.73	0.04	16.14	18.86
Current Smoker of Other Tobacco Products	0.34	0.13	37	123.1	3.83	0.37	0.09	0.59
Daily Tobacco Smoker	21.15	0.65	1,934	7,673.9	2.09	0.03	19.88	22.43
Number of Manufactured Cigarettes Smoked per Day	9.66	0.32	768	3.5	3.22	0.03	9.03	10.29
Number of Hand-rolled Cigarettes Smoked	11.14	0.31	1,475	5.6	3.04	0.03	10.53	11.75
Age at Daily Smoking Initiation in 4 Categories	18.45	0.14	2,981	11.5	3.07	0.01	18.18	18.73
Former Daily Tobacco Smokers Among All Adults	9.10	0.43	923	3,302.6	1.87	0.05	8.25	9.96
Former Tobacco Smokers Among Ever Daily Smokers	28.61	1.26	923	3,302.6	2.33	0.04	26.13	31.09
Time Since Quitting Smoking in Years	12.41	0.39	1,189	4.5	2.63	0.03	11.64	13.18
First Daily Use of Tobacco Within 5 Minutes of Waking	22.94	1.70	432	1,760.3	3.16	0.07	19.61	26.27
Current Tobacco Users	29.22	0.78	2,684	10,599.3	2.43	0.03	27.69	30.75
Uses Only Smoked Tobacco	83.06	1.00	2,152	8,803.8	1.92	0.01	81.09	85.03
Smoking Quit Attempt in the Past 12 Months	48.99	1.85	1,077	4,575.7	3.13	0.04	45.37	52.62
Visited a Health Care Provider in the Past 12 Months	34.47	1.50	894	3,218.1	2.28	0.04	31.52	37.41
Health Care Provider Asked about Smoking	60.65	2.33	578	1,952.3	2.04	0.04	56.08	65.22
Health Care Provider Advised Quitting Smoking	53.19	2.37	505	1,712.3	2.03	0.04	48.54	57.85
Use of Pharmacotherapy for Smoking Cessation	8.89	1.42	84	406.7	2.68	0.16	6.10	11.67
Use of Counseling/Advice or Quit Lines for Smoking Cessation	5.56	1.00	58	254.3	2.06	0.18	3.59	7.52
Quit on Your Own	88.89	1.75	957	4,067.1	3.34	0.02	85.46	92.32
Use of Other Methods for Smoking Cessation	2.52	0.55	34	114.4	1.33	0.22	1.44	3.60
Plans to Quit Smoking Some Day but not in next 12 Months	36.97	1.63	787	3,319.1	2.53	0.04	33.76	40.17
Exposure to SHS at Work	30.13	2.05	404	2,013.2	2.61	0.07	26.11	34.15
Exposure to SHS at Home	43.65	1.36	3,738	15,755.7	6.14	0.03	40.99	46.32
Exposure to SHS in Government Buildings/Offices	3.70	0.38	283	1330.1	3.33	0.10	2.95	4.44

Table C5 (continued): Sampling Errors of key indicator for adults ≥ 15 years and over living in rural areas

Indicator	Estimate	Standard Error	Un-weighted Count	Weighted count in 1000s	Design Effect	Relative Error	Lower Limit	Upper Limit
Exposure to SHS in Health Care Facilities	1.87	0.21	182	673.8	2.02	0.11	1.45	2.29
Exposure to SHS in Restaurants	7.38	0.53	573	2,656.3	3.29	0.07	6.35	8.41
Exposure to SHS on Public Transportation	4.94	0.48	315	1,772.7	4.07	0.10	3.99	5.89
Exposure to SHS at Outside Market	51.80	1.07	4,121	18,736.3	3.74	0.02	49.71	53.89
Last Brand of Cigarette Purchased - Krongthip	54.88	2.44	518	2,559.4	2.33	0.04	50.10	59.66
Last Cigarette Purchase at Grocery	95.96	0.67	924	4,475.4	1.12	0.01	94.66	97.27
Total Monthly Expenditures on Manufactured Cigarettes	510.83	19.04	969	4.7	3.23	0.04	473.52	548.15
Last pack purchased had pictorial warning	96.91	1.06	475	2,089.9	1.86	0.01	94.83	99.00
Noticed Anti-Smoking Information in Newspapers or in Magazines	22.51	1.03	1,718	8,162.7	4.96	0.05	20.50	24.52
Noticed Anti-Smoking Information on Local TV	72.95	1.15	5,970	26,449.2	5.54	0.02	70.69	75.21
Noticed Anti-Smoking Information on Radio	33.75	1.26	2,785	12,238.0	5.86	0.04	31.27	36.22
Noticed Anti-Smoking Information on Billboards	35.75	1.53	2,738	12,964.7	8.42	0.04	32.75	38.76
Noticed Anti-Smoking Information on Leaflet or Sticker	35.89	1.45	2,821	13,014.6	7.47	0.04	33.06	38.73
Noticed Anti-Smoking Information on Internet	5.09	0.52	230	1,845.8	4.55	0.10	4.08	6.11
Noticed Anti-Smoking Information in Public Campaign Activity	14.44	1.21	984	5,234.3	9.73	0.08	12.07	16.81
Noticed Anti-Smoking Information Demonstration Board	30.34	1.36	2,171	10,996.9	7.19	0.04	27.68	33.00
Noticed Anti-Smoking Information Somewhere Else	0.83	0.26	57	292.4	6.78	0.32	0.31	1.34
Noticed Health Warning Labels on Cigarette Packages	80.29	0.80	6,340	29,112.8	3.30	0.01	78.73	81.86
Thinking of Quitting Because of Health Warning Labels on Cigarette Packages	66.71	1.76	1,455	5,980.9	3.09	0.03	63.25	70.16
Noticed Health Warning Labels on Raw Tobacco Packages	21.36	2.31	312	1,691.8	6.69	0.11	16.82	25.89
Thinking of Quitting Because of Health Warning Labels on Raw Tobacco Packages	14.99	1.68	224	1,187.7	4.62	0.11	11.71	18.28
Noticed Cigarette Advertisements in Stores	6.12	0.67	404	2,219.4	6.33	0.11	4.82	7.43
Noticed Cigarette Advertisements Anywhere Else	1.90	0.26	139	666.8	2.92	0.14	1.39	2.41

Table C5 (continued): Sampling Errors of key indicator for adults ≥ 15 years and over living in rural areas

Indicator	Estimate	Standard Error	Un-weighted Count	Weighted count in 1000s	Design Effect	Relative Error	Lower Limit	Upper Limit
Noticed Sponsorship of Sport or Arts Event	1.15	0.26	71	416.7	4.91	0.23	0.64	1.66
Noticed Cigarette Promotions - Clothing/item with brand name or logo	5.69	0.49	361	2,062.4	3.70	0.09	4.73	6.65
Noticed Other Promotion	1.59	0.23	109	576.4	2.74	0.14	1.14	2.04
Believes that Tobacco Smoking Causes Serious Illness	98.32	0.22	8,064	35,653.4	2.48	0.00	97.88	98.76
Believes that Tobacco Smoking Causes Strokes	78.25	0.96	6,416	28,372.7	4.48	0.01	76.37	80.14
Believes that Tobacco Smoking Causes Heart Attacks	74.54	0.97	6,064	27,024.4	4.04	0.01	72.65	76.43
Believes that Tobacco Smoking Causes Lung Cancer	97.11	0.24	7,933	35,210.4	1.67	0.00	96.64	97.58
Believes that Tobacco Smoking Causes Mouth Cancer	90.18	0.63	7,295	32,697.9	3.64	0.01	88.95	91.41
Believes that Tobacco Smoking Causes Larynx Cancer	90.34	0.62	7,364	32,754.4	3.67	0.01	89.11	91.56
Believes that Tobacco Smoking Causes Impotence	64.05	1.14	5,113	23,222.5	4.64	0.02	61.82	66.29
Believes that Tobacco Smoking Causes Emphysema	88.48	0.75	7,226	32,079.4	4.57	0.01	87.00	89.96
Believes that SHS Causes Serious Illness in Non-Smokers	94.41	0.40	7,639	34,233.2	2.49	0.00	93.63	95.19
Believes that SHS Causes Heart Disease	63.70	1.01	5,285	23,096.9	3.64	0.02	61.71	65.68
Believes that SHS Causes Lung Illness in Children	89.49	0.60	7,228	32,448.4	3.16	0.01	88.31	90.67
Believes that SHS Causes Lung Cancer in Adults	89.77	0.57	7,232	32,551.9	2.94	0.01	88.65	90.90
Believes that SHS Causes Emphysema	80.97	0.87	6,583	29,352.0	4.06	0.01	79.26	82.68
Believes that SHS Causes Low Birth Weight	68.46	1.00	5,490	24,814.4	3.82	0.01	66.50	70.42
Believes that SHS Causes Premature Birth	58.14	1.11	4,706	21,078.4	4.19	0.02	55.96	60.32
Pictorial Warning #8 Most Makes Smokers Want to Quit	30.55	2.08	304	15,11.6	2.11	0.07	26.49	34.62
Pictorial Warning #7 Most Influences Non-Smokers to Not Smoke	35.01	1.18	1,376	7,342.2	2.62	0.03	32.70	37.32
Believes Manufactured Cigarettes are More Harmful	42.70	1.21	3,841	14,922.1	4.71	0.03	40.33	45.07
Daily Manufactured Cigarette Smoker	9.74	0.46	768	3,533.3	1.99	0.05	8.84	10.64
Daily Hand-rolled Cigarette Smoker	15.45	0.66	1,475	5,604.7	2.73	0.04	14.16	16.74
Daily Smokeless Tobacco User	4.39	0.34	464	1,592.0	2.22	0.08	3.73	5.05
Average Price per Pack of Manufactured Cigarettes	44.07	0.56	969	35.5	5.85	0.01	42.97	45.16

Appendix D: Technical and Survey Staff

Consultants

Organization	Position
1. Action on Smoking and Health Foundation, Thailand	
Prof Dr Prakit Vathesatogkit [1)]	Executive Secretary of Action on Smoking and Health Foundation, Thailand (ASH Thailand)
2. Thai Health Promotion Institute	
Dr Hatai Chitanondh	President of Thai Health Promotion Institute (THPI)
3. Ministry of Public Health	
Dr Suwit Wibulpolprasert	Senior Advisor on Disease Control, Office of Permanent Secretary , Ministry of Public Health
Dr Prapont Tangsrikiatkul	Deputy Director of Department of Disease Control (DDC)
Dr Pongpisut Jongudomsuk	Director of Health Systems Research Institute (HSRI)
Dr Viroj Tangcharoensathien	Director of International Health Policy Program, Thailand (IHPP), Bureau of Policy and Strategy, Office of Permanent Secretary, Ministry of Public Health
Dr Panuwat Panketu	Director of Bureau of Non Communicable Disease , Department of Disease Control, Ministry of Public Health
Dr Churit Tengtrisorn	Deputy Director of Bureau of Tobacco Control, Department of Disease Control, Ministry of Public Health
Associate Prof Dr Wichai Aekplakorn	Director of National Health Examination Survey Office (NHESO), HSRI
4. National Statistical Office	
Mrs Jirawan Boonperm	Director-General of National Statistical Office
Ms Rajana Netsaengtip	Director of Economic Social and Opinion Statistics Bureau 2
Ms Oraphin Matthew	Director of Policy Statistical Techniques Bureau
Dr Malee Wongsaroje	Director of Information and Communications Technology Center (ICT Center)
Mrs Somsri Wasintham	Chief of Provincial Information and Communication Technology Support group
5. Faculty of Public Health, Mahidol University	
Associate Prof Tharadol Kengganpanich	Statistician
Associate Prof Dusit Sujirarat	Statistician
6. World Health Organization	
Dr Sawat Ramaboot	Advisor to WHO Country Office
Dr Chai Krittiyapichatkul	National Professional Officer on Tobacco Control

Note: [1)] Chair of consultant team and consultant of GATS Working Group

GATS Working Group

Name	Organization	Position in GATS
Assistant Prof Dr Lakkhana Termsirikulchai	Faculty of Public Health, Mahidol University	Chair of working group
Core Staffs [1]		
Dr Sarunya Benjakul	Department of Disease Control, Ministry of Public Health	Principal Investigator
Assistant Prof Dr Mondha Kengganpanich	Faculty of Public Health, Mahidol University	Co- Principal investigator
Ms Chitrlada Touchchai	National Statistical Office	Co-investigator
Ms Hataichanok Puckcharern	National Statistical Office	Co-investigator
Ms Areerat Lohtongmongkol	National Statistical Office	Co-investigator
Mrs Wanpen Toaditep	National Statistical Office	Technical Staffs
Mrs Siriporn Kulboonyiam	National Statistical Office	Technical Staffs
Ms Yupawadee Boohchanasap	National Statistical Office	Technical Staffs
Mr Apichat Thunyahan	National Statistical Office	Technical Staffs
Mr Bunpot Teemuangsong	National Statistical Office	Technical Staffs
Mr Saroj Nakju	GATS Office	Coordinator
Mr Nuttapon Theskayan	GATS Office	Coordinator

Supporting Staffs	Organization
Assistant Prof Dr Supawan Manoksunthon	Bureau of Non Communicable Disease, DDC
Dr Nawarat Petcharoen	Bureau of Non Communicable Disease, DDC
Ms Salinee Sensatian	Bureau of Non Communicable Disease, DDC
Ms Siriporn Kaopoothai	Health Information Systems Development Program Office (HISO)
Ms Naiyana Bpraditsittigon	International Health Policy Program (IHPP)
Ms Wanpen Tinna	Health Systems Research Institute (HSRI)

Note: [1] Most core staffs take role as field supervisors (FSs), except Ms Hataichanok Puckcharern

Field Staffs

1. Northern Region

1.1 Provincial Technical Officers (PTOs)

- Mrs Punnapa Rattanaburi
- Mr Kajorn Rattanaburi
- Mr Perasak Pensiripan
- Mr Kavesak Gunjear
- Ms Supattra Sarapun
- Ms Tueanchai Panboon
- Mrs Songkran Vongsa
- Ms Piyanuch Tugaew
- Mr Adisak Jinavil
- Mr Warayut Piyaphanee
- Mrs Pantipa Laohatongthip
- Mrs Ruangvipha Vongsaroj
- Ms Tongngam Aussawamekagul
- Ms Kamolthip Chantavarang
- Mr Phanupan Piluk
- Mr Jirawat Thammarak
- Mrs Theraporn Vichitpanya

1.2 Field Interviewers (FIs)

- Ms Piyamas Boonmekhum
- Mr Yuttasak Tayapong
- Mr Nuttapol Taubon
- Mr Chatre Sukcharoen
- Mr Somsak Charoenkhunmueang
- Mr Apinya Charoenchaikittikul
- Ms Piyanuch Sannog
- Mr Chanon Gassomboon
- Mrs Puangpaka Thanutkul
- Ms Wilaiwan Mahawansri
- Mr Jirapit Singpun
- Mr Apichat Chaiya
- Mr Sukij Chaowwong
- Mr Sombat Yhamnongtao
- Mr Nirut Kumaeam
- Ms Jittra Rutragan
- Mrs Siriprapha Kadsanit
- Mr Chan Jitjamsai
- Mr Pongpun Pruchyasakul
- Mr Nopparat Chanrug
- Mrs Khanogtip Vongkasum
- Ms Thong Sukmueang

2. Northeastern Region

2.1 Provincial Technical Officers (PTOs)

- Mrs Khwanlak Siripopamporn
- Mrs Prapassorn Kathong
- Mr Manoon Sawisit
- Mr Sumit Chatchawan
- Mr Suphan Srihayra
- Ms Chorrak Intanon
- Mrs Sanyakorn Nasungnern
- Ms Yupared Chuawongyad
- Mr Suphun Chatpaengta
- Mr Somjit Raksrithong
- Mr Tosaporn Wongla
- Mrs Jiraporn Tienpitak
- Mrs Thitarporn Phasaweth
- Mrs Yupaporn Moonut
- Mrs Wimonporn Hnoosut
- Mrs Kanlapat Mahipan
- Ms Naparat Thannarat
- Mr Nopphadon Paoyaosuk
- Mr Thammasak Srisongkram

2. Northeastern Region (Cont)

2.2 Field Interviewers (FIs)

- Ms Busara Hongthai
- Ms Kavarin jaikaewairi
- Ms Nichapak Jindapee
- Ms Janya Swamechai
- Mr Niwat Inhorm
- Mr Adisak Raksasi
- Ms Ratanaporn Nathamplong
- Mr Panupat Atthachon
- Mr Suwit Napho
- Ms Rapeepan Boonpa
- Ms Wanida Kumkangwal
- Mrs bannasorn Chaichawan
- Mr Sumrit Phapol
- Mr Kawi Nimnual
- Mr Prachaup Srinate
- Ms Wanrudee Praserichai
- Ms Uraiwan Nuangwanna
- Mr Narin Nomrawee
- Ms Kantaporn Prapong
- Mr Yutthapong Meesri
- Mr Putipong Thongon
- Ms Supitcha Suphanthamart

3. Southern Region

3.1 Provincial Technical Officers (PTOs)

- Ms Supakul Rachpibul
- Mr Sitichai Tansiri
- Mr Nikom Comleang
- Ms Prapai Pukngarm
- Mr Songpol Narkrod
- Ms Ubonwan Kaeoiat
- Mr Theeratham Sawattham
- Ms Mukdarat Pechtnoo
- Mr Thanes Suwattikul
- Mr Thamolwan Naphatthaluang
- Ms Taepa Markkong
- Ms Methini Chumniturakarn
- Ms Chaluay Sannichart
- Mr Weerasak Sonchareon

3.2 Field Interviewers (FIs)

- Mr Withan Deenu
- Mr Winyoo Pislangam
- Mr Kriangsak Paensuwan
- Mr Priwan Sravaree
- Ms Jiraporn Kasorn
- Ms Piangjai Sudwilai
- Mr Somrak Saengarvut
- Mr Adinan Kaew-on
- Ms Anong Rachsiri
- Mr Yostiya Haggayanon
- Ms Sunisa Ruangtip
- Mr Supop Suwanno
- Ms Napat Isaparo
- Mr Prasit Balang
- Ms Nisara Rodphai
- Mrs Kanda Rakkoeng
- Mr Rossalan Benno
- Ms Kodchakorn Make
- Mrs Areeya Satirak
- Mr Santi Satirak

4. Central Region

4.1 Provincial Technical Officers (PTOs)

- Mrs Nichaporn Sangsakul
- Mrs Natchanok Sumetyachan
- Ms Suttiya Tongsai
- Ms Wanna Kaewbuadee
- Ms Maneerat Sandtuppar
- Ms Raphatsha Phuthakorn
- Mrs Anchalee Tharnskulmatar
- Ms Kanchana Pajariyapong
- Ms Pimporn Horasith
- Mrs Nuanchan Muangsangthum
- Mrs Nutcharat Lapboon
- Mr Somsak Peerachairat
- Ms Jerapa Varadul
- Mr Yothin Mekarun
- Ms Sudarat Jongsiriruk
- Ms Raweewan Booyakalampa
- Mr Krisnapong Nipattachot
- Ms Sidarat Tharasombat
- Mr Soontorn Fugsil
- Ms Paphopsorn Timsriklum
- Mr Lamol Kerdubol
- Ms Sutinee Keyata
- Ms Muttawan Chaisuwan
- Mrs Nisra Pheetawee
- Mrs Athtthan Changphueak

4.2 Field Interviewers (FIs)

- Ms Wararat Chantawad
- Ms Nattanan Junsri
- Ms Chanoknan Thunnthong
- Ms Siriphat Ratanasanguanwongs
- Mrs Thayaluck Bumrungpetch
- Ms Saowanee Paoin
- Ms Lamai Ritthiherm
- Mr Jedchan Lorprasert
- Mr Peeraphat Khuntong
- Mrs Prajin Klibpan
- Mrs Wannapa Boonmakul
- Acting sub Lt.Watchara Thongma
- Ms Saysunee Phonpai
- Mr Nirutth Owatthananawakhun
- Ms Pucharee Ngachur
- Ms Wandee Wutiwong
- Ms Nittaya Wongsa
- Mr Paruehas Suthipongphan
- Ms Wattana Phalahan
- Ms Ngamta Muangthong
- Mr Samatcha Wisanwong
- Mr Sakkarin Seesom
- Ms Kannika Klinkong
- Mrs Uraiwan Nitsawang
- Mr Thanavat Satanont
- Mrs Pranom Sukyu
- Ms Yupin Jongdee
- Ms Ratchanok Ninpradub

5. Bangkok Metropolis

5.1 Provincial Technical Officers (PTOs)

- Mr Attachai Sanitsanom
- Mr Panuwat Karunratchathorn
- Mr Wasit Srisengchoti

5.2 Field Interviewers (FIs)

- Mr Jirapat Sangpap
- Ms Rungruedee Kaewkalong
- Mr Winai Ausub
- Ms Chonlatee Wungdeephongam
- Ms Nuchari Chittra
- Mr Kittipong Monmol
- Mr Sripai Srisutham
- Mr Eakarat Pantee
- Mr Sirichai Wongplang
- Ms Patamporn Ouamaram
- Ms iyanuch Mahakotr
- Mr Ruangsin Sae Tang
- Ms Arisara Wannawat
- Ms Jureerat Kongnoy
- Ms Suchada Prakobun
- Ms Yupin Phonyiam

Appendix E: Glossary and Abbreviations

GATS	Global Adult Tobacco Survey
FCTC	World Health Organization Framework Convention on Tobacco Control
MPOWER	2008 WHO publication with six key strategies on Tobacco Control
	Monitor tobacco use and prevention policies
	Protect people from tobacco smoke
	Offer help to quit tobacco use
	Warn about the dangers of tobacco
	Enforce bans on tobacco advertising, promotion and sponsorship
	Raise taxes on tobacco
NSO	National Statistical Office
PSUs	Primary Sampling Units
SSUs	Secondary Sampling Units
PSO	Provincial Statistical Office
FSs	Field Supervisors
PTOs	Provincial Technical Officers
FIs	Field Interviewers
Adults	Population who aged 15 years and over
SES	Socioeconomic status
PHW	Pictorial Health Warning
Tobacco Products	Two types of tobacco products;
	1) Smoked tobacco: manufactured cigarettes, hand-rolled cigarettes, others smoked tobacco such as pipe, cigar, khi-yo, cheroots, water pipes, hookah, and others 2) Smokeless tobacco: snuff by keeping mouth/nose, chewing tobacco, betel quid with tobacco, and others
Smoking frequency	Classified into three categories, i.e., 1) Daily smoking means smoking at least one tobacco product every day or nearly every day over a period of a month or more 2) Occasional smoking (/less than daily) 3) Never smoking includes tried once or twice in lifetime
Current smoker	Smoker who daily and occasional smokes any tobacco product
SHS	Second-hand smoke
Prevalence (%)	Statistical concept referred to the number of occurrences of tobacco use that are present in a particular population, aged 15 years and over at a given time
Quit attempt	Current tobacco smokers who tried to quit during the past 12 months and former tobacco smokers who have been abstinences for > 12 months

Interest in quitting smoking	Current tobacco smokers who are planning or thinking about quitting smoking within the next month, 12 months, or someday
HCPs	Health Care Providers include various health professions such as medical doctors, nurses, pharmacist, health workers etc.
Exposure to secondhand smoke	Includes smoking by respondents and saw somebody smoke, smelled the smoke, or saw tobacco butts inside (indoor areas) the public places during their visit in the past 30 days, i.e., ○ *Government Building: covering indoor areas which are non-smoking areas by the national smoke free laws* ○ *Health Care Facilities: covering indoor areas of both public and private health care facilities which are non-smoking areas by the national smoke free laws* ○ *Restaurants: covering food and/ or beverage selling place inside the building, not include place in front of any building and wayside* ○ *Public Transportation: All public transport with both air conditioner and non air conditioner* ○ *Outside Market: means a place provided for vendors to shows and exchanges goods and services, on a regular or temporary or specific-day basis*
Exposure to secondhand smoke at home	Emphasize inside the respondent's home, not include areas outside such as patios, balcony, garden, etc. that are not fully enclosed
Exposure to anti-smoking information	Respondents who have noticed information on various media in the last 30 days about the dangers of cigarettes smoking and those encourage quitting
Thinking of quitting because of pictorial health warning on cigarettes package	Current tobacco smokers who thought about quitting smoking in the last 30 days because of the pictorial health warning on cigarettes or shredded tobacco package
Awareness of cigarettes advertising, promotion and sponsorship	Respondents who have noticed cigarettes at point of sale, free gifts or discount offers on other products when buy cigarettes, or any advertisement or signs promoting cigarettes in stores where cigarettes are sold in the last 30 days, or who have noticed any advertisement or signs promoting cigarettes of cigarettes company, sponsorship of sporting event or other that in store where cigarettes are sold in the last 30 days
Beliefs about the dangers of tobacco smoking	Respondents who believe that tobacco smoking causes serious illness and specific diseases, i.e., stroke, heart attack, lung cancer, mouth cancer, larynx cancer, impotent, and emphysema
Beliefs about the dangers of secondhand smoke	Respondents who believe that breathing other smoke causes serious illness and specific disease in non-smokers, i.e., heart disease in adults, lung illness in children, lung cancer in adults, emphysema, low birth weight (< 2,500 grams), premature birth (28-34 weeks)

Pictorial Health Warning	Nine color-based of pictorial health warning on cigarettes packages includes cigars as following;	
	 **Picture 1**: Cigarette Smoke Harms People Nearby	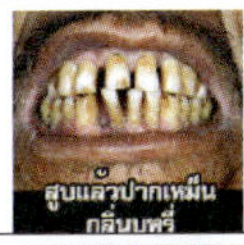 **Picture 2**: Smoking Causes Your Breath to Smell
	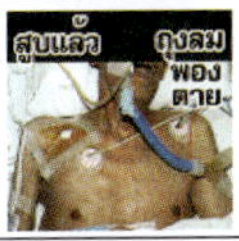 **Picture 3**: Smoking Causes Fatal Emphysema	 **Picture 4**: Cigarette Smoke Causes Lung Cancer
	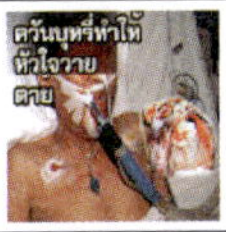 **Picture 5**: Cigarette Smoke Causes Fatal Heart Failure	 **Picture 6**: Cigarette Smoke Leads Your Life to Death
	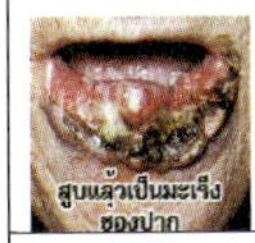 **Picture 7**: Smoking Causes Oral Cancer	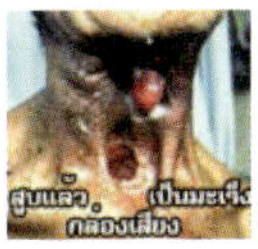 **Picture 8**: Smoking Causes Laryngeal Cancer
	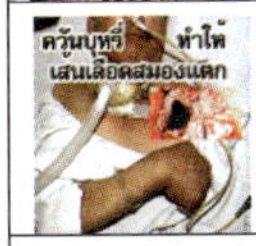 **Picture 9**: Cigarette Smoke Causes hemorrhagic Stroke	
	Two black and white color-based of pictorial health warning on raw tobacco pack using for hand-rolled cigarettes and smokeless tobacco use as below;	
	 **Picture 1:** Smoking causes laryngeal cancer	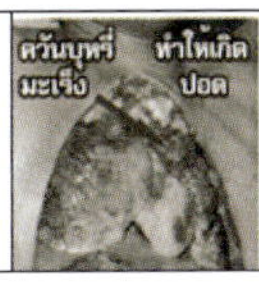 **Picture 2:** Cigarette smoke causes lung cancer